Bach and the Dance of God

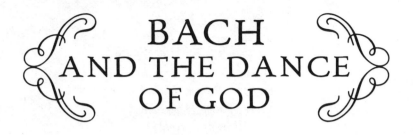

BACH
AND THE DANCE
OF GOD

Wilfrid Mellers

New York
Oxford University Press
1981

First published in 1980
by Faber and Faber Limited
3 Queen Square London WC1N 3AU
Printed in Great Britain
by BAS Printers Limited
Over Wallop Hampshire

© *Wilfrid Mellers, 1980*

British Library Cataloguing in Publication Data

Mellers, Wilfrid
Bach and the Dance of God
1. Bach, Johann Sebastian
I. Title
780'.92'4   ML410.B1
ISBN 0-19-520232-5

Contents

Preface

This book and its companion volume, *Beethoven and the Voice of God,* have been thirty years in the writing and are a distillation of analysis classes given throughout my career as university teacher. Originally the analyses were presented orally, at a piano, the spoken word being intimately related to the sound of music. Though this method has obvious advantages over presentation in written form, there's something to be said for a written script which can be reread and an analytical-interpretive comment which can be checked by reference to both text and score — and, if desired, to recording. In the published books the music examples are no more than pointers or momentary alleviations; the analysis can be *fully* intelligible only if read with a score at one's elbow.

As a writer about music I have learned, as have most of us, from Schenker, Tovey and Réti, among others. I suppose I take more risks than they did in that, starting from a fairly — sometimes very — detailed description of what happens in musical terms, I proceed to relate these musical events to their physiological and psychological consequences. Nowadays any attempt to talk about music's 'meanings' in other than technical terms is often deplored; yet it seems to me self-evident that description that goes no further than musical facts can never be more than a trivial occupation. Since music is made by human beings, any musical judgement, however technical, is also psychological: it is not merely improbable, but totally impossible, that musical events could be separable from human experience — thoughts, feelings, actions — conceptualized in other than musical terms. Verbal comment and comparison is entirely valid so long as it stems from a careful delineation of the musical facts; and such subjective elements as enter into one's commentary on music are neither more nor less damaging than those that occur in reference to any human activity. I cannot prove that my account of a problematical work like Beethoven's op. 101 is unequivocally *right*. I can however demonstrate that it is a possible, even probable, deduction from a given sequence of musical events; and I could point to other accounts which would be demonstrably *wrong* in that they did not take account of those musical facts. In any case, if it is worth while to write about music at all—and clearly I believe it is—one has no choice but to have the courage of one's musical and human convictions. Musical analysis cannot and shouldn't be a science, since music itself isn't. Responsibly carried out it may, however, be an aid to human understanding; and is perhaps most fully justified in approaching, with humility, the greatest music so far created by Western man.

Being detailed, the analysis in these studies doesn't make for easy reading, but if it weren't detailed it couldn't be an adequate basis for philosophical and theological extension; and if it weren't thus extended it would be pitifully inadequate to Bach and Beethoven, neither of whom doubted that their music had 'meanings' discussable in terms simultaneously musical, theological and philosophical. Certainly, teaching, and therefore verbalizing about, the music of Bach and Beethoven over thirty years has helped me to respond to and enjoy their art more deeply; and I like to think that I've helped my students in helping myself.

W.M.
November 1979

University of York

ACKNOWLEDGEMENT

'Dame Algebra', an extract from 'A Reminder' from *Collected Poems* by W. H. Auden on page 251 is reprinted by permission of Faber and Faber Limited.

I

PRELUDE

Dancing, bright lady, then began to be
When the first seeds whereof the world did spring,
The fire, air, earth and water did agree
By Love's persuasion, Nature's mighty King,
To leave their first disordered combating
And in a Dance such measure to observe
As all the World their motion should preserve . . .

For that true Love, which Dancing did invent,
Is he that tun'd the whole world's Harmony,
And linked all men in sweet Society.

SIR JOHN DAVIES: *Orchestra*, 1596

There is a stone face beside a road with an inscription saying 'The true portrait of the Holy Face of God of Jaen'; if we really knew what it was like, the key to all parables would be ours and we would know if the carpenter's son was also the Son of God.

Paul saw it as a light which hurled him to the ground; John saw it as the sun when it blazes with all its force; Teresa of Leon saw it many times, bathed in a tranquil light, and could never determine the colour of its eyes.

We have lost these features just as one may lose a magic number made up of customary digits, just as one loses for ever an image in a kaleidoscope. We may see them and be unaware of it. A Jew's profile in the subway is perhaps that of Christ; the hands giving us our change at a ticket window perhaps repeat those that one day were nailed to the cross by some soldiers.

Perhaps some feature of that crucified countenance lurks in every mirror; perhaps the face died, was obliterated, so that God could be in all of us.

JORGE LUIS BORGES: *Parables*

If the lion were to ascribe thee a face, he would imagine the face of a lion, the ox would imagine that of an ox, the eagle, of an eagle. O Lord, how marvellous is thy face, which youths cannot conceive but as youthful, men as manly, the aged as aged! . . . The face of faces is veiled in all faces, and seen in a riddle. Unveiled it is not found until one has entered, beyond all visions, into a state of secret and hidden silence, in which nothing is left of knowing or imagining a face. For so long as this obscurity is not reached, this cloud, this darkness . . . so long can thy face be encountered only veiled. This darkness, however, reveals that it is here, in the transcending of all veils, that the face is present. And the more densely the darkness is felt, the truer and closer is the approach, by virtue of the darkness, to the invisible light.

NICHOLAS OF CUSA: *De visione Dei*, vi

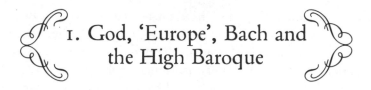

1. God, 'Europe', Bach and the High Baroque

For many primitive peoples the origin of life is a sound: it is the *voice* of God—his laugh, hum, gibber, croak or chuckle—that stirs creation in the void. Why primitive peoples should believe this may be implicit in the cry of the newborn babe who, separated from the mother as he struggles into an alien world, yells for mammalian security, yearning to be again part of Nature, the mother of all creation. The baby's cry, according to Géza Róheim, is the 'only form of permitted crying which gains sympathetic attention and earns symbolic gratifications'; indeed we may even smile at, or gently laugh with, the baby's tears. Many authorities from Darwin onwards have pointed out that in this respect the utterance of the human infant resembles that of the beasts. Both speak a language pre-existent to consciousness, which consciousness must and does obliterate. None the less it is to our peril that we forget this language, which links us to Nature. Jakob Boehme regretted that in his day (and we are his heirs) 'no people understands any more the sensual language, and the birds in the air and the beasts in the forests do understand it according to their species. Therefore man may reflect what he has been robbed of, and what he is to recover in the Second Birth, for in the sensual language all spirits speak with one another.' The linguist Jespersen tells us that 'men sang out their feelings long before they were able to speak their thoughts'; Susanne Langer remarks that 'the beginnings of language are not natural adjustments of ways to means, but purposeless lulling instincts, primitive aesthetic reactions and dream-like associations of ideas'. Lulling invokes the cradle, and a magical return to the womb.

We may still observe, among primitive peoples, the origins of music in the cries of infants, the yells of created Nature. Eskimo children, for instance, take empty tubs used by their parents for the storage of whale oil and blow into them rhythmically, creating an interplay of sonorities. While these breathing exercises are practised by children as a game, the procedure is also, for the Eskimos, of deep ritual significance. All the time God is pouring out life into animate Nature; what would happen if, one day, he had no puff left? Humbly the Eskimo recognizes his part in the ultimate mystery, which is Being itself: his rhythmically patterned exhalation is a cry, a sigh, that pays back to God the tribute of the breath of life. Similarly the African bushmen who live in the Kalahari desert create a weird music by emulating the twitters, yawps, barks, grunts and grizzles of birds and beasts; in becoming, in sound and movement, their totemic creatures, they employ disguise and illusion as a propitiatory act, conquering their fear of the unknown in making a gesture of reverence to the creatures on whom they rely for subsistence. The music they make is an aural mask that complements the visual masks they may wear; in being metamorphosed into Nature, aurally, visually and corporeally, they acquire some of the attributes of divinity. The Australian aborigine, in the silent emptiness of the outback, likewise uses magical, pre-articulate syllables to invoke natural phenomena — the sun, moon, cloud or water on which his minimal existence depends. The magic vocables, shouted against the 'everlasting' drone of the didgeridoo and accompanied by the beating of sticks, dramatize the basic facts of his life: the ticking of his pulse, the thudding of his heart. Through song and dance he would remain whole, hale and holy as part of the cosmos; and much the same is true when at a more sophisticated level song and dance become an act of affirmation rather than of propitiation.

For the African pygmies or Australian bushmen wild creatures are unknowable, feared yet depended on; for the South Plains Indians, however, the horse, if not fully domesticated, is an intrinsic part of social life: the Indian may perform dance-songs that affirm his and the horses' phallic dominance, an expression of pride in his ability, however inadequately, to master Nature. Often these horse chants are 'tumbling strains', to use the phrase coined by Curt Sachs; beginning on a high note, they descend wildly in a cry that creates an effect of uncontrolled libido, driven none the less by the drum's or rattles' regular, furiously pounding beat. Though the cry has become assertive, even aggressive, its relationship to the baby's yell is unmistakable; and although the chants have words, they are not articulate. Some say that the words once had meanings which have been forgotten. In any case, the meanings were magical; what is left is the 'sensual speech', a 'music of the vowels'.

Yet if music began as a communal rather than individual appeal to the Great Mother, a desperate protest against separation, it entails a paradox: the act of parturition — of being born — is itself a move towards consciousness. To be conscious is to be aware of differences and distinctions, to separate subject from object; and in the strict sense 'sub-ject' is that which is injected under or within the self, 'ob-ject' is that which is thrown against or across one's path.

Dualism is inherent in awareness; and this is why the communal and magical origins of music are complemented by a search for identity. The American Indian must get his tribally sanctioned songs 'right' because they are the law; mistakes could bring ruin to the crops and destruction to the community. But he has also his own song, which usually comes to him in a dream (see Curtis in Bibliography); and this song is his soul, his identity, his attempt to answer King Lear's sublime question when he asks, reduced to the state of 'unaccommodated man', 'Who is it that can tell me who I am?' Articulate language probably entered primitive art as part of the search for identity: the Name is sacred because it is synonymous with man's awareness, God's child though he may be, of his own existence and of the existence of objects in the external world. In this light we can understand why God, who ontologically is the Unnameable, became equated with Logos, first as the original breath of life, then as the articulate Word. 'Homo intelligendo fit omnia', wrote Vico in 1744. Understanding is at once human and divine, for as St. John told us long ago, 'In the beginning was the Word, and the Word was with God, and the Word was God. All things were made by Him and without Him was not any thing made that was made. In Him was life; and the life was the light of men. And the light shineth in darkness; and the darkness comprehended it not.' We must grow towards comprehension; *infans* means unable to speak, and to evolve beyond the infant's cry is to learn to speak the identifying Name. Logos is God because the gift of consciousness—knowing that one knows and who one is—is the pearl without price, distinguishing us from inanimate Nature and brute creation. We can still find evidence of this in the naming games beloved of children; and the close relation between the naming game and the Sacred Riddle is also significant, for the riddle seeks a magic (and cheating) answer to the duality which is consciousness. A riddle, like consciousness itself, is a paradox—a pun in which differentiations and contradictions do not need to be resolved because they are, or seem to be, momentarily one.

In so far as naming games and riddles effect magic through incantation, usually involving regularly periodic alternations of pitch, we may relate them to the evolution of syllabic chant, which is still man's oldest, unbroken musical-poetic tradition. The Maori of New Zealand are dependent on trees for almost everything—food, clothes, shelter, transport. When the Maori shaman clasps a tree in his arms and 'names' its god in a strange ululant chant halfway between speech and song he creates an incantation, dependent on repetition, order and rhythmic alternation, which induces trance and rapture; and this process is extended, but not radically modified, in the religious chants of antiquity and of Christian Europe. In the chanting of Tibetan monks, of Japanese Zen Buddhists, or Ethiopian or Islamic priests or of Christian priests of the Coptic, Greek, Russian, Roman or Anglican church there is an equivocation between the Word as consciousness and the Word as an act of holistic union. In singing, or even in participating vicariously as silent congregation, we are consciously thanking God for the gift of consciousness and are at the same time handing the gift back to him, renewing ourselves in surrendering the self—a more complex version of the Eskimo's returning to God of the gift of breath. The meaning of *incantare* is to charm, to cast a spell, and *cantare* is to sing. In Christian Europe no less than in remote Tibet the chant is sung in a dead, hieratic language wherein the pre-articulate vocable survives alongside the language of consciousness.

The dance-songs of primitive peoples depend on the rhythms of the human body and on the 'sensual speech' that relates us to Nature; religious chant from remotest antiquity to the present day relates consciousness of the Word to the rhythms of breathing and speaking. Both musics, if they employ instruments at all, regard them as literally instrumental: agents that extend the human voice or body, or channel the voice of God. Nor is there much distinction in kind between instruments sacred and profane; the holy trumpets of Tibetan priests are gigantic versions of amorously phallic flutes, while the sacred drums of the Yoruba are larger and more imposing versions of the 'speaking' drums of social communication, except that they may be patriarchally male as well as female and womb-like, as drums commonly are. Now both primitive song-dance and religious chant, though they exist within time, seek to deny it. In religious ceremonial or in secular fiesta, today as at any time in history, we are released from linear, chronological time and re-enter circular, mythological time wherein, as Octavio Paz has put it, time is 'not succession and transition, but rather the perpetual sound of a fixed present in which all times, past, present and future, are contained'. We may refer to fiesta and religious ceremonial as art, but not as works of art; and it is significant that most primitive peoples—and some fairly sophisticated ones, such as the Balinese— have no linguistic term to denote art in our sense. The work of art occurs only when we accept the burden of consciousness unequivocally, or as nearly so as we can make it; and the work metaphor makes a point, in contrast to the eternally *present* activity of *homo ludens*. To accept consciousness is to accept past, present and future as differentiated, and therefore to accept the facts of temporal progression and of death.

This is an achievement that first flowered with the Greeks. Pythagoreanism and Orphism possibly inherited from ancient shamanistic cults of Thrace their separation of soul from body and their consequent guilt about sex. Not surprisingly, later Greek thought played a significant part in the rise of Christianity which, more than any other religion, attempted to confront mortality and guilt, associating both with an event presumed to exist in historical time—the Crucifixion of Christ. This equation between guilt and time is a peculiarly European phenomenon, which radically transformed our notions of art as communication. When in the fourteenth century the European Renaissance decisively ousted medieval theocracy in favour of man's stumbling search for self-responsibility, the tintinnabulations of religious and ecclesiastical *cloches* were gradually replaced by the clicking of secular and civic clocks; and the way was open to Locke's statement that 'duration is one common measure of all existence whatsoever'. The apparently final acceptance of linear time as an absolute made possible the development of ratiocinative logic. Consciousness of being conscious enabled man to evolve a language of intellectual abstraction, separate from the metaphorical, sensual language of poetry; and this in turn made feasible the scientific exploration of Nature. When once we know, we wish to *know how*; the modern tag 'knowing how things tick' provides the revealing link between intellectual enquiry and clock, pendulum and temporal progression. Though there is no development precisely comparable in the visual arts, the discovery or rather the enthusiastic investigation of visual perspective is a parallel phenomenon, which made possible the exploration of literal (photographic) representation. Primitive man draws, paints and sculpts to effect practical ends by magical means, whereas modern man makes visual artefacts in order to 'freeze' a moment existing in historical time; although this too is a magic act, it is without practical consequence. Music itself cannot convey intellectual concepts or can do so only vicariously in collaboration with verbal language; nor, except at a very crude level, can it imitate reality in the way painting can. This may be why music has, throughout the centuries, preserved closer ties with the old magical notions of art than have literature and painting; and it may be why only in Europe, not the Orient, has music made a potent if equivocal attempt to embrace and to transcend man's most crucial development in consciousness. As we might expect, the growth of European music from ritual into art is manifest in a technical development—the evolution of harmonic perspective—which has no parallel in the East. Significantly, it emerged at about the same time as the investigation of visual perspective.

The timeless quality we have observed in primitive song-dance and in religious cantillation is inseparable from their purely melodic-rhythmic nature. A corporeal beat, endlessly repeated, destroys time even as it measures it, while a melodic-rhythmic pattern, insidiously reiterated, effaces the identity it would seem to establish, so that, participating, we are unaware of beginning, middle or end, and enter a timeless state of trance. Complementarily a purely melodic, monodic line will tend to become independent of metrical stress, moving in additive rather than divisive rhythms; and this asymmetry will be encouraged by the association of chant with the inflections of the spoken word. This flexibility is not affected by the fact that chants may sometimes be sung heterophonically at several different pitches simultaneously; indeed (as Peter Crossley-Holland tells us), Tibetan monks, chanting at what appears to our ears and to scientific computation to be a multiplicity of different pitches, are unaware that they are not uttering the same note. Most *ad hoc* polyphony or homophony in non-Western music is more accurately termed heterophony, and is certainly not harmonic in our 'European' sense. The great watershed in European history, musically as in every other way, occurred during the Renaissance, when harmony was recognized as the musical consciousness of duality wherein two or more notes bear to one another different vibration ratios. The forms of music may then become gradations of tension and relaxation, *existing in time*. The Renaissance technique of suspension epitomizes this, for the note suspended on the strong beat is resolved on the weak; a concept impossible except in reference to linear and chronometric time. The suspended dissonance, stimulating complex vibrations, to varying degrees excites or hurts; thus the awareness of time implies not only an awareness of beginnings, middles and ends, but also of passion and of pain. The nature of music, intelligible yet untranslatable, has safeguarded it from a rigid separation of the sensuous and intellectual faculties such as occurred between metaphorical poetry and ratiocinative prose. None the less, by way of its new harmonic techniques European music could reconcile its seeds in the 'sensual speech' with the purgatorial experience of modern, Faustian man, making aural his mental strife, his desire to control his own destiny, in a complex ordering of the stresses and counterstresses of linear and harmonic organization.

It is in this context that we can best understand the crucial position in European history of J. S. Bach who, rooted in his Baroque present, looked back to a medieval past, and at the same time anticipated the future — which is ourselves. One may suspect that his appeal is almost primeval, for in his music one is seldom totally divorced from a motor rhythm which, like that of 'primitive' musics, is regular, reiterated, non-developing: as unremittent as the turning earth, as continuous as the surging sea. It is not fortuitous that Bach's music may be jazzed, swung, or rocked more readily than that of any other classically trained European composer; its rhythm is close to Nature, viscerally rooted in the human body, moving in temporal units around the speed of the pulse, which feels right for a remarkably high proportion of Bach's music, irrespective of the pace of the figuration. Over this earth-beat independent polyphonies sing and wing, often transcending, sometimes even contradict-ing, the beat, so that the lines induce ecstasy, as does religious chant. But the rhythmic energy and linear ecstasy of Bach's music are more potent than those of primitive song-dance or religious monody because its 'many voices', sounding together, bring with them varying degrees of tension and relaxation, and collaterally a sense of progression. The 'ecstasis' that Bach's polyphony evokes is the more miraculous because his apprehension of human anguish — manifest in his use of dissonance — is so intense. The simultaneously temporal and atemporal nature of Bach's music is thus exactly mirrored in the simultaneously harmonic-vertical and linear-horizontal character of his technique: in this sense he may be said to be the supreme composer of the Christian Cross, itself a metaphor at once vertical and horizontal. I shall have much to say of this in later chapters; here I need only point out that, given its philosophical basis, Bach's music remains consistent in approach and technique, despite the diverse functions it fulfilled. The larger part of his output has explicit relationships with the myths, dogma and liturgy of his church. Even when he composed in purely instrumental terms, however, he employed the same musical imagery in similar ways; for him all music was a 'harmonious euphony for the glory of God and the instruction of my neighbour'. This made a difference to Bach's treatment of the fashionable conventions of his day, dominated by the opera house and the dance.

Post-Renaissance man, believing in his potential if not absolute Perfectibility, naturally thought that human actions were worth imitating. This is why in the seventeenth century music's centre of gravity shifted from the church (ecclesiastical polyphony) to the home (secular polyphony — the madrigal), and from there to the opera house; and it is also why early opera composers were obsessed by the myth of Orpheus, a non-Christian man who, through Reason and Art (his lute-lyre), challenged the gods in controlling Nature (the birds and beasts) and even in confronting death itself. Most heroic operas took their themes from classical mythology rather than from

Christian tradition; and all dealt with the attempt of man⁄as⁄hero to play God in ordering and controlling men and Nature. All such attempts were doomed, since man is not God, but mortal and fallible; any solution to this dilemma can be no more than wish⁄fulfilment, as is the device of the *deus ex machina* who descends from 'above' to put right the mess made by blundering mortals.

In Baroque opera there are three interrelated facets of musical technique; Bach was trained in, and became expert in the use of, all of them. The first, which represents the public or social life, is the metrical order of the dance, originally derived from the dances of the court masque, which were literally a symbol of human solidarity in the here⁄and⁄now. Men and women, measuring *time* as they beat the earth with their feet, create concord within a clearly defined system of harmonic order and tonal relationships. By Bach's day this public order of the dance had been stabilized into what we call binary form: usually a sixteen⁄ or thirty⁄two⁄bar tune over fundamental diatonic harmonies, modulating to the dominant, with a second half usually mirroring the first and returning to the tonic. Significantly the form may be called 'architectural', its proportions being as symmetrically disposed as the buildings erected by the god⁄presuming aristocratic monarch. The architectural metaphor suggests how binary dance⁄forms measure time metrically and measure space harmonically and tonally, thus imposing man's will on chaos.

At the opposite pole to this public life of the dance is the private life of recitative, sung⁄spoken to a rudimentary harmonic accompaniment. *Recitativo secco* was 'dry' because it wasn't clearly differentiated from the speech in which human beings normally conversed as they lived out their private lives. Recitative may, however, *become* differentiated from speech when human beings are 'beside themselves' with passion, driven by love, hate, madness, despair or transports of joy; then it is sublimated into lyrical arioso, accompanied not merely by the basic harmony of the continuo, but by obbligato instruments also. In aspiring to arioso men, 'beyond' themselves, at once fulfil and transcend their humanity. Bach always sets Christ's words as arioso.

Between the extremes of the public life of the dance and the private life of recitative and arioso stands the mediator of aria. In Baroque opera, arias are private in that they're usually sung by individuals, with lyrical lines that often spring from physical gestures, reinforced by often impassioned harmonic tensions in their relationship with the continuo. At the same time an aria is public in that each aria —of love, of rage, of bellicosity and so on —has and is controlled by a given dance rhythm, often with allegorical intent. Formally, the structure is not binary, like the actual dances, but ternary. A symmetrical (often thirty-two bar) melody is stated, in its particular dance rhythm with conventionally disposed harmonies and tonality, usually ending in the key in which it began; this is followed by a middle section in a related key, often the relative, which serves as architectural balance rather than dramatic contrast; and the aria is completed by a literal repetition of its first section, modified only by traditional, usually improvised, ornamentation. A da capo aria thus does not grow or evolve; it is, or at least it would be, concerned with absolutes of experience, so that most heroic arias, even if fast and furious, are meditation after the event rather than events in action. Private passion is disciplined by public necessity: dance rhythm and tonal symmetry are imposed on what might be mere whim. Arias are thus concerned with the heroic ideal of civilization, which of its nature must be a compromise between individual wilfulness and social good. Only when singing arioso are the characters in Baroque opera unabashedly uttering the heart's truth — a procedure which, of course, is prone to threaten civilization.

It is hardly an exaggeration to say that all the forms and conventions of high Baroque music derive from these three fundamental elements of heroic opera, in manifold interrelationship. Bach never wrote an opera, though he employed these techniques in church music no less than in secular cantatas. How he adapted secular techniques to his sacred purposes we'll discuss in detail in later chapters. At this point it will be helpful to examine how Bach's music differs from that of more representatively high Baroque contemporaries (such as Handel and Telemann).

The most important instrumental form of the period was the concerto grosso, which owes its pre-eminence to the fact that it is an instrumental microcosm of the techniques of heroic opera. Its title implies *concerted*: people working and striving to make a coherent whole (civilization). None the less, concern for the whole must imply respect for the individual; this is the difference between civilization and oligarchy. In the classic form of the concerto grosso the private-public dichotomy is not between a soloist and a band but between a group of soloists (the *concertino*) and the tutti (*concerto*), thus resembling the relationship between singers and orchestra in Mozartian rather than high Baroque opera. This is not surprising since the concerto grosso, being less rigidly tied to the ceremony and economy of specific courts, survived longer than *opera seria*, gradually merging into sonata-styled music. A concerto grosso is an experiment in private relations which fit into, because they help to create, a public whole. So the forms of concerti grossi are closed, but not so closed as those of heroic operas, in which there is little ensemble work because they're directly concerned with a conflict between public morality and private passion. In effect the arias—of love, rage, terror or what else—are saying 'Look what's happening to *me*, a private man or woman impossibly placed in this public situation'.

In a concerto grosso there is a move *towards* resolving the tension between private and public values. The norms are still those of defined diatonic tonalities in given relationships—tonic, dominant, subdominant, relative, sometimes mediants—in socially sanctioned, time-measuring, space-enclosing dance forms. But the basic binary structure is often extended, the second 'half' of the mirror getting longer than the first, embracing more movement (modulation), more variety of figuration and rhythm, tending towards sonata; while the ternary forms often used for slow movements may occasionally introduce into the middle section dramatic contrast, even conflict, thereby potentially threatening an authoritarian view of the world, which the rhythmic uniformity and tonal stability of the style reflect. Most typical is the form often used for finales—the modulating rondo. A rondo, being a sophisticated form of round dance, is basically a circular, closed form appropriate to the old society. But if the thematic permutations and tonal modulations of the episodes effect the recurrences of the rondo theme, it is breaking out of its circle, moving towards 'development', growing through conflict towards self-knowledge, towards all the features of the new sonata style. One sees this if one compares the concerti of Handel and Vivaldi. Handel's genius consists in a tension between social expectation and the realities of experience; but in assuring us that he wants 'civilization' to prevail, he created the supreme classical prototype—technically brilliant, emotionally mature—of the concerto grosso. Vivaldi's case is more ambiguous, for in introducing relatively 'low' material from peasantry and urban artisans, he opened the form democratically: street tunes and rustically droning bagpipes jostle with the elegance of aristocratic social intercourse, often with ironic effect. Complementarily, the structure is loosened.

But if Handel is the most classically representative of concerto grosso composers, Bach is the greatest; and his concerti are at once archetypal—in that they most profoundly reveal the human impulses behind the evolution of the form—and unique. This is typical of his status among the composers of his time, all of whom were men of faith in that they believed in, and employed musical conventions that reflected, an autocratic world. But Bach, born out of

as well as within his time, was a composer of faith in a different and
fundamentally religious sense; from this springs, as we've seen, his music's
synthesis of horizontal and vertical, linear and harmonic, metaphysical and
physical, elements. This remains true even in secular, aristocratic-autocratic
music composed for a mundane lord and master, as in the Brandenburg
Concertos, which were written to grace the Margrave's courtly ceremonial.
Technically the difference lies in Bach's more developed polyphony and
counterpoint, even in works based on the celebration of human solidarity
through the dance. This is clear even in the first concerto, which is closest to
the old, aristocratic-autocratic world. It's scored for 'royal' horns and oboes,
instruments of the chase, plus strings; its first movement's themes tend to be
arpeggiated, earthy, stable. At the same time the many-in-oneness of the
counterpoint, the terraced groupings, the antiphonal dialogue and soli and tutti
and the relatively wide-ranging modulations in the middle section become an
interchange between groups, a metaphor for social organization. And the
slow movement subtly and profoundly modifies the metaphor: although it is
still dialogue, the solo lines, if operatic, are Passion music as well as
passionate music. Over the beat of the pulse they break the time-barrier; from
the physical they become metaphysical, so that social experience becomes
'universal'. The close on the dominant carries us back from this metaphysical
excursion to the courtly world, and to a movement similar to the first but,
being in 6/8, more dance-like. The human excitation of the modulatory middle
section is also a release: so in a sense the manners of the first and second
movements are fused. But Bach ends with his feet firmly on the Margrave's earthy
earth: with a conventional suite of dances, social music for dancing to, if
distanced, and perhaps universalized, by the linearity of Bach's technique.

The pattern suggested by the first three movements of this concerto is
followed, with many variations, by the other concerti. The fifth carries the
private-public dichotomy and synthesis to its farthest point. The key is heroic
D major, the soloists are flute, violin and harpsichord. The first Allegro begins
in C time, with arpeggiated trumpet-style themes reflecting power and glory: a
tactful tribute to the Margrave's majesty. But the soloists' interplay in complex
and syncopated cross-rhythms complicates this extroversion, as the music
moves through spacious modulations to dominant, relative and subdominant.
Demisemiquaver scales introduced by the harpsichord in bar 47 are a hint of
things to come; though immediately sequential modulations to B minor, A
major and F sharp minor still the polyphony to repeated quavers, with
sustained pedal notes. The original theme returns in the dominant, rather as in

a sonata development, then in the tonic again. As the texture subsides into homophony the solo harpsichord grows increasingly prominent. Being a harmonic instrument, the harpsichord is most capable of human passion, through its capability for varied tone colour, vibrant sonority, and for exciting passage-work and excruciating dissonance. What happens here is that the individual, represented by the harpsichordist, gradually takes over from the whole, first in whirling scales, then in exploding chains of diminished sevenths, ultimately in an immense solo cadenza. The idiom of this cadenza strikingly resembles that of Bach's orgiastic Chromatic Fantasia, probably giving us a notion as to how he improvised when most 'carried away'. Significantly, however, this riot of keyboard passion and dexterity becomes, from its obstreperously sensual source, an ecstasis. As the individual takes over, he also takes off, in Dionysiac abandon; momentarily the cadenza highlights the individual life, and the human becomes divine. No other composer of Bach's period ever risked so much, allowing the irrational to have its fling, even in the midst of rational order. That Bach could do so makes his order the more to be valued; we heave a sigh of relief when the final tutti simply and briefly brings us back to the everyday world. At the same time we know we've been eternally privileged to travel with Bach on that wild excursion.

The slow movement is again Passion music, a trio sonata which translates operatic convention into religious ritual: it is a free canon, three in one; yet in its suspensions is also, as Bach indicates, humanly *affetuoso*, in B minor — Bach's key of suffering, the relative complement to D major's glory. The gigue is a modulating rondo which effects a synthesis of the dance rhythm's corporeality with the potential heavenly grace of the lyrically winging polyphony.

The third concerto has a similar pattern, though in detail it is very different. For this time there is no overt dichotomy between concertino and tutti; or, rather, there are no soloists because all the players are soloists. The strings are divided into three groups of three, again forming a complex metaphor for social organization that may, given Bach's numerological proclivities, have religious implications too, as a trinity of trinities. At first each group has its own thematic material, riddled with brave arpeggios and brilliant scales. But the density of the texture is compromised by antiphonal badinage between the groups; and the structure is elaborately cyclic, if not developmental. This music, though apparently heavy and stocky, earthbound, generates 'intimations of immortality', and it is completely transformed in the second and last movement. Some think that Bach intended a slow movement to be improvised by a soloist or two, ending with the cadential chords he briefly notated. It seems more likely that the absence of a slow movement was intentional, in that the second movement makes explicit what in the first movement is only implicit. This is not a contrast between individual and group, but rather a working together of individual beings that itself produces ecstasy. The first movement's secular clichés of prancing arpeggios and whirling scales become airborne in an expanded binary form having a second half much longer than the first. The music is a flying, a floating, in fast but long-spanned lines in 12/8—a quaternity of trinities which Bach (as we'll see later) usually associates with heavenly aspiration.

In the Brandenburg Concertos, then, Bach radically reinterpreted a public convention of his day. There is another genre of his work wherein such reinterpretation is yet more fundamental. Since this takes us to the very heart of the Bachian experience we must examine it in greater analytical detail. I refer to his dance suites for the ostensibly improbable medium of solo cello: a monophonic music wherein a man has created a dance of God.

2. Voice and Body: Bach's Solo Cello Suites as an Apotheosis of the Dance

Listening to Bach's dance-dominated music we cannot but be aware that, however he may have started from the Baroque view of dance as human and temporal order, he reinvoked its ancient religious-magical implications. The impulse to project unconscious myth into movements of the body and into sound is perennial, surviving even in today's industrialized societies in the danced games of children wherein, through the interaction of the basic types of line dance and circle dance, duality is healed. Such collective enterprise is an act simultaneously social and religious. 'Whosoever knoweth the power of dance,' said the Dervish poet, 'dwelleth in God'; 'we don't merely dance,' say the Witoto, 'we tell tales at the festival'; and the Zuni Indians inform us that 'we dance for pleasure and for the good of the city'. In many high civilizations, such as the Chinese, dance, associated with music, was considered essential to the preservation of the cosmos.

Bach cannot have been aware how radically his idea of dance differed from that current in the eighteenth century; the evidence is simply audible in his work, and nowhere more impressively than in the suites for solo cello. They were written around 1720 when Bach, living at Cöthen, served a secular court rather than an ecclesiastical authority. And just when his music had of necessity to be dance-oriented, he became fascinated by the technical problem of writing music for melody instruments unaccompanied. For Bach, a technical problem was also spiritual: he would start with the instruments of his age, which were admirably developed to perform concerted, harmonized music accompanying social dancing, and would demonstrate that it was possible to create for them monodic music which did not cease to be dance in becoming also an act of praise. For such an experiment the evolution of Baroque stringed instruments was ripe. Although the bass instrument still survived in a solo capacity, viols had been superseded by the violin family. The chest of viols had roughly corresponded to the natural ranges of the human voice — treble, alto, tenor and bass; and the method of playing the instruments, with the bow resting in the upturned hand, made for flexible, vocal-style rhythm, without aggressive accents. The violins were not newly invented instruments. In the sixteenth century they'd been regarded as of low provenance, suitable for rowdy and jocund entertainment, while the viols were reserved for 'serious' music, usually polyphonic, though sometimes extending dance forms into large-scale pieces. Changing needs relegated the viols to history and transformed the violins into representative instruments of the Baroque era — because they could sing lyrically, like human voices, but with a range and agility beyond human resource; because their tone could be humanly expressive or ceremonially brilliant, penetrative through the large halls or chambers wherein music of the heroic world was likely to be performed; and because they were as well adapted for the execution of dance metres as they were for lyrical melody. The changed technique of bowing, with the bow held from above and therefore more capable of metrical accent, is pertinent.

If we think of the Baroque age as the triumph of post-Renaissance humanism, we can accept the sexual symbolism of bow and string as all-embracing. The instrument is passively female, the bow actively male; together male and female result in creation. As Herbert Whone has put it:

> In the perfect balance of bow and violin lies the principle of here and now awareness. . . . As in a male-female relationship, over-aggression in the male, or lack of response from the female, can destroy harmony. . . . In terms of the violin, the tightness of egotism (in the Post-Renaissance world) can be seen in the tension of the string, and the new love can be seen in the relationship between the bow and the string. Bow and violin, in this new state, are two reciprocal parts of a whole. Whether we see the word 'violin' as coming from 'vol' (German root) or 'vil' (Italian root), the violin is essentially to do with the will. The playing of the violin is the enactment of life itself. The bow, operating on the right side, the side of power, stimulates the universal female womb (the left side), giving life to all the potential forms within it, symbolized by the fingers of the left hand. With the substance wooed by the will, and the ensuing form vitalized, the work is complete — a perfected man in whom every second of consciousness, like every second the bow is on the string, is a second in time and eternity.

Bach's music for solo violin and solo cello is the ultimate manifestation of this 'humanization' of an instrument. The cello, even more than the violin, becomes a projection of a total human being. Its timbre is closest of all instruments to that of a wide-ranging male voice; physically, it calls for

movements of arms, trunk and shoulders, so that to play a cello is at once to
sing and dance within time. Moreover, a solo line can seek maximum
independence, while implying maximum density of harmony, epitomizing
the technical features whereby Bach's music reveals, as we have seen, its
simultaneously physical and metaphysical nature. In his solo violin works
Bach sometimes spells out the harmonies in multiple stopping, even to the
extent of creating the illusion of a four-part organ fugue for solo fiddle. In the
solo cello suites, he is more austere, and in a sense more profound. He writes
few quasi-fugato passages, and adheres strictly to the conventions of the dance
suite of his age. A high proportion of the writing is purely monodic; when
harmonies are stated in multiple stopping, their function as accompaniment to
melody is usually clear. The suites are thus central to Bach's achievement: the
music springs from the dance and from the corporeal act of playing the cello,
yet in the process earthbound temporality is sublimated into continuous line.
As a human being *dances* and *sings* through the physicality of a cello, he
becomes a dancing god. In the words of the Gnostic hymn of Jesus:

> But as for Me, if thou wouldst know what I was:
> In a word I am the Word who did dance
> All things, and was not shamed at all.
> 'Twas I who leapt and danced.

Or as Spenser put it, 'Form is Soul, and doth the Body make'. If Bach
composed the suites as home music, it must have been with divinely endowed
performers in mind. It's not merely acoustical accident that makes this secular
music sound overwhelmingly impressive when played in an ecclesiastical
building.

    Bach keeps to the sequence of dances as it had been established by the
seventeenth-century French lutanists and harpsichordists who had adapted
them from the dances of the Renaissance court. He employs the French
language for his elegant title-page, whereas he had used Italian terminology for
the solo violin works. The fourth suite, in E flat major, will serve as our point
of departure. It opens — as do all the suites, on the precedent of the French
lutanists — with a prelude which is not strictly a dance, but rather a loosening-
up exercise: an example of Bach's metamorphosis of a technical problem into
spiritual experience; for having begun with the physical nature of the cello as a
monodic instrument capable, through the spreading of chords across the strings,
of simulating harmonic textures, it flowers into cantilena that sunders the
barriers of metrical time. It becomes religious music, in a sense that will become

manifest when we discuss the closely related arioso in the *St. John Passion*, which is also in E flat major, a key often used by Bach to symbolize, with its three flats, the peace of mind that flows from the Trinity.

For the first nine bars the music is earthbound, a low tonic pedal being affirmed on the first beat of each 4/4 bar. There is no apparent melody, let alone a theme; but the gravely falling arpeggiated chords move in steady quavers effecting, at the top of each group, a slow decline from tonic to flattened seventh to subdominant 6/4, and so to dominant seventh dissonantly elided with the tonic pedal:

Ex. 1

In the ninth bar the E flat triad is reinstated, lower in register, but in bar 10 the bass moves for the first time, its scalewise descent from E flat to D to C echoing the earlier descent in the top line, now stably on the beat instead of off the beat on the second quaver. The C minor arpeggio unfolds as the bass moves down another third to A natural, which acts as sharp seventh in effecting a modulation to the dominant. The almost immobile character of the opening has thus been undermined; and over the next thirteen bars the energy increases with modulations from the dominant to its minor, to subdominant, to relative minor (C), and to *its* subdominant minor (F) —traditionally the key of *chants lugubres*. Throughout these modulations intervallic tension rises steadily, beginning with the plunge through a major seventh between bars 26 and 27 and embracing diminished fourth and diminished seventh in the F minor passage. This harmonic momentum causes the bass to push up from E natural to F, in bar 35, rather than to fall; and although the tonic is reinstated by way of arpeggiated dominant sevenths, the gravely articulated quavers now rise, as well as descend, in slowly tumultuous waves. And the reassertion of the tonic is not in fact a return home, for a first inversion tonic leads to an extended passage built on diminished sevenths, dominant sevenths and tonic triads in G minor, until there's a cadential half-close on the dominant ninth:

Ex. 2

This acts as a dramatic, even rhetorical climax, though passion is disciplined because the last four bars have re‑established the pattern of falling arpeggios. The silence that then occurs is itself action; after the cumulative animation, it seems almost inevitable that the line should now spurt in stepwise‑moving semiquavers, in a three‑bar phrase of vast span. This relapses into the falling quaver arpeggios, still in G minor, until written‑out turns are incorporated into the semiquaver flow, culminating in a spread dissonance of a dominant minor ninth, followed by a swirling downward scale. The quaver arpeggios are reinstated with a firm cadence in G minor, but have acquired, from the semiquaver surge, mobility instead of immobility. Thrusting both up and down they move flatwards from G minor to F minor, then flatwards again to B flat minor and to the flattest E flat minor, their movement agitated by semiquavers. The Neapolitan cadence on a first inversion of the chord of F flat is an explosion, which resolves, cadenza‑like, on to a perfect cadence (balancing the earlier cadence into G minor) moving back from dominant to tonic of the original E flat major:

Ex. 3

At this point there's a six‑bar da capo of the opening, which sounds stable after the piece's momentous evolution. To conclude, there's another and longer cadenza of running semiquavers, descending from the D above middle C to the low E flat, which forms the bass of a quadruple‑stopped tonic triad.

The asymmetrical structure of this prelude contributes to its momentum. The first forty‑eight bars swing like a pendulum, unbroken, generating eleven modulatory bars moving from dominant major to its relative G minor, cadencing on the diminished seventh of its dominant. Passages of semiquaver arioso alternate with the pendulum of the arpeggios, producing, after thirteen bars, a full close in G minor. The next twenty bars modulate widely, but cadence in the tonic major by way of its dark, Neapolitan‑enhanced minor. Ten more bars round off the piece with a truncated da capo and an arioso‑like cadenza. The prelude thus effects a tragic alternation of repose and movement, oscillating between two types of figuration (quaver arpeggios, semiquaver scales and turns), polarized on two keys, E flat major and G minor. Later, when we analyse the *St. John Passion*, we'll see that in that work G minor would seem to 'represent' the tragic turbulence of human life, E flat major the

certitude of Christian grace, the Godhead incarnate in man. There is a specific
parallel with the bass arioso (no. 31) of the Passion, since that sublime
movement employs earth-weighted, descending quaver arpeggios in E flat
simultaneously to suggest a purgatorial pilgrimage, falling tears and
enveloping wings. There too the stillness of the drooping arpeggios generates
action, which promotes tension, which ultimately flowers into lyrical release.
In the context of Bach's music as a whole we may, indeed, hear the coda to this
cello prelude as a resurrection.

For Bach, it seems, music and theology are inseparable, as are pedagogic
technique and spiritual allegory. This is not belied by the second movement
which, being a dance, has a stronger pull to the earth, for here too the physical
is complementary to the metaphysical. The first dance of the French suite was
traditionally an allemande, which had gradually replaced the courtly pavane.
Rousseau says that an allemande '*se bat gravement à 4 tems*', while Thomas Mace
had described it as 'heavie, fitly representing the Nature of the People whose
name it carryeth, so that no Extraordinary Motions are used in dancing it'. In
the event, the earthiness of allemandes was modified by their linear and
rhythmic complexity, so that for Bach as for Couperin they became serious,
even at times sacramental. This allemande offers relief after the prelude's tragic
grandeur yet proves, as it evolves, a comparable kind of music. The theme
begins with an offbeat leap up a fourth; flows into scalewise lyricism
undulating down from the E flat above middle C to G on the bottom stave;
and counterpoises this surging melody with four bars of quasi-two-part
polyphony. The line bounces up a seventh, down an eleventh, up a tenth, the
figure being repeated in free sequence to cadence in the tonic in the middle of the
sixth bar:

Ex. 4

The answering clause echoes this alternation of flowing scales and prancing
leaps, but is more exuberant (modulating to the dominant) and more
extended (covering ten bars). The first half of the binary structure thus has the
conventional sixteen bars, but divided as six plus ten, not eight plus eight.

After the double bar it seems at first that Bach will repeat the six-bar phrase,
starting from the dominant; but the semiquaver scales flow longer and
cadence, with the widest leaps thus far, in the tonic's relative, C minor. In the

answering phrase the cantilena takes off from the beat, as scales mingled with written-out trills carry us to C minor's dominant and subdominant. The return to the tonic brings a quasi da capo; but there is hardly any literal repetition as the sweeping phrases, sometimes tied across the beat, are expanded to seventeen bars. Though this is not among the more complicated of Bach's allemandes, its dance-like character is thus modified by a kind of linear sublimation. It's always about to be airborne, and is a slighter piece than the prelude mainly because its harmonic implications are more straightfor-ward.

The next dance in the suite, the courante, had two forms, at different speeds. French courantes exploit rhythmic contradiction and ambiguity, Italian courantes flow in graceful quavers, in 3/4. In the cello suites Bach's courantes are usually Italianate, probably because he wants them to serve as foil to the allemande's gravity. This courante from the E flat major suite doesn't emulate the prelude's and allemande's equilibrium between earthly rhythm and heavenly melodic flight; however, the dance's earthiness is equivocal, largely because of its metrical trickiness. The first four bars are triggered off by a descending fourth on the beat, inverting the allemande's offbeat rising fourth. The phrase is jolly, modulates conventionally to the dominant, but then unexpectedly breaks into quaver triplets:

Ex. 5

This produces a slightly tipsy effect when, after eight bars, the phrase is extended, with gaping leaps through an eleventh. Four bars of sequential quavers bring back the triplets with double stops on the strong beats — an almost risible hiatus. Octave skips and a medley of quaver, semiquaver and triplet scales lead to a perky full close, accented on the second beat in the dominant.

After the double bar the opening phrase is imitated literally in the new key. The sequential passage is, however, extended through fifteen bars, closing in the relative C minor. The remaining twenty bars merely return to the tonic, with occasional touches of subdominant. The character of the music is none the less changed, for the line flows with more flexibility, interweaving its quavers, triplets and semiquavers. The tipsiness acquires a faint flavour of the allemande's levitation, flowing scalewise, suddenly leaping through a seventh, an eleventh, a fifteenth. Bach seems to be reminding us that experience cannot be categorized. In his divine comedy hilarity may at any moment turn into exaltation; too highly developed a sense of human dignity may lead to an ungodly self-importance.

The sarabande was the oldest of the masque dances, said to have been introduced into France from Spain in 1588. Originally fast and considered lascivious, it slowed to a courtly grace during the seventeenth century, acquiring its characteristic stress on the second beat. By Bach's time it was not only ceremonial but also solemn, sometimes even sacral, a marriage or altar dance: he creates vast if modified sarabandes for the final choruses of both the *St. John* and the *St. Matthew Passions*. Not surprisingly therefore, the sarabandes are always the centre of emotional gravity in the cello suites; that from the E flat suite transports us back to the passionate and Passion-laden aura of the prelude. That the music is sensuous is manifest in the fact that its harmonic texture is explicit, for it makes considerable use of multiple stopping. Yet if this harmonic richness implies duality, it is still subservient to the gravely arching line, which moves scalewise from fifth to flat seventh and resolves by way of a double appoggiatura. The phrase is imitated a fourth lower, but instead of cadencing thrusts sequentially from subdominant to its relative (F minor), and to its subdominant (B flat major). The dotted rhythm, as often in sarabandes, should probably be played with the dots nearly doubled, creating an effect at once ceremonial and tense.

This section expands the conventional eight bars to twelve, which are answered after the double bar by a twenty-bar period. Beginning with a literal repetition of the scalic rise to the flat seventh of the new key, this modulates directly to C minor, and then to its subdominant, with resonant triple stopping:

Ex. 6

Grandly leaping, the double-dotted rhythm returns to the tonic and its enhanced dominant. Subtle metrical ambiguities occur between the arioso line, the conventional sarabande stress on the second beat, and intermittent metrical disruption caused by offbeat triple stopping—for instance the dominant on the last beat of bar 22. This is a Passion aria, rather than arioso: it contains the duality created by written-out, not merely implied, harmony as well as the tight-lipped pride of ceremonial rhythm and metrical ambiguity, yet absolves these qualities in lyrical song. Such a purgatorial progress is epitomized in the last bar, wherein the rising arpeggio, balancing the declension at the end of the first half, implies triumph, while the dissonant sharp seventh reminds us of our 'crucial' pain. Though courtly and sensual, this dance clearly is also devotional. The final resolution on the high E flat is ambiguous; either it hangs in the air on the third beat or we hear it as a cross accent in duple time.

After the emotional climax, at once high and deep, of a sarabande, Bach habitually brings us back to the ground with galanteries such as minuets, or with rowdier dances such as bourrées and gavottes. The first bourrée from the E flat suite accepts its earthiness without quibble, being melodically simple, rhythmically regular and tonally rudimentary. Beginning conventionally on the upbeat, it modulates in twelve bars to an equally conventional dominant. It is, however, no routine affair; and its piquancy springs from the contrast between the upbeat semiquaver runs, the metrical angularity of the second bar's *ta ta-ta ta* rhythm, and the three weighty crotchets that conclude the phrase with a descending octave. Moreover, after the double bar, this simplicity is compromised. Modulation to the relative C minor prompts a dominant seventh arpeggio, which seems to give energy, even a certain wildness, to the originally sturdy leaps:

Ex. 7

While the tonal scheme remains basic, the figurations are combined in patterns complex because ambiguous, over thirty-six bars—three times as long as the first section. Something like a climax occurs when the *ta ta-ta ta* rhythm is diminished to quavers and semiquavers. The originally gawky rhythm becomes slightly hectic; when it bursts into a rising dominant seventh arpeggio in the tonic (balancing that in C minor in the first section) it sounds unbridled, almost a belly-laugh. The coda is a free da capo, modified by a cross-rhythm with dotted crotchets on the second beat—an effect at once witty and exciting:

Ex. 8

In this context the regularity of the final five bars is the more satisfying.

In the second bourrée or trio there is no modulation and a minimum of rhythmic variety. Double stops suggest a rustic hurdy-gurdy, without evoking a beer-garden in some pre-conscious Eden, as later musette trios in Mozart, Schubert and Mahler often do. It is, however, dreamy as compared with the straw-booted solidity of the first bourrée which, when played da capo, sounds more disturbed and disturbing than we'd suspected. The two bourrées are each in binary form but together form a classical scherzo and trio. Admitting to this duality, they are the most 'modern' movements in the suite, and the least musically substantial.

The concluding dance in the suites is usually a lively gigue, which originally came from England and was described by a contemporary French authority as 'vive et un peu folle'. Commonly gigues are in a lilting 6/8, which was the Italian convention. French and German gigues were sometimes more complicated, however, and we can find traces of this in the cello suites, though not in this particular E flat gigue. If a lightweight piece, it is not, however, as simple as it looks. For one thing it is notated in 12/8 rather than 6/8, which suggests that Bach thought of it as more airborne, melodically wider-spanned, than a conventional gigue. For another thing the first section runs to ten instead of eight bars, making a disquieting effect because of its unexpected descent, in the middle of the second bar, from the seventh to the low tonic. This faintly comic hiatus is only momentary, for the quavers then flow evenly to their expected dominant cadence. After the double bar the frustrated phrase is extended, from the dominant, through several keys, the modulation to G minor being so long sustained that it has something of the effect of a middle section in a sonata movement. There's tension between the quavers' buzzing around a nodal point (as in Couperin's Le moucheron) and their desire to spring upwards in arpeggio. A da capo, which might almost be styled a recapitulation, begins in bar 27, modulating flatwards to the subdominant instead of sharpwards to the dominant. We touch on the subdominant's relative, F minor, and its subdominant, B flat minor; but upward leaping arpeggios take over from the fly-like nagging and buzzing, sailing back to a merry tonic major. Despite the 12/8 time signature, there's little exaltation in this gigue, though the downward bump in the last bar is hilarious:

Ex. 9

I suggested in reference to the courante that with Bach hilarity and ecstasy may be interrelated. This may be why the gigue, without aspiring to the heights and depths of the prelude, allemande and sarabande, makes a satisfying conclusion to the suite. Despite its dancing facility, it has a dramatic structure with beginning, middle and end, polarized on the same E flat major-G minor axis as the prelude. It doesn't deny the prelude's purgatorial experience, though it brings us back to our everyday world, wherein we chug rather than float along, sometimes lumpishly reaching heavenwards, sometimes ignominiously slipping on the banana skin which, as mortals, we're all liable to encounter. In comically complementing the tragic prelude, the gigue rounds off a cycle of experience.

The Christian Trinity and Passion cast both their light and their shadow on this secular dance music. The D major suite, on the other hand, begins as a celebration of the visible, audible and tactile world, in the key of trumpets and of resonating open strings, and gathers spiritual under- and overtones. It is the last, greatest and grandest of the suites; and Bach must have intended it to be such, since he gave it imposing dimensions and scored it for a five-stringed cello, tuned conventionally in fifths, with an extra E on top. The prelude immediately affirms the cello's physical nature, for it starts as an exploration of reverberating open strings, sonorously swinging in 12/8. Yet although the resonance is sensuous, the wide span of the clauses overrides any hint of the cloddishness that makes the 12/8 E flat gigue fallibly human. Here sonorousness flows from the open strings, at first in echoed repetitions, the quavers surging like the sea, rotating around the open pedal notes, yet aspiring upwards. So vast is the range of the piece that, as we see in the noble calligraphy of Bach's wife Anna Magdalena, the composer calls on the bass, alto and soprano clefs.

The first twelve bars of unbrokenly rocking quavers move sharpwards from tonic to dominant, at which point the open string pedal notes are re-established on the dominant A. The next ten bars repeat the pattern of rotations and soarings, balancing the sharpwards modulation with a subdominant modulation to G and its relative E minor. The open string pedal is reaffirmed on the high E (the instrument's extra string); and the quavers swing cyclically up the fifths from E minor to B minor to F sharp minor, still singing, if slightly agonized because of the altitude. Tonal excitation is reinforced at bar 41 by upward-lunging arpeggios, balanced, however, by tonal declension back to B minor, D major and the subdominant G. The open-string resonance booms on the low G (bar 54), then sweeps back to the tonic, with dominant enhancement. At bar 70 high Ds ring like celestial trumpets, until the rising exaltation creates an upward-swirling dotted figure, exploding in cascades of semiquavers sweeping in an immense descent, then undulating in waves across the strings:

Ex. 10

The intrusion of flat sevenths leads to a diminished seventh approach to the open A string (bars 88–90). The reverberating As change to tonic Ds, with a climax closing in a triple-stopped chord sequence moving chromatically from the dominant seventh of A, to first inversion G minor, to a chromaticized 6–4 cadence in D:

Ex. 11

These are the only bars in this long piece in which the quaver pulsation is halted. A coda of arpeggiated waves stretches over four octaves in defining a IV–V–I peroration.

What makes this prelude so powerful is the seeming inevitability of its unfolding. It starts from the physical fact of playing the cello—especially this large instrument with its five strings. Corporeal motor rhythm carries all before it, yet the line grows from within so that when, after seventy-eight unbroken bars, the quavers seethe into semiquavers, it feels like the process of birth itself. A technical exercise has become a paean of praise; the triple-stopped cadence and coda shout hosanna. So although the prelude celebrates human sensuality and the physicality of the cello it becomes no less profoundly a religious piece than the Passion-fraught E flat prelude. With Bach the celebration of Nature's creativity is a manifestation of the divine. The 12/8 gigue of the E flat suite is as much about our fallibility as about our aspiration; this 12/8 prelude, however, demonstrates how man's sensual nature may contain, *in potentia*, celestial bliss.

To cap this tremendous piece Bach creates a dance movement, an allemande, that carries us as far beyond the thump of human feet in an act of social solidarity as the prelude takes us beyond technical experiment. We have noted that, after the sarabande, the allemande is usually the most serious, and certainly the most complicated, of the dances in a French suite; but not even Bach wrote an allemande more imposing in its continuous lyrical span. This D major allemande is a supreme example of Bach's cantilena, comparable with the cornucopias of Nature's fecundity that embellish Baroque churches with birds, beasts, twining tendrils and filigreed foliage: a riot of sensuality that paradoxically, since it seems without beginning, middle or end, takes us outside time and space. None the less the emotional effect of the allemande depends on the fact that its passion is disciplined; one might equate its freedom with soaring melodic arabesque, its discipline with latent body rhythm and with the pull of harmonic roots that define the metre. One senses the rhythm more as a slowly swaying two than as a gravely paced four, since the swing of the pendulum is underlined by double-stopped chords, two to each bar. The melody sings resonantly in the tenor register with an upbeat approach to a D major triad. The sensuous third, at the top of the chord, flows into cantilena in demisemiquavers (with a written-out turn) only to be held back, on the third beat, by a sustained quaver appoggiatura. Another turn leads into more undulating demisemiquavers, and a written-out trill. The second bar begins with the D major triad now elevated to first inversion, and repeats, more urgently, the pattern of forward melodic flow retarded by harmonic suspension:

Ex. 12

Bar 3 takes us back to the D major triad in root position, lifts it high in ringing sixths, in a ceremoniously dotted rhythm, the thrust of which not only releases more lilting figuration, but also provokes modulations to dominant and relative minor. Pulsing on, reinforced by trills and triple stops, the lyrical line is again checked by the dotted rhythm. When the arabesques spurt again, trill-garlanded, they modulate decisively to the dominant. Stopped chords thin out in the last two of the eight noble bars; cantilena flows luxuriously, though the pattern of forward pulse halted by sustained notes in dotted rhythm is not abandoned.

The tempo at which this eight-bar period is played is critical. It must be leisurely enough for the arabesques to be articulated clearly, but not so slow that body rhythm disintegrates. Given the right tempo the transformation of earth rhythm into a heavenly flight occurs with apparent inevitability, so that we know that the last bar's descent through a dominant arpeggio has brought us to earth only so that we may fly again. This happens in the second 'half': which begins with an echo of the initial bar, but is extended through twelve enormous measures, without much literal repetition. The forward thrusts are now underlined by quadruple stopping; and modulate up the cycle of fifths from E to B to F sharp minor. After bar 15 the multiple stopping disperses as the cantilena soars to the high A. With the return to the tonic the bass also rises, stabilizing the rhythm to approach a IV—V—I cadence. Only at the end of the penultimate bar is the burgeoning of demisemiquavers dammed by a double-stopped chord in dotted rhythm, on the dominant. This is resolved in arabesques which exactly balance the dominant arpeggio at the end of the first section; the return to earth is, however, the more assuaging because of the distance the music has travelled. Throughout, the texture is dense in a manner typical of allemandes; yet at the same time the lines sing ecstatically, culminating in the swirling roulades and immense skips of the final two bars. No piece of Bach lives more 'amphibiously', as Sir Thomas Browne put it, in the worlds of spirit and of flesh.

This the courante doesn't attempt; instead it bounces exuberantly in its persistent metrical pattern ♪♫♪♪ . The gaiety is, however, complicated by the fact that, after the modulation to the dominant, the rhythmic figure is succeeded by running semiquavers, as though melody would escape from metrical domination. This music, though not as tipsy as the rhythmic surprises of the E flat courante, is uneasily hilarious. It comes as a relief when the rhythmic pattern is reasserted for the dominant cadence at the double bar. The second part, being twice as long as the first, exaggerates its effect. The first ten bars return to the tonic and stay there through the sequence of flowing semiquavers. Modulations to dominant and relative occur with the reappearance of the characteristic rhythm, seeming more comic as the cello's skips between registers widen. The long passage of running semiquavers beginning in the thirty-second bar sounds like chuckling; the return to the original rhythm in upward-bouncing arpeggios is almost a guffaw:

Ex. 13

The piece is an overflow of corporeal energy, godlike only in the sense that Bach's laughter might be called Jovian.

The sarabande *is* both human and divine—not because it's a ceremonial dance that, like the E flat sarabande, becomes a Passion aria, but because it reveals the sacramental significance of human love. The most overtly harmonic because the most multi-stopped movement in the cello suites, the sarabande's body-movement is evident from the stressed second beat of the first bar and is referred to recurrently. At the same time it's the most melodic movement in the suites, in that it has a sublime tune, one that looks superficially Handelian. That Bach notates it in 3/2 instead of 3/4 indicates not that it should move slower, but that its manner is grand and courtly. Gravely sensual, the repeated F sharps press up, resonantly spaced in the middle register, to the high B, modulate to the dominant, only to droop, in the answering clause, in sighful pairs of crotchets and dissonant appoggiaturas:

Ex. 14

The heart-easing effect of this eight-bar period depends on its equilibrium between the stately rise from the repeated notes in sarabande rhythm and the weeping descent in paired crotchets, which brings balm.

Only after the double bar are the implications of this evident. A repetition of the opening figure leads to more animated figuration and to a modulation to E minor instead of major. Dissonant suspensions move grandly to E minor's relative, G major, which is also subdominant to the D major tonic. Drooping crotchets phrased in pairs (first heard in bar 7) acquire almost the status of a second subject—a sighful descent transformed into plangent song. Falling in sonorous parallel sixths, these crotchets return to the tonic with a hint of dominant; melody sings suavely; harmony, ripe with sequential dominant sevenths, melts the heart:

Ex. 15

and although the second-beat sarabande rhythm reappears, decorated, in the next bar, there is no strict da capo. The caress of a dominant seventh on the last beat of this bar re-establishes the luxurious parallel sixths, which cadence on multi-stopped suspensions. The last bar begins with an upward-resolving appoggiatura, C sharp to D, balancing the falling appoggiatura in bar 8. In context it's at once an exquisite pain and a release. What has happened in this second part (again three times as long as the first) is that sensual harmony and corporeal rhythm have dissolved into lyrical song; melodic proportion and harmonic evolution are identified. If this sarabande-aria is a love song it reveals once more how for Bach there can be no distinction between love sacred and profane.

The prelude, allemande and sarabande are the high points of this D major suite, and perhaps of the cello suites as a whole. What follows roots us again in our everyday world, much as, at the end of the excursus of the Goldberg Variations, Bach brings us back, in the quodlibet, to the pieties and impieties of his domestic hearth. The D major gavotte is not quite hearth music, though it lives up to D'Alembert's description of gavottes as being of '*une gaieté vive*', if not exactly '*douce*'. Conventionally, it begins on the offbeat of its 2/2 metre. Each offbeat phrase opens with repeated note crotchets that prompt stepwise-moving quavers; each beat is stockily emphasized by triple or quadruple stopping. The repeated notes, in the stolid rhythm, sound in context almost like a parody of the sarabande's initial phrase; or perhaps it would be truer to say that the gavotte reveals the common sociability which, in the sarabande, had been 'sacramentally' transcended. In the gavotte men and women lumpishly if lovingly dance together; in the sarabande human love offers a glimpse of heaven. There is one essential quality—apart from the thematic correspondence—that relates this peasant-like piece to the sarabande's sublimity: it has a tune so powerfully memorable that it has almost acquired the status of a pop number. Though simple, this tunefulness is far from simple-minded, as is evident when, after the double bar, Bach modulates to E minor and B minor, and underlines the return to D with ponderous quadruple stopping:

Ex. 16

There are no class distinctions in Bach's music, which finds most people worthy of respect as members of the family of God.

The second gavotte or trio is again in musette style, quietly complementing the first gavotte in being devoid of sharpwards modulation. The first four bars are a decorated version of the repeated F sharps, flowing into smooth scales harmonized in two parts. The figure is repeated after the double bar, modulating to the subdominant, then back to the tonic; the original four bars are repeated literally. The final eight bars are all in the tonic, the thematically significant F sharp acting as a bagpipe drone.

The concluding gigue is neither grand nor sublime; yet neither is it innocent. Like the gigue of the E flat suite, it rather returns to the ambiguously merry/melancholy world in which we habitually live. Its 6/8 rather than 12/8 metre, its arpeggios alternating with stepwise movement, give it a peasant/like virility that relates back to the gavottes; development, however, is more extended, and both tonally and rhythmically more sophisticated. In the middle of the fourth bar the bouncing quavers pause on a low D, then gather energy around the open A string, recalling the bagpipe drone of the gavotte. This releases semiquaver figuration covering two and a half octaves, modulating conventionally to the dominant. After the sixteenth bar the original phrase is repeated in the new key; the next twelve bars, though without further modulation, transform the bounding figure into repeated quavers, decorated with semiquavers rocking in thirds, an effect that is, paradoxically, both exuberant and nagging:

Ex. 17

The countrified theme is modified in the relative minor, after the double bar, in an extended passage that again uses the note F sharp as a drone. Wide skips hint at F sharp minor, but lead through flowing scales in the subdominant to the tonic and a modified da capo. The music seems to be approaching a songfulness recalling the grandeurs of earlier movements; but the lyricism is dampened with a return of the chugging, repeated-note figure with its rocking accompaniment—a noise which, if exciting, is far from celestial. Falling scales reappear in the penultimate bar; the final plunge is through a tonic arpeggio landing, like the allemande's, on the low D. Even more than the gigue of the E flat suite, this movement has incorporated into the binary form ternary elements which suggest the dynamism of sonata. This is its realism, its truth to 'dualistic' experience.

The relationship between the E flat major and D major suites is exactly complemented by that between the suites in C minor and C major. Detailed analysis would duplicate points already made; a few general comments are, however, pertinent. C minor, for Bach, tends to be a key of pain, borne with imperturbability; and the C minor is the toughest, gravest suite, for which Bach employed a scordatura tuning (the A string flattened to G) in order to darken the sonority. The prelude is secular in being in two sections on the analogy of a French overture, the first part ceremonial in duple time, the second part a triple-metre dance. But the multiple-stopped chords, dotted rhythms and upthrusting scales of the first section acquire tragic pathos, in the Greek sense; and even the 3/8 dance is strenuous rather than blithe. It builds, over a tonic pedal, to a tremendous climax on a diminished seventh, cadencing through chromatic appoggiaturas:

Ex. 18

The allemande preserves the tough spaciousness of the prelude and also refers to the convention of the heroic overture, multiple-stopped chords on the strong beats being linked by swinging scales and thrusting dotted rhythms. Similarly the courante is darker and more sinewy than the other courantes, being notated in the French manner in 3/2. The texture is dense, the rhythm complicated, for the Italianate grace that Bach favours for the other courantes would here be inappropriate, especially since the courante precedes a sarabande which is one of the most extraordinary, and profound, movements in Bach's work.

For the first time in this suite there is no multiple stopping. Yet although entirely monodic, the sarabande is harmonically powerful, even anguished, because its widespread arpeggios frequently involve dissonant intervals such as the diminished fourth, augmented fifth and diminished seventh. The painfully spread melody incorporates so many chromatic appoggiaturas that it remotely resembles—especially since the leaps become, in displaced octaves, vast— Schoenbergian atonality:

Ex. 19

Paradoxically, however, the level quaver movement remains calm, almost disembodied: physical (harmonic) anguish dissolves in metaphysical (melodic) grace. The music is a purgation; the blood of Christ drains, as it were, from his cross-suspended body as the line, pallid in tone, is stretched almost—but not quite—to breaking-point. Not surprisingly this strange and wonderful music casts a shadow over the earthier flavour of the remaining dances. The gavotte, though vigorous, is hardly jolly, for its texture is thick, its rhythm stumping; and although the second gavotte is an alleviation, flowing in triplets, it's still in the minor, with metrical oddities that flutter the nerves rather than provoke laughter. Even the final gigue, if lightweight, doesn't deny the intensity of this sombre suite: it's a German gigue in a dotted 3/8, rather than an Italian gigue in flowing 6/8. The irregular rhythms—for instance the dotted crotchets tied across the bars—are at once witty and disturbing.

For Bach C major tends to be a key of contentment rather than, as with D major, a key of triumph. In conceiving the C major suite as the most sensuous of the set he must have been influenced by the resonance this key offered him from its open strings. The prelude is in continuous semiquavers, mingling scales with arpeggios. Increasingly, however, arpeggios dominate, creating, as they reverberate over the open pedal notes, a sonority resembling massed strings or voices, or even a peal of bells. Eventually the resonance blows up in a cadenza of cascading scales and multiple-stopped chords, separated by silences:

Ex. 20

This piece, though the most sensuous and rhetorically extrovert in the suites, is also the one that profits most from performance in ecclesiastical acoustics.

The allemande, hardly less grand than the prelude, also exploits open strings and multiple stopping. The initial scale rising through a fourth generates its own diminutions; its cross accents are urgent as well as animated. Yet although this is the most physical of the allemandes it remains noble, even hymnic, in manner. Even the agilely corporeal courante, with its bounding arpeggiated theme, is intensified by chromaticism and by a darkening to the minor in the approach to the cadence. Similarly the sumptuous sarabande extends its spacious melodic span and ripe multi-stopped harmonies from the first section's eight bars to sixteen in the second section, thereby affording scope for tonal exploration —to the *minor* of the dominant —as well as for a spatially and temporally expanded line. The remaining dances are no longer grand, though the bourrée's bucolic vigour is as memorable as it is energetic; while in the 3/8 gigue rhythmic irregularities create high comedy, mirthful in both the modern and the medieval senses.

Bach's fusion of the apparently contradictory principles of religious monody and secular dance, as revealed in his suites for solo cello, defines the heart of his sublime and unique achievement. In all his music the density of texture is inseparable from the fact that each line, while making sense as an independent melody, contains harmonic implications that suggest or even create polyphony and tonal movement existing in time. We may most conveniently examine the nature of Bach's polyphony, in relation both to ecclesiastical polyphony and to then modern dance, by way of his forty-eight preludes and fugues in all the major and minor keys, a work that was composed as a pedagogic *demonstratio* but became a microcosm of Bach's musical-philosophical world.

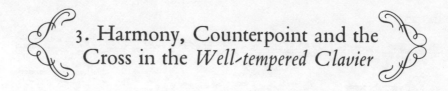

3. Harmony, Counterpoint and the Cross in the *Well-tempered Clavier*

The genesis of the *Well-tempered Clavier* was a set of eleven preludes that Bach composed for Wilhelm Friedemann's *Clavierbüchlein*. He extended them and added others, in 1722 presenting them as a set of 'preludes and fugues in all the tones and semitones, both with the major third of Ut, re, mi and with the minor third of Re, mi, fa. For the use and profit of young musicians who are anxious to learn, as well as for the amusement of those who are already expert in the art.' These twenty-four preludes and fugues were so successful that between 1738 and 1742 Bach completed a second set of 'twenty-four new preludes and fugues'. These may have been conceived as an entity, as the first set was not; both were simultaneously absolute music and pedagogic texts. The pieces were demonstrations of the laws of counterpoint, as inherited by Bach from tradition; they were keyboard exercises exploring various types of figuration without reference to any specific keyboard instrument; and they were an investigation of the possibilities of temperament, the systems of tuning that made feasible modulation to most, and eventually to all, keys of the chromatic scale. Again, we observe Bach's position between past, present and future. The contrapuntal skills he demonstrates were already archaic, if not obsolete; the keyboard figurations and dance rhythms he explores were contemporary, high Baroque in spirit; while the potential of fully equal temperament was to be revealed only in the future. For the common belief that the '48' were composed to demonstrate the virtues of equal temperament—the division of the octave into twelve equidistant semitones—is incorrect. Many methods of tuning were being investigated in Bach's day, their purpose being to facilitate modulation to the remoter keys. Few of them, however, were systematic and most compromised: the purity of some intervals—especially the harmonically important thirds—could be preserved only by sacrifice of modulatory freedom, with the result that some 'foreign' keys were more out of tune than others. This was not all loss. Keys acquired character from their relative degree of in- or out-of-tuneness; in strict equal temperament we cannot hope to understand why F sharp minor was for Bach a key of transcendent

suffering or for Couperin a key of paranormal intensity, nor why Bach notated
the eighth prelude of Book I in E flat minor, its fugue in D sharp minor.

Marpurg tells us that Bach tuned his own keyboard instruments before use,
seldom taking longer than a quarter of an hour over it. He seems — though the
text is somewhat obscure — to suggest that Bach empirically decided on a
tuning appropriate to the piece. Certainly for the first volume of the '48' there
can be no absolute system, since the pieces were written over a considerable
period of time, for various instruments that called for different tuning
techniques. The second volume, being conceived as a whole, may imply a
more systematic (and equal) temperament, though scientific system mattered
less than inherent philosophy. Tuning, in classical antiquity and in the
Middle Ages, through the seventeenth century and up to Bach's day, had
religious implications. According to Boehme the soul itself is 'a tuned
Instrument of the Harmony of God', a part of God's Kingdom of Joy, 'which
God's spirit would play upon'. The notion harks back to Philo's *Quod Deus
immutabilis sit* (quoted by John Hollander), which compares the soul to a lyre
tuned in 'knowledge of moral opposites . . . Such a soul is the most perfect
instrument fashioned by Nature . . . And if it be well adjusted, it will produce
a symphony the most beautiful in the world, one which has its consummation
not in the cadences and tones of melodious sound, but in the consistencies of
life's actions.'

If this applies to music in its metaphysical-moral origins, still more is it
pertinent to the harmonic music of the Renaissance. The more tones involved,
the more complex will be their relations one to another, and the more difficult
an ideal in-tuneness becomes. Musicians of the Renaissance called chromatic
notes — which ultimately made temperament necessary — *musica ficta*. It was
the 'fictitious' nature of the thirds, sharpened — especially on the cadential
seventh of the scale — for reasons of harmonic congruence, that put them in
'false' relation with the mode. In this sense it is not fanciful to say that
temperament is a musical allegory of the Fall and is, like Adam's *mea culpa*,
simultaneously a sign of evil and of potential grace. Only through the false
compromise of temperament, and in particular the distortion of the third
which a harmonically oriented music calls for, can music embrace the
dualism which is post-Renaissance man's agonized awareness of his fallen
state. Yet only after this fall can he find redemption in an equilibrium between
music's horizontal (melodic) and vertical (harmonic) manifestations.
Seventeenth-century English poets were obsessed by metaphors comparing the
difficulty of tuning lutes and keyboard instruments to the yearning of the

separated soul for in-tuneness with God; George Herbert relates the metaphor specifically to the Crucifixion:

> The Crosse taught all wood to resound his Name,
>   Who bore the same.
> His stretched Sinews taught all strings, what key
> Is best to celebrate this most high Day.
> Consort both heart and lute, and twist a song
>   Pleasant and long:
> Or, since all musick is but three parts vied
>   And multiplied,
> O let Thy blessed Spirit bear a part
> And make up our defects with His sweet Art.

In *Deniall* Herbert symbolizes out-of-tuneness between man and God by defective rhyme, which the last stanza rights:

> Therefore my soule lay out of sight,
>   Untun'd, unstrung:
> My feeble spirit, unable to look right,
>   Like a nipt blossom, hung
>   Discontented.
> O cheer and tune my heartless breast,
>   Deferre no time;
> That so Thy favours granting my request,
>   They and my mind may chime
>   And mend my rime.

Seventeenth-century poets usually imply that, since the Fall, getting in tune with God is likely to hurt: as Clemant Paman puts it, 'Screw thee high My heart: up to The Angels' key. What if thy Strings all crack and flye? On such a Ground, Musick 'twill be to dy.' Similarly it would seem that Bach, whose compositional technique is, we've suggested, a cross between a melodic horizontal and a harmonic vertical, compromised with tuning in the interests of spirit. He needed temperament to explore the ramifications of passion and pain inherent in his harmony, yet knew it was a betrayal of the intervallic purity on which religious monody, and the melodic essence of his own art, had been based. When once the Fall has happened and (in musical terms) we've experienced the delights and despairs of harmonic duality, it would be naive to hope that we could again be fulfilled in justly intoned monody. Henceforth,

any perfection we seek cannot evade compromise between divine demands
and human needs. In admitting that the technical dubiety of temperament is
also moral, Bach's harmonic polyphony becomes a *demonstratio* of the
workings of Christian grace more revealing than any theological text. This
should be evident in our analyses of pieces from the '48'.

Equivocation between past, present and future extends in this music to the
practical question as to the instrument on which the pieces may most
appositely be performed. *Das wohltemperierte Clavier* should not, of course, be
translated as the *Well-tempered Clavichord*, though it often used to be. *Clavier*
simply designates a keyboard instrument; and those available to Bach were
clavichord, harpsichord, pedal harpsichord and organ. A few of the pieces
can work effectively only with the sustaining power of the organ; some, with
percussive and arpeggiated styles, clearly suggest the harpsichord; many can
be most convincingly played on the clavichord; one or two even prophetically
suggest the fortepiano, the new instrument which Bach came into grudging
contact with at the court of Frederick the Great. Which instrument is
appropriate to a piece depends on the music's relationship to past, present and
future. In any recital of these preludes and fugues on a single instrument, some
pieces 'fit' more readily than others. But to have reflected on the most suitable
instrument for each piece is not a waste of time, since such reflection bears
directly on interpretation. We will keep these practical problems in mind
during the course of our analyses, which will attempt to demonstrate the
workings of 'Christian grace' through Bach's linear-harmonic polyphony,
starting with pieces that are superficially most archaic in concept, moving
towards those that are closest to Bach's Baroque contemporaneity.

The D sharp minor fugue from Book I opens with a theme notated in
common time:

Ex. 21

We don't, however, hear it metrically and, asked to write it down from
dictation, would be nonplussed as to where to insert bar-lines. The quietly
rising fifth with which the subject begins is an interval which, we've noted,
was traditionally a synonym for God, since it's the most absolute consonance
after the octave, which is hardly an interval at all. Around this fifth the theme
undulates in stepwise movement, descends to the tonic, rises through a fourth

(which is the fifth inverted), and declines scalewise, tied across the bar, to the tonic. Of its nature this theme, enclosed within God's fifth, has a minimum of momentum and of temporality, and is without rhetorical accent. It sounds as impersonal as plainsong. Through it breathes the voice of God, or life itself, without our volition.

Yet that Bach is not anonymously creating liturgical incantation becomes evident as soon as the theme is answered in the third bar. For a two-part texture inevitably creates the duality of harmony; and to monophonic plainchant duality is anathema. The 'answer' at first, however, tries to evade the tension and pain inherent in duality. It's a tonal rather than a real answer; starting on the fifth it ascends a fourth to the upper tonic, but modifies the stepwise undulation to a more 'open' minor third. It then strictly follows the thematic pattern, while the original voice flows tranquilly up the scale, graduating from the bare fifth and octave (bar 3) to more sensuous thirds and sixths (bar 4). This also involves an upward movement tonally, for bar 5 cadences, with the B sharpened, into A sharp minor, the dominant. There is still little sense of metrical pulse, the bar-lines having no accentual significance; indeed, up to this point the music could be high Renaissance polyphony of Palestrinian vintage. The lines are individually indistinguishable from plainsong: timelessly 'spiritual', yet creating from their concurrence a sensuously pleasing euphony. None the less, the simultaneous appearance of two parts, however metrically fluid, does imply a *latent* temporal pulse; and at the point of cadence there is the first dissonant suspension—a relatively mild major second—moving from strong to weak beat.

The modulation to the dominant proves, as in Palestrina, to be no real modulation, for in the next bar it subsides back into the tonic. Yet the subsidence is not mere relaxation, for it happens by way of a 'crucial' suspension of the interval of a tritone: the *im*perfect fifth which, complementing God's perfection, has symbolized the Devil from the Middle Ages onwards. In this context it doesn't seriously disturb the level flow of the music, centred in the middle register of the keyboard; but the fact that it is there affects our response to the richer texture from the entry of the third voice. This sings in the 'real' form, but an octave lower, while the two higher voices flow upwards in parallel thirds, an interval which the Middle Ages had considered dissonant but which in the Renaissance became an incarnation of sensuous bliss, to the extent that composers of the Burgundian school could create longish compositions consisting mainly of chains of 6–3 chords, indulging in this softly sensuous excitation like a cat purring in sunlit semi-slumber:

Ex. 22

The level, stepwise quaver movement also recalls the seventeenth-century *scène de sommeil*, wherein the operatic hero, distraught by fallen man's crassness, cruelty and rapacity, dreams a wish-fulfilment wherein a god rights human wrong. Traditionally, such a scene was in common time, moving by step, in quavers, at roughly the speed of the human pulse. In Bach's passage triadic euphony is tinged with the tender pain of chromatic alteration, as in the suspension on the first beat of bar 10; while in bar 11 — the first measure that is transitional rather than strictly thematic — there's an explicit secularization of the ecclesiastical gravity with which the fugue had opened. For the first time the unhurried quavers are flustered by semiquavers, in a rhythm derived from the figure in the aborted cadential approach to the dominant in bar 5. The semiquavers now rise in rich parallel sixths, while the bass transforms the music's diatonic or modal simplicity into descending chromatics. Now chromaticism had epitomized in musical terms the death of the Middle Ages and the birth of the modern world; for traditional vocal modality was undermined by the 'false' notes introduced in order to attain, in a two-or-more part texture, the harmonic satisfaction of the major third, especially at cadential points. Ever since — from Gesualdo's despairingly sensual and flagellating madrigals to the lament of Purcell's dying Dido, to the death-invoking ululations of Wagner's Tristan — chromatics have been associated with sensual deliquescence and with moments of harmonic sensation which, being momentary, disrupt continuity of line and regularity of pulse.

Of course, in this single bar there is no such disintegration. The texture, owing to the chromatically drooping bass and the more varied figuration, is merely a bit more animated: a process continued in the next (tonal) appearance of the theme in the bass, since the quaver figuration of the upper parts creates the occasional sob of an augmented fifth (bar 12). On the whole, however, the increasingly sensuous quality of the music moves in a positive rather than negative direction, especially when, in bar 15, the step-rising quavers are no longer restricted to the compass of a fifth, but soar upwards in parallel tenths, cadencing, in bar 17, on the piercingly suspended dissonance of a major seventh:

Ex. 23

Implicit here is the Renaissance discovery that any bliss experienced within the senses, since it is dependent on time, must also entail pain. Yet in Bach's fugue these physical occurrences modify but do not destroy the music's metaphysical calm. The ascent through a ninth to the high B is an angelic flight as well as a sensual liberation; and the suspended E sharp, against the bass's F sharp, is unobtrusive because it is without agogic accent. It does, however, lead the music to its first authentic modulation: a house-moving from tonic to dominant which concludes the fugue's first section, in so far as it is valid to speak of sections in music so essentially continuous.

We may sum up the events of these eighteen and a half bars as the gradual secularization of a religious, plainsong-like impulse. In the next section Bach seeks to counteract this 'humanization' by a return to (archaic) contrapuntal law; the richer the music grows harmonically and texturally, the more necessary it becomes to assert the eternal principles of many-in-oneness. The theme thus enters in stretto in the alto and treble, at two beats' distance, over an upthrusting quaver bass that breaks into semiquavers:

Ex. 24

The declining tail of the subject is now splintered by a quaver rest, agitating the theme slightly with a syncopation, as the music presses to the dominant of the dominant (E sharp minor). At this point the theme, its rising fifth changed to a fourth, enters in stretto, at the distance of only one beat. This contrapuntal

complexity inevitably subverts rhythmic regularity, for the accents don't
conform with the bar-lines. It also supports a good deal of tonal movement so
that—with broken entries of the theme over a continuously moving bass—
we're carried through C sharp minor to a luminous resolution in F sharp
major, D sharp minor's relative. This significant tonal event also has linear
consequences, since it coincides with the first appearance, in the treble, of the
theme in inversion:

Ex. 25

The major apotheosis isn't, however, of long duration, for the music subsides
by way of B major to its relative, G sharp minor, and so back to the tonic.
Throughout this passage the quaver movement is continuous, though the
harmony grows increasingly emotive, with sobbing chords of the augmented
fifth in bar 33 and with semitonically dissonant passing notes in bar 38.
Increased emotional heat prompts more semiquaver movement also, until the
return to the D sharp minor tonic brings with it a sonorous entry of the theme
in the bass, in inversion, but with the original godlike fifth instead of the
substituted fourth. And again greater harmonic plangency is countered by
more rigid contrapuntal control. The inverted theme is answered in stretto at
two beats' distance and then, moving to G sharp minor, at one beat's distance,
but with the inverted theme modified so that it flows in dotted rhythm:

Ex. 26

Back on D sharp, though not *in* the tonic, there's a triple stretto at one beat's
distance, with the subject *rectus* with rising fourth, followed by the *inversus*,
with falling fifth. In both cases the entries proceed from bass to alto to treble.
Tonality veers between G sharp minor and B major, returning to A sharp
minor by way of a chain of suspended seconds, familiar from the instrumental

textures of the trio sonata rather than from strict ecclesiastical polyphony.

Once more this harmonic emotionalism prompts a contrapuntal response. The theme appears resonantly in the bass, in augmentation, answered in the treble at the original speed but by inversion, and then by the alto in the augmented form.

Ex. 27

Semiquaver figuration and syncopation increase the animation as the augmented theme soars higher. This melodic ascent is balanced, however, by the tonal descent in a cycle of fifths from C sharp minor to F sharp minor to B minor. The bass line leaps with unwonted agitation through sevenths, until chromaticism, first hinted at in bar 12, invades all three parts in a passage of near-romantic voluptuousness:

Ex. 28

This resolves in the subdominant but immediately veers to the dominant, at which point the augmented theme enters in the treble, ringing like a celestial trumpet over the alto (which has the dotted rhythm extension of the theme) and a bass line that remains agile. This creates a consummation, if not, given the level and impersonal nature of the counterpoint, exactly a climax, and subsides into a not strictly thematic coda. The treble declines through arpeggiated fifths both perfect and imperfect; the lower parts descend in parallel thirds. From its low C double sharp the treble finally climbs scalewise through a ninth, reflecting the 'liberated' scale of bar 15. Alto doubles treble in warm parallel sixths, bass falls in contrary motion through scalic fourths. The final cadence resolves, inevitably, on a *tierce de Picardie*, since the 'feel' of the subject, despite its chromatic extensions, is archaically modal. The bass's falling fifth, defining the final dominant-tonic cadence, not only serves its conventional harmonic function; it also affirms thematic identity as an inversion of the subject's original godly fifth.

In this sublimely beautiful piece, therefore, Bach creates a fugue which seems retrospective—in the modal, plainsong-like contours of the subject itself; in the absence of the duality of a countersubject; in the impersonal flow of the non-metrical rhythm; in the disposition of the three parts in the middle of the keyboard: yet within its 'spirituality' the music becomes increasingly 'humanized'—in euphonious triadic harmonies, in sensual chromatics and augmented intervals, in a gradual expansion of range in the part-writing. This 'humanization' is in turn counteracted by increasing complexities of contrapuntal control, a many-in-oneness assimilating all aspects of the texture to the single theme, in stretto, in inversion and in augmentation. The ultimate consummation is the appearance of the augmented theme in the treble: a contrapuntal event that has been prompted by the harmonic evolution. Personal emotion is thus objectified. No piece from the '48' is in its total effect more profoundly an experience of the numinous, more ineffably calm, more impervious to the slings and arrows of outrageous fortune. Yet it is so precisely *because* its tranquillity embraces so much of human stress and distress. That is why its peace 'passeth understanding'; there is nothing to understand in the quietude of a cabbage.

The fact that Bach notated this piece in the recondite key of D sharp minor is worthy of comment. Why did he do this, when he notated the prelude in the more normal E flat minor? It may well have been a way of symbolizing the music's extraordinarily numinous character, for if, in the Baroque period, E major was traditionally a key of heaven because it was the sharpest, most 'upward' key in common use, Bach's pedagogic investigation of temperament might well reserve the sharpest key possible within the chromatic system for an experience that miraculously marries the physical with the metaphysical. Difficulty of intonation would enhance the sense of mystery; and that the theme itself is diatonic, even modal, makes the equivocation even more piquant.

An analytical account of music must, if it takes account of the human impulses that create musical events, bear directly on interpretation. Thus the tempo of this fugue is determined by the subject's self-enclosed neutrality, its avoidance of metical accent. It must breathe gently and inevitably: so the apposite speed is clearly that of the human pulse. Similarly, since harmonic expressivity is inherent in polyphonic flow, performance must be unrhetorical; play the counterpoint equably and the 'expression' will reveal itself. This is true of most of Bach's music, but nowhere more critically so than in this fugue. Level pulse, dynamic neutrality and quasi-vocal polyphony bear too on the question of the appropriate instrument. An early Baroque or even a Renaissance organ could create the right radiance of sonority; still more suitable is the clavichord, whose ethereality of tone could also reveal the emotional nuances which we have seen to be latent beneath the apparently unruffled surface. The piano also can be beautifully adapted to the fugue, as Rosalyn Tureck's performance demonstrates. The more aggressive and percussive sonorities of the harpsichord, on the other hand, are fatal to it. On that instrument a piece that counts among the wonders of European music can even sound tedious.

My comments on Bach's employment of the tonality of D sharp minor were speculative; that contemporary theorists regarded F sharp minor as a key of peculiar significance is an indisputable fact. Seventeenth-century lutanists termed it '*le ton de la chèvre*'; and for keyboard instruments tuned in the mean-tone system it offered comparable difficulties. Couperin, like the lutanists, associated F sharp minor with obscure emotional states; for Bach it became a key of heightened, especially purgatorial, suffering. The F sharp minor fugue from Book I is in four parts, and is therefore capable of greater harmonic density than the three-part D sharp minor. The subject seems to have some of the spiritual character of the D sharp minor theme: it moves by step and avoids metrical accent, the first dotted minim being tied across the bar. The emotional flavour of the fugue is none the less very different; and the difference may be defined in terms of its harmonic character. The D sharp minor, despite the range of experience latent within it, is 'absolute'; the F sharp minor dramatically evokes a human situation. By comparison with Bach's overtly religious music we may, indeed, establish that the F sharp minor fugue is concerned with the Passion, both that of the historical Christ and of the Christ-figure potential in everyone.

Examining the theme itself we note that the stepwise movement and lack of metrical accent which seem to relate it to the D sharp minor subject are soon belied. For whereas the D sharp minor theme, enclosed without harmonic movement in its rising fifth and falling fourth, exists outside time, the F sharp minor theme is action in time:

Ex. 29

It strains upward by step; transmutes its minor third to major; sharpens its fourth to make a cadential leading note to the dominant; declines to the tonic by way of the flattened fourth and third, with a cadential trill. The answer at the fifth, and in the dominant, again thrusts upwards and sharpwards, from C sharp to G sharp; but it is accompanied in the original voice by a descending countersubject. Phrased in pairs of drooping quavers, this is one of Bach's musical synonyms for tears, and is almost literally a sigh since the pairs of quavers often descend, as appoggiaturas, from dissonance to consonance. By the end of the alto's entry the duality inherent in the fugue is established: whereas the D sharp minor has one theme only, and only the briefest episodes, the F sharp minor springs from a tension between the upthrusting, tonally aspiring subject and the countersubject's descending lament. The contrariety is unmistakable, even though the countersubject is, in essence, an inversion of the subject.

A transitional bar built on the thrusting scale with sharp seventh leads to the third (tonic) entry in the bass. The weeping countersubject is now on top, the first note of each of its pairs clashing with the bass line's thematic notes:

Ex. 30

A promised relaxation into the relative A major comes to nothing; activity is intensified with a real modulation to the dominant, with acute suspended seconds. In bar 13 a chromatic alteration of G sharp to natural stabs dissonantly towards a cadence in the subdominant, B minor. The suspended G natural in the alto bumps into the bass's F sharp; semitonic suspensions coruscate until the treble enters, not with an independent part, but doubling the alto in parallel thirds. This again is a harmonic device; and as tenor and bass sing the countersubject in weeping parallel tenths, the texture grows almost luxuriantly dense. The tonic minor is by now reaffirmed, but another transitional episode based on the upthrusting scale in stretto modulates decisively to the dominant. A repetition of the chromatically altered G, an octave higher, functions as a Neapolitan cadence leading back to the tonic, with chains of suspended seconds in the upper parts and a 'weeping' bass in which the pairs of quavers are occasionally inverted:

Ex. 31

Again activity increases effect, with an unobtrusive inversion of the subject in the alto, a cadence to the dominant; again upthrusting scales, in the upper parts, rise to the fugue's highest note (B) which, in declension, releases the only semiquavers to agitate the pulsing quavers (bars 28–29). At the same time the subject reappears in the tenor, the countersubject drooping above it. Four bars later the bass inverts the theme, so that all is now a descent. Anguished aspiration turns into lament, as of weepers at the Cross. Again the weeping is in parallel thirds and tenths, with suspended seconds and ninths. The tonality too relaxes, from F sharp minor to passing modulations to A and D major, in an astonishingly rich, Romantic-sounding passage of descending sequential dominant ninths:

Ex. 32

With no alteration to the harmonies and an only slightly more opulent disposition on the keyboard this is almost identical with another celebrated keyboard weeping, also in F sharp minor—that of Granados's *Girl with the Nightingale*. After this subsidence the theme returns *rectus*, but low in the treble register. Its aspiration is muted; the weeping parallel sixths between alto and tenor are stabilized by the bass's dominant pedal. Equilibrium of emotion justifies the final *tierce de Picardie*, though the chromaticized diatonicism has none of the latent modality of the fugue in D sharp minor.

In this fugue, as compared with the D sharp minor, the 'humanization' of a spiritual impulse has gone further, since the harmonic implications of the theme itself give density to the texture. Thus the Neapolitan flattened G (bar 13) is a harmonic device within a linear texture; while the romantically sequential ninths of the closing section are a harmonic rather than contrapuntal consummation. It's significant that whereas in the D sharp minor fugues Bach employs every kind of contrapuntal device, in the F sharp minor there are no diminutions or augmentations, few stretti, and only one inversion that serves a structurally harmonic purpose in initiating the coda. In being thus harmonically humanized, the music becomes dramatic, if not exactly theatrical. It celebrates the Godhead become Man, equated with us weeping; in this sense it belongs with Bach's Passion music, whether or no he thought of it in theological terms. He probably didn't; for although his mind functioned analogically, he cannot be categorized as either a medieval or a Baroque allegorist. Indeed Bach's supreme greatness lies in the fact that he overrides chronology and history; this is why no other composer used his contemporary materials in the same way. Telemann's fugal textures never mysteriously prophesy Granados, as Bach's do here; and the parallel between Bach and Granados is not merely surprising, and certainly not arbitrary. It exists because, nearly two hundred years later, the Spanish composer discovered in the dialogue of the girl lover and the nightingale an analogy for the relationship of body to soul, of love human to love divine, which is psychologically true at any time and place. Bach is at once within time and without it.

Regarding performance, the theme's latent urgency suggests a tempo rather faster than that appropriate for the D sharp minor; yet it must not be too fast, both because the quaver movement is equable and also because the harmonic density needs time in which to tell. It would not be amiss to treat the dotted minim of the F sharp minor as equivalent to the minim of the D sharp minor. The fugue's 'Romantic' character, inherent in its luxurious harmony, suggests a degree of rubato, especially in the sequential ninths in the coda. This fugue, like the D sharp minor, is probably clavichord music, for that instrument is best attuned to its (Greek) pathos. Being passionate music, it also goes well on the harpsichord, in a fairly simple, unmodified registration. On Baroque organ the dissonances could be more effectively sustained than on any other instrument; although the music's fervency would be dampened, continuous line could be achieved, without aggressive twang.

The D sharp minor fugue, as we saw, has an almost stressless theme, in level movement, at approximately the speed of the pulse; its dynamics are neutral.

Within its quietude it contains depths of sorrow and heights of joy; yet in total effect it's a hymn universalized, without rhetorical accent or subjective distress. Superficially, the F sharp minor fugue seems comparable, for it moves by step, without metrical accent, in a consistent figuration. Yet the subject itself implies movement in time, its 6/4 pulse suggesting body rhythm as the D sharp minor's 4/4 does not; and also in space, since the essence of the undulating theme is its modulatory energy, thrusting sharpwards. Moreover, the D sharp minor has no real countersubject, while the F sharp minor has a countersubject which, inverting the stepwise rise of the subject, renders incarnate the tension of a sigh, a flagging of limbs and drooping of head. Despite its continuous texture, the fugue has a beginning, middle and end, the sequential ninths of the coda achieving a harmonic resolution of the energy polyphony has generated.

For a further stage in the process of humanization and temporalization let us consider the C minor fugue from Book II; here is the exposition and first episode:

Ex. 33

The theme, presented in the alto, resembles that of the D sharp minor in that its contours are vocal, calmly relaxed. Again it rotates around the godly interval of a fifth, and is rounded off by a stepwise descent. It differs from the D sharp minor subject only in that its triadic basis is more conspicuous, giving it, at least incipiently, a more harmonic bias. In the treble's entry, however, the third is changed to second in a tonal answer; and the descending scale creates a chain of suspended seconds in trio-sonata style. This faintly disturbs the serenity; and we soon become aware that, for all its vocal character, the theme's arpeggiated brevity tends to a more sectional treatment than do the subjects of the D sharp and F sharp minor. After the third (real) entry in the bass, strict thematicism is succeeded by an episode in flowing semiquavers. This modulates authentically to the dominant, whereas the tinge of dominant in the exposition had been a momentary feint; but then immediately, by way of the subdominant, to a no less clear transition to the relative. Though this semiquaver episode is free it is not athematic: the falling fifth which sets the semiquavers in motion is derived from the subject, and is inverted in the treble's imitation, while the upward scales are inverted diminutions of the theme's declining scale. The rocking quaver thirds (bar 6) that form a tailpiece to the semiquavers may also be construed as a permutation of the triadic opening notes of the subject; this again emphasizes the fugue's tendency to fragmentation.

With the fourth and last entry in the bass the relative major gives way to tonic minor. On the other hand the music's growing animation is not cancelled, for the theme is again significantly modified. The first two notes descend neither through a third nor a major second, but through a chromatic semitone, to the sharp seventh, the leading note. This gives the originally relaxed theme a degree of tension, reinforced by the fact that the leaping fifth in the alto's semiquavers is changed to a minor sixth, contracting to a tritone and then to a fourth. So of the four expositional entries of the theme only two are identical; and the three versions grow progressively more tense. During the next episode the bass hints at the theme, with fourths and diminished fifths substituted, often in dotted rhythm, for thirds. The treble and alto twine above in sequential suspensions, moving to the subdominant minor. The chromaticized version of the theme returns in the alto; but the effect of this passage is harmonic rather than contrapuntal, attaining a small climax in its Neapolitan (G flat) approach to the subdominant cadence (bars 11–12). In the next bar the flattening tendency is contradicted as the music swings two degrees sharpwards to the dominant minor; the subject's opening motive is now transformed into a clearly defined harmonic progression — subdominant, dominant, tonic — in the bass. This dominant close on three-octave Gs (bar 14) definitively concludes a section wherein a vocal-seeming, spiritual theme has gathered harmonic momentum and textural sensuousness, and has done so by increasingly free thematic transformation.

To this humanization the music reacts in a manner comparable with, though more extravagant than, that of the D sharp minor: the cadence is followed by a strict contrapuntal passage wherein the treble sings the theme in its original version with third and fifth, answered in the tenor in augmentation.

If this seems like an attempt to recover the fugue's initial certitude, it is undermined by the bass entry, with the chromaticized version of the theme in inversion, the falling fifth translated into a leaping sixth:

Ex. 34

Stretti occur, one with the tonal version of the subject at the original pitch, the other with the major third turned minor, inducing a return to close-textured sequences. Harmonic intensity is here inseparable from contrapuntal growth; in bar 18 chromatic alteration creates sequences and false relations so cluttered that some editors have ironed out the harmony by the addition of A flats and D flats to effect a straightforward modulation from F minor to A flat major. The angularity of harmony here is surely, however, a consequence of angularity of line, which leads, as the tonic is re-established, to the delayed introduction of a fourth part, chanting the original version of the theme in augmentation in the bass:

Ex. 35

Again, however, this thematicism proves harmonic rather than linear in effect, since the stable bass entry provides support for the upper parts' tightly chromaticized figuration. When the bass sings the sharp-seventh version of the theme at the original speed the chromaticism communicates itself to the other parts also; the treble climbs upwards and the tenor clashes dissonantly with the bass. The tailpiece to the bass theme changes the thematic descent through third and fifth to two falling fifths, tonic, subdominant, dominant, tonic, with apparent cadential finality.

So the first section, ending with the landmark of the modulation to the dominant, has been balanced by a second section, that returns even more decisively to a cadential tonic. Yet this is not a conclusion; Bach appends a coda consisting of a series of now overtly rhetorical stretti. The original version

of the subject in the alto is answered by the chromaticized version in the treble;
the tenor echoes with the opening motive, the third changed to a diminished
fourth, followed by a perfect fourth:

Ex. 36

This momentarily gives the impression of a *tierce de Picardie* which turns,
however, into a brief modulation to the subdominant minor; the tenor
fragments the theme to a *diminished* fifth followed by a *diminished* fourth. Moving
down the fifths we touch on B flat minor, subdominant of the subdominant,
releasing a cadential roulade of demisemiquavers, which become an approach
to a fierce diminished seventh cadence to the tonic. The bass has the
chromaticized version of the theme in inversion, exploding into a cadenza-like
arabesque on a G minor diminished seventh—an aggressive enhanced
dominant to bring the final cadence back to the tonic. The penultimate bar is a
chain of upthrusting semitones, the 'leading' note progression which had
initiated the dramatic-harmonic recreation of the originally serene, lyrical
theme. The bass's final descent through a fifth from G to C is thematic but, in
context, powerfully and unambiguously also fulfils its harmonic, dominant-
tonic function.

Despite the vestiges of counterpoint surviving in the last bars, the style of the
music is now closer to a Baroque organ toccata or fantasia than to a vocally
conceived fugue. In the course of this comparatively brief piece we have witnessed
a microcosmic version of the historical process whereby ecclesiastical
polyphony had been metamorphosed into the secular, incipiently theatrical
rhetoric of the Baroque. Instead of continuity of rhythm and consistency of
figuration we have a *sectional* style, in which linear and harmonic material is
recreated in time. Whereas the polyphonic evolution of the D sharp minor and
F sharp minor fugues almost necessitates a *tierce de Picardie*, the sturdy harmonic

conclusion to this fugue is resolutely minor. A major apotheosis would not, according to Baroque precedents, be impossible; here, however, the minor triad seems fitting, because it is acoustically less resolved and reminds us of the process of 'becoming' which the fugue has undergone.

The shape of the theme suggests much the same tempo as that of the D sharp minor, though the increasing activity will make the fugue sound faster as it develops. The sectional structure suggests the use of a Baroque organ, with discreet changes of registration as the textures are modified from Renaissance polyphony to Baroque rhetoric. The piece works well on the harpsichord, which can readily emulate the sonorities of a Baroque organ. The clavichord is too self-effacing to cope with its dramatic potential.

In this C minor fugue experience is in process; in the A minor from Book II the old principle of contrapuntal unity itself becomes a theatrical gesture. Here the theme is characteristically rhythmic and harmonic rather than lyrical:

Ex. 37

This is, of course, a Baroque cliché which vigorously survives in Mozart's *Requiem*. The most famous example is the chorus 'And with his stripes' from Handel's *Messiah*, which reminds us that it is not fanciful to hear it as a scourging motive in Bach's theme too. The first two aggressively detached notes assert the fifth and third degrees, followed by the sixth, though not until the plunge through a diminished seventh of A minor in the second bar can we be certain that the tonality is not C major (in which case the first two notes would be third and tonic). The second part of the subject, after silence, is a diminution of the same motive, a tone lower; this time the figure is extended to jab through a descending major seventh. The tonal answer moves sharpwards to the dominant, accompanied by a spurting countersubject of demisemiquaver scales, lurching into a syncopated rhythm and a sizzling trill. In place of unfolding lyricism we have bodily gestures; and the power of the fugue springs from a tension between these gestures' disruptiveness and a drive towards wholeness, if hardly towards song. The first statement and answer modulate to the dominant and subdominant; the tonic returns with the third entry in the treble. Fragmented thematic gestures then take over from full entries; sequences reiterate the diminished section of the theme, with prominent tritones; the shooting demisemiquavers are briefly broken, then surge more continuously into the relative major. This affirmation is emphasized since the diminished segment of the theme, with its cadential trills, rises through a cycle of fifths from C to G to D to A to E, the first three keys major, the last two minor.

The rise is offset by equally rapid tonal descents from E minor to A minor to D minor, though forward thrust is maintained with the demisemiquaver lashings extending from treble through alto to bass. Dissonant suspended sevenths mark a return to the tonic, which however serves only to initiate still bolder sequences wherein the cadential trills, beginning on the bass's low E, thrust remorselessly up through two and a half octaves to arrive at the B flat above middle C, splattered by broken demisemiquavers and savage arpeggios:

Ex. 38

Yet although the line seethes upwards, the tonality falls back through its cycle of fifths — from A to D to G minor and from C to F to B♭ major; this last triad signalizes the long-delayed return of the full fugal subject, in D minor. It's soon transformed into its tritonal diminution, with the syncopated but swirling scales in the bass much extended. Again the segments of the theme are fragmented, yet modulate to the relative. The final return to tonic minor lets loose a flood of demisemiquavers swirling from bass to alto to treble, ascending to the highest note of the piece (B natural), then crashing in an immense descent over a diminished seventh, which is all that survives of the theme:

Ex. 39

The passage is at once exciting and frightening. The last two bars, returning to the diminished segment of the theme and its thrusting trills, dam the flood as though by a conscious act of will, and with an almost triumphant foot-stamping. This fugue is the polar opposite to the D sharp minor, which is a (vocally conceived) apprehension of the numinous that incorporates sensuality within its radiance. The A minor, on the other hand, is the most unambiguously physical of the fugues in the '48', though its physicality threatens to blow up and to embrace 'other modes or experience that may be possible'. Though conventionally Baroque and superficially Handelian, the piece could hardly therefore have been composed by Handel.

Some editions give a *tierce de Picardie* for the final triad. As with the C minor fugue, this is possible in accord with Baroque convention, and makes a point in emphasizing the sense of triumph. The minor triad is probably better, however, for although we've come through turbulence, the tightness of the textures tells us it's been a matter of touch and go. If there's a victory, it has not been easy; and the unease conditions the tempo. The lashing demisemiquavers must be as fast as they can be clearly articulated, while the detached crotchets and quavers must have a heavy gravity, in the scientific sense. A fast tempo will be more easily managed on a harpsichord than on a Baroque organ, though the piece sounds well on either. The clavichord would be unequal to its savagery.

The C major fugue from Book I will serve as a retrospect of the ground we've covered, for in no other single fugue are sacred and profane elements held in surer equipoise. The theme, like that of the D sharp minor, moves entirely by step up a fifth, followed by leaps of fourth and fifth and a threefold descent through fourths, down the scale:

Ex. 40

But it is more affirmative because unambiguously diatonic, without modal implications; nor has it the D sharp minor's metrical neutrality, for its structure is lucidly ordered in its repetitive patterns of rising and falling fourths, both scalewise and intervallic. The real answer produces the expected modulation to the dominant; and the semiquaver countermotive now smilingly rises, instead of falling. The semiquavers, still grouped in fours, make passing dissonances with the tenor entry of the theme, back in the tonic. The bass entry survives a touch of subdominant occasioned by the tenor's B flat, and is in stable tonic major when, in bar 7, the stretti begin.

Although this fugue is of considerable contrapuntal ingenuity, stretto is the only device it employs. The tight thematic interrelationship of every aspect of subject and countersubject (if the descending scale can be graced with this name) is emphasized as each entry treads on the feet of its predecessor, until an old-fashioned principle of linear unity becomes an incipiently dramatic technique. As the rising entries proliferate they increase the dissonance and the complexity of texture; gritty semitonic clashes and grinding false relations lead to a full close in the relative minor:

Ex. 41

But the stretti are immediately resumed in the tonic major, in still more rapid sequence, and modulate to the dominant, the entry now fortified in parallel thirds. Once more stretti pile to a climax on the highest note thus far — a B flat in acute false relation with the tenor's B natural (bar 18). An acrid suspended seventh leads to a canonically induced cadence from D minor to major. As usual, stretti overlap the harmonic resolution, carrying us back in a descending cycle of fifths from D to G to C major. Passing dissonances of major seventh and minor ninth are still fairly fierce (bar 20), but are increasingly absorbed in the lines' songfulness, and sustained by a long dominant, and then tonic, pedal. This tonic pedal supports a plagal-flavoured coda-cadence wherein flattened sevenths are still in false relation with the sharp leading notes. The subject's rising stretti continue to soar; semiquaver scales flow in contrary motion, reaffirming the fugue's characteristic equipoise; in the final bar and a half the plagal flat sevenths are cancelled when the rising scales appear in double diminution, aspiring through B natural to resolve on a C major triad, two octaves above middle C. The piece ends on its highest note; and since the concluding demisemiquaver scales are an inversion of the scalewise falling fourths that form the tailpiece to the subject, one can say that the only downward-tending feature of the fugue is ultimately liberated.

The structure is wonderfully balanced, dividing the twenty-three stretto entries into exposition, extension and coda with invisible seams. The exposition covers bars 1 to 6. The extension is made up of three sections covering two entries of the theme in two parts, each followed by a full entrance of the theme; these sections cover bars 7 to 14, 14 to 19, 19 to 24. The coda (bars 24 to 27) contains one three-part stretto, followed by a cadence (in which all the figuration is freely thematic) over a tonic pedal. This long pedal note can function adequately only on an organ; and a Baroque organ can best reveal the music's fusion of serenely aspiring 'vocal' line with dissonantly clotted harmony. None the less, the clavichord is probably the most suitable instrument, especially since the prelude to this fugue is indisputably clavichord music. No other instrument can so effectively create the radiant euphony apposite to the fugue, while at the same time doing justice to its expressive dissonance. The speed that suits the evanescence of the clavichord's tone is also appropriate to the music's steady movement, which should be slightly faster than the pulse since the stretti stimulate drama, however latently. Though the first fugue of the '48' is not the greatest of the series, a case might be made that it is, in its balance between heavenward flowing lines and sensuously resonant harmony earth-rooted by pedal notes, the most representative. And its representative qualities lend themselves more readily to the clavichord than to any other keyboard instrument.

We have examined a sequence of fugues from the '48' in which old-fashioned contrapuntal unity has been subjected to gradually increasing degrees of secularization, appending some comments on the C major fugue as retrospect. We will now consider a series of preludes, most of them paired with fugues already discussed, and will discover in them an opposite but complementary process. For Bach's preludes usually eschew rigorous contrapuntal procedures in favour of two then fashionable conventions: the secular dance movement, usually in binary form but occasionally in the form of a ternary aria da capo, and the loosening-up exercise based on a single type of keyboard figuration. Frequently, however, Bach reinterprets these conventions; if the fugues tend to secularize the spiritual, the preludes spiritualize the secular.

Thus the companion piece to the D sharp minor of Book I is, as we've already intimated, notated in a very flat E flat minor, and is explicitly a dance. This dance, however, being a sarabande, is traditionally solemn, possibly associated, like the chaconne, with marriage, a union at once sexual and sacramental. A glance at the score suggests that the music is dominated by body movement: it opens with three regular chords to a bar, notated in 3/2 rather than 3/4; and the theme is arpeggiated rather than stepwise-moving. Closer examination, however, reveals a characteristically Bachian equivoc-ation within the music's physical theatricality. Thus, though it's a binary dance movement, the full close in the dominant is not defined by a double bar; and although the first 'half' covers the conventional sixteen bars, they are not conventionally divided into eight plus eight. Throughout these sixteen bars quietly breathing chords are sustained on each beat, with a melody usually poised above them, occasionally answered by a second voice which will grow more potent during the second half. The two voices may be thought of, operatically, as man and woman. A duet is inevitably duality; but in so far as this is a marriage dance, duality seeks unity.

During the first bar, over the softly repeated E flat minor triad, the soprano melody lifts upwards, arpeggiated through the triad, only to descend through a noble fifth to the subdominant triad:

Ex. 42

The song has been sundered; but aspires again, from the subdominant, with the same arpeggiated figure, which this time falls through a tenser diminished seventh to a dissonantly ornamented D natural, with a tonic appoggiatura in the accompaniment. Drooping through a sixth on to the third beat of bar 3 the line becomes baroquely decorated; returning to a tonic triad which proceeds to relative major, the melody is transferred from soprano to baritone, whose descending arpeggio inverts the soprano's original motive. A second baritone entry falls through a diminished, not perfect, octave, modulating to the subdominant minor (bars 6–8). But the next descent moves back to the tonic, with diminished seventh appoggiatura, while the arabesques in the soprano are extended. The dialogue between the baritone line, which always descends through arpeggios in dotted rhythm, and the soprano line, which grows more convoluted in ornamentation, increases momentum in figuration, rhythm and tonality. The soprano wings through modulations to the dominant and to the dominant's relative, with an effect at once sensual and levitational:

Ex. 43

Although the regular minim chords are unbroken, their temporality is effaced
by the soprano's twining arioso, the contours of which seldom coincide with
the metrical beat. Thus the high G flat that effects the modulation to the
dominant's relative major occurs on the second beat; and although a second
beat stress is not unexpected in a sarabande, we no longer feel this stress as a
body rhythm. Metrical accent is transcended in lyrical flexibility (bar 13).

The shift to the dominant in the fourteenth bar is by way of a cadential trill,
echoed by an alto arabesque in the next bar. Though the dominant cadence
occurs where expected, in bar 16, it does not impose finality. On the contrary,
as the soprano melody extends *through* the bar, the baritone assumes the more
energetic role. 'He' begins with a rising instead of falling arpeggio, which
modulates to the subdominant minor by way of a plunge through a seventh:

Ex. 44

The rhythm of the baritone arioso conflicts with the dotted rhythm of the
soprano, who is driven up, by the baritone's thrusts, to cadence in A flat
minor. The regular chordal pulse has now dissipated; what remains is a two-
part dialogue in free canon, between male voice and female voice. The canon
starts with descending tritones, in a dotted rhythm that now sounds lacerating
rather than ceremonial, if we hear a distant echo of flagellating Passion music
in the passage. Lyricism returns, however, when the baritone resumes his
declining, dotted-rhythm arpeggio, with sighing appoggiaturas from the
soprano. Again, a diminished seventh descent in the baritone releases whirling
arabesques in the soprano; and time-denying semiquaver scales explosively
climax on the Neapolitan chord of F flat:

Ex. 45

This shatters the slow pulse of the accompanying chords which, over the two
previous bars, have tried to re-establish themselves. As in an opera, indeed, the
Neapolitan chord precipitates a solo cadenza in a lashing dotted rhythm, with
tritonal and diminished seventh writhings that mount to a written-out double
appoggiatura — C flat, A natural, B flat.

This cadenza, approached by the 'tritonal' canon, is so dramatic, even
theatrical, that the passage has somewhat the effect of a ternary middle section
within the extended binary form. That the rhetorical convention of the
Neapolitan cadence has prompted the quasi-vocal solo line irregularly to spurt
in arioso reminds us again of the specific significance of arioso in Baroque
opera. Operatic characters, we recall, sing in arioso rather than in 'dry'
recitative, when 'beside' or 'outside' their merely human selves. So perhaps we
may say that, in this passage from the E flat minor prelude, intensity of natural
human feeling is also an approach to the *super*natural: once more the physical
and metaphysical are identified.

This climax is not, however, a consummation. The written-out double
appoggiatura on to B flat looks as though it's going to resolve by way of a
cadential 6–4 on to the tonic. Yet again cadence is interrupted: the bass moves
not to the tonic, but to a first inversion of the subdominant, with piercing
suspended dissonance in the arioso, now transferred to alto. The slowly
pulsing chords resume in the subdominant minor, but the arioso, flowing
from alto to tenor to bass, is asymmetrically extended, grinding towards a
diminished seventh return to the tonic. The diminished seventh again
explodes in a cadenza, breaking the time barrier of the bar-line. Again an
apparent 6–4 cadence is delayed, though not this time frustrated, by the
substitution of the warmly enveloping flat seventh for the straight tonic:

Ex. 46

Though this momentarily implies subdominant minor, the last four bars unfold over a tonic pedal. The arioso, back in the soprano, soars freely across the beats, subsides on the sharp seventh, acutely dissonant with the pedal note, and is reiterated on the last quaver of the penultimate bar. (Some editions anticipate the resolution on this quaver, but the D natural reading is the more authentic and convincing.)

The first sixteen bars of the sarabande-prelude proceed without structural division. The second part covers twenty-five instead of sixteen bars, the irregularity being created by the delayed cadences. They in turn are produced by the music's attempt to transcend body rhythm in melodic lines that are at first fragmented but which grow, elaborately ornamented, in flexibility and in continuity. This evolution towards continuity is prompted by the interplay of two voices in dialogue; over the body rhythm of a dance, the operatic interaction of arioso lines creates, out of duality, a Passion music of transcendent ecstasy. The prelude is no less a religious piece than its companion fugue; only whereas the fugue celebrates the universal Godhead's impact *on* mankind, the prelude celebrates the Godhead inherent *in* man. In this sense the prelude is Protestant, the fugue Catholic, bearing to one another a relationship similar to that between the *St. John Passion* and the B minor Mass.

The tempo of this prelude is naturally that of a sarabande, though slower than that of a sarabande danced, owing to its linear and harmonic complexities. The lines must suggest the freedom of arioso; on the other hand the slow swing of the pendulum must be unbroken, for the essence of the piece lies in its equipoise between the temporal and the atemporal. This is clearly clavichord music; no other instrument could suggest a lute-like texture for the chords, and also a 'speaking' subtlety in the quasi-vocal dialogue. The piece can also sound well on harpsichord, if the convolutions of the lines are plastically handled. The organ is not appropriate to the plucked-string effect of the accompanying chords, though it can negotiate the melodic dialogue effectively.

The E flat minor prelude is a dance that is also operatic arioso. Our next prelude, the F sharp minor from Book II (not the companion to the Book I F sharp minor fugue we analysed) is formally an operatic aria da capo. Even more than the E flat minor prelude, however, it 'spiritualizes' its operatic humanity in a manner peculiar to Bach: in no other classical Baroque composer can one find cantilena so long sustained, so sensuous yet so apparently disembodied. The opening bar melodically establishes a tonic

triad, both in the syncopated soprano voice and in the rising tenor; and
reaffirms it in the second bar by a kind of 'ghost' canon in middle register:

Ex. 47

But the second half of bar 1 dissolves syncopation into stepwise moving
triplets; and the momentum is enhanced in bar 3, since the initial syncopated
fourth is twice repeated in diminution, with a passing dissonance on the last
quaver between sharp seventh and tonic resolution. The autograph
occasionally intersperses the undulating triplets with a semiquaver followed by
two demisemiquavers, which some editors straighten into level triplets. I
suspect that what is implied is extreme freedom of nuance: the triplets will not
always be equal, the *ta ta-ta* rhythm never rigid.

During the first eleven bars, indeed, there is no break and virtually no point
at which the presence of a bar-line is definitive. The melody sings in its
convolutions of semiquavers, triplets and demisemiquavers, the fluidity and
irregularity dissipating any sense of time-dominated metre and weakening the
pull of harmonic roots. Again, as in the D major cello suite's allemande
(which I compared to the fecund cornucopias that float from the pillars of
Austrian Baroque churches) line aspires heavenwards from metrical and
harmonic sensuality. The forward flow here modulates to the dominant but is
delicately disciplined by the appearance of a falling scale in dotted rhythm, first
in the tenor, then later in the bass:

Ex. 48

This stabilizes, but does not dam, the melodic flow, which in bar 13 returns to
the original syncopated fourth dissolving into triplets, echoed by a pseudo-
canon in the tenor.

This turns out to be not the second half of a binary structure, but the middle of an aria da capo. In embryonic sonata style, it also contains faint hints of development, for the dominant modulation is immediately balanced by a subdominant modulation, with a demisemiquaver turn at the end of the linear roulades. From there the music moves to the relative, A major, semiquavers and triplets unfolding together to create a warmly enveloping sonority. Although the line is unbroken, the texture is now more homophonic, as we move in sequence between E and A major (bars 15–22). When the original syncopated figure returns, the harmonic and tonal evolution continues, for the music strains upwards in a cycle of fifths from E to B to F sharp to C sharp, all minor, and so back by way of the syncopated rhythm over a falling chromatic bass, to a half-close on, not in, the dominant:

Ex. 49

At this point one imagines, perhaps even plays, a brief, quasi-operatic cadenza which, echoed by the bass triplets, leads into a da capo. This begins strict, but is modified in bar 3 to produce a modulation to the subdominant, as in a sonata recapitulation.

The da capo has fourteen bars to the aria's twelve; even more than in the exposition the cantilena is unbroken and apparently barless. Again a harmonic event—the substitution of a Neapolitan G natural (bar 34) as an approach to a tonic cadence—precipitates cascading triplets extending over eight bars. This Neapolitan had been touched on in the sequences of the middle section; now it has become harmonic drama in its own right, and its consequences are lyrical. For by the time we're back in the tonic at bar 36 the diminished syncopations are agilely leaping through major and minor sevenths and tritones over the lower parts' rich harmonies. In bar 39 the triplets begin to surge in an unbroken descent which is to cover ten bars, culminating in a written-out double appoggiatura (D natural to B sharp over the dominant triad) in the syncopated rhythm:

Ex. 50

In the last bar downward-flowing triplets in the tenor balance the treble's upward triplets, and the syncopated motive resolves on to a major triad. The soaring of this Baroque line would not be so balm-dispensing if it didn't embrace those suspended dissonances, that richness of texture, that Neapolitan stab; only the 'crucial' crisis of the double appoggiatura in bar 41 seems to make possible the triplets' contrary motion running down to the *tierce de Picardie*.

The E flat minor prelude is basically a dance, from the slow rhythm of which unfold melodies of operatic intensity, at first fragmented, gradually growing in lyrical range. The F sharp minor prelude is basically an operatic aria in which, however, metrical periodicity dissolves in melodic cantilena of immense span. In both cases the initial secular impulse—the social solidarity of a dance or the human expressivity of an aria—seeks, and in the F sharp minor prelude finds, a transcendental consummation. The parallel between the F sharp minor prelude and the Benedictus of the B minor Mass is not fortuitous. The prelude is also a musical synonym for the state of blessedness, and could be so only because (as its tonality indicates) it doesn't evade pain. This prelude works well on any of the keyboard instruments available to Bach. The organ delineates its proliferating lines lucidly while depersonalizing its passion; the harpsichord stresses its emotional plangency, the clavichord its introspective intimacy.

The C minor prelude from Book II is a very different kind of piece, which interestingly complements its fugue. That, we noted, has an old-fashioned, religiously vocal theme which is progressively and sectionally transformed into the rhetorical, theatrical and instrumental world of the Baroque. The prelude is representatively classical Baroque in two ways. First, it's a simple binary structure with a first section modulating to the relative major and a second section returning to the tonic minor; secondly, it evolves from keyboard figuration rather than from a lyrical theme. But if, in the fugue, quasi-vocal counterpoint is rendered harmonically dense, rhythmically potent and instrumentally virtuosic, in the prelude Baroque motor-rhythm and figuration seek polyphonic discipline; for the texture is that of a two-part invention, the closely wrought thematicism of which depersonalizes humanistic passion.

Contrapuntal unity is manifest in the first two bars, which are in double counterpoint: the upper part of the second bar imitates the lower part of the first bar, while the lower part imitates the upper:

Ex. 51

The right hand consists of semiquaver wriggles around a descending scale; the left hand quavers ascend in parallel tenths with the upper part, bouncing through octave, fifth, and two sixths. Bars 3 and 4 abandon the imitation but move sequentially upwards, first diatonically, then chromatically. In bars 5–6 the rise both in pitch and in harmonic impetus is counterpoised by a scalewise descent in parallel tenths, each beat filled out with the semitonic wriggle. The music stabilizes in the relative major, by way of a touch of subdominant. For the rest of the first half prancing sixths create a rising arpeggio in the top part and a rising scale in the lower, though the bass diatonically descends. A clear IV–V–I cadence, with additional parts brought in to fill out the harmony, concludes with a falling E flat arpeggio.

This first half has comprised twelve bars, asymmetrically divided into 2 + 2 + 3 + 3 + 2. The second part runs to sixteen bars, the extension occurring because the second section explores the harmonic-dramatic implications of the first. There is little strict imitation, and no direct repetition of the original material in the new key. None the less the first measure after the double bar hints at an inversion of the opening bar. Instead of falling through the scale the crotchet beat of the upper part moves from tonic E flat to F to A flat, decorated by the semitonic wriggle with A naturals, while the bass stalks in quavers through a basic dominant-tonic progression.

The next bar is not strictly imitative, though it transfers the wriggle to the left hand, and adds a trill to the right hand's falling arpeggios. Bars 15–16 repeat the pattern of the two previous bars sequentially; the appearance of D flat on the last beat of the sequence carries us flatwards to the subdominant minor, the left hand repeating the wriggle in middle register, with leaping sevenths. This heating-up process continues when the line moves chromatically between D flat,

C and B natural; the quaver bass is also chromaticized on each strong beat, leaping through sixths and sevenths. All these elements gel in bars 19–20, for each bar reasserts the downward diatonic scales decorated with the wriggle and, in the other hand, embellishes with the wriggle a rising arpeggio in quavers.

The music proceeds from F minor to A flat major, to B flat minor, and back to F minor. Sharpened cadential sevenths in the right hand impart energy and disturb the rhythmic regularity, since one hears the cadential quavers phrased across the beats. This is the point of greatest momentum; the next bars return to the tonic by way of the relative, through three strictly sequential, tranquilly ordered bars, with rising scale and falling octave in the bass's quavers. The coda adds richness with an additional part. In the penultimate bar the bass's rising quavers are chromaticized and the semiquavers, released from the nag of the wriggle, fuse the downward scale of four tones with a diminution of the motive with which the bass began after the double bar. Characteristically, increased harmonic tension leads to more fulfilled, songlike contours in the figuration. The final bar makes a firm 6–4 approach to the tonic triad; the bass rises through a tonic arpeggio, to balance its fall at the end of the first half. This kind of figuration works best on the harpsichord, to which instrument, as we've already noted, the fugue too is best suited.

So whereas the C minor fugue, starting from sixteenth-century polyphony, grows freer as it becomes contemporaneously Baroque, the C minor prelude disciplines Baroque improvisatory figuration with contrapuntal rigour. The A minor prelude from Book II—as the complement to a fugue which is, we saw, of the high Baroque in being harmonic, rhythmic and rhetorical in character rather than linear—does something comparable, more extra-vagantly. This prelude is also a two-part invention, and this time the two halves are strictly symmetrical, consisting of sixteen bars each, the first ending on the dominant, the second in the tonic. Binary form is reinforced by contrapuntal rigour, since the piece is in double counterpoint throughout, and the second half begins as a mirror inversion of the first. Yet the theme itself is one of the most chromatic Bach ever created; so much so that the music almost tends to atonality, or at least modulates so fluidly that it is often difficult to determine the key.

The bass of the first bar leaps an octave, descends down the chromatic scale, phrased, probably, in weeping pairs of quavers across the beat. The upper part opens with a swirl of rising demisemiquavers, descends through a fourth, alternates rising thirds with falling tritones, the last of them syncopated over the beat. The second bar inverts this, the weeping quavers being in the right hand an octave higher, the left hand having the original upper part, two octaves lower. Bar 3 is transitional in the sense that the left hand balances the falling chromatics with rising diatonic scales, pressing through the sharp seventh to a dominant modulation:

Ex. 52

The upper part embellishes the descending chromatics with a demi-semiquaver inverted mordent, with leaping sixths and persistent syncopations that misplace accents. Bars 4–5 repeat bars 1–2, in the dominant; in bar 6 the rising scale in the bass momently re-establishes the tonic to conclude with bouncing octaves, tied to the leaping and chromatically shifting sixths. This figure is treated canonically, falling in descending sequence through D, G and C major. Bach now returns to his original double counterpoint, with the two motives widely separated. Bars 10–11 have the diatonic (sharp seventh) scales in the upper part, the ornamented, syncopated descending chromatics in the lower, followed by the original motive moving sequentially from D to G and back to A minor. The next two bars again disrupt tonality, proceeding in rapid sequences through A minor to D, G, and C, all major. Disintegration is held at bay, however, since the texture is strictly canonic. The last bar of the first half swoops on to the dominant by way of demisemiquaver scales:

Ex. 53

The second half—and this time it really is such—begins with a mirror inversion of the opening bars: the right hand has the original left hand part upside down, the left hand has the original right hand part, also inverted. After two bars the diatonic scales descend in the right hand, though the left hand figuration is no longer inverted. The canonic patterns remain consistent, and chromaticism is so extreme that no key centre is defined until the sequential modulations to D minor in bars 23–24. In the next bar the original double counterpoint is resumed in the *rectus* form, answered *inversus* in the following measure. In bar 27 the lower part's rising diatonic scale leads, through rising and falling chromatically altered sixths, to a discreet climax in which the sixths mingle with unstable tritones:

Ex. 54

This passage has no strict parallel in the first half; and even when in bar 30 symmetry between the parts is reaffirmed, both parts now move up, and then down, instead of in contrary motion. The final bar, though not strict, has the effect of an inversion of the closing bar of the first half, as the demisemiquaver scale in the left hand shoots up beneath the mordent on the tonic A.

To comment on the tight contrapuntal organization of this prelude is not to describe its musical effect, which depends on a precarious balance between the sensual disturbance of the total chromaticism, with its nervously fluctuating harmonies and unstable modulations, and the cool, almost geometric control of the mirror counterpoint and architectural symmetry. This anticipates the 'fugal universe' of Bach's last years; and here is a case in which the prelude indissolubly belongs to the fugue, to which it profoundly modifies our approach. Having heard this prelude, we cannot accept the fugue's subject as the Baroque cliché it initially seemed to be. Recognizing that the prelude's chromatic sensuality and rhythmic dislocation have been counterbalanced by mathematical double counterpoint of uncompromising rigour precisely because these two poles of experience, sensual and intellectual, have become one, we also recognize that the fugue's physicality is seeking a metaphysical release. The fugue's final whirring demisemiquavers abortively seek what the prelude has attained; and the miracle of the prelude is precisely that, for all its timeless symmetries, it contains the fugue's wildness within it.

This bears on the speed at which the prelude should be played. It *can* be performed rapidly, in which case the chromaticism sounds hectic; or it can be played slowly, thereby emphasizing the chromaticism's weeping expressivity. But it surely should be played at a moderate tempo, so that extravagance of passion sounds *sub specie aeternitatis*. This music gives aural reality to the cliché that describes an experience as being 'outside time', 'beyond good and evil', for it renders incarnate in sound, not one man's distress at a particular time and place, but *lacrimae rerum*, universalized through the crucible of Bach's imagination. The piece works well, if differently, on any keyboard instrument. The Baroque organ colours the chromaticism beautifully, while preserving impersonality; the harpsichord clearly delineates its linear and rhythmic complexities; the clavichord simultaneously reveals emotional nuance and rarefied linearity. On balance, it's probably harpsichord music, since its complementary fugue is indisputably so.

The famous prelude to the C major fugue of Book I is in some ways the simplest, in other ways the subtlest, piece on which we've commented. The *Well-tempered Clavier* is, among other things, a pedagogic work; and this prelude is pedagogic at a rudimentary level, both as an exercise in harmonic progression (Bach's original sketch was merely a chord sequence) and as a loosening-up exercise for the fingers. The figuration, which recalls the broken chords of the lutanists' preludial movements, is derived from the natural behaviour of the hands playing this chord sequence on a keyboard: lying nearly under the ten fingers, it spreads the chord in rising arpeggios, sustaining the two lowest tones with the left hand:

Ex. 55

There would seem to be no theme. The broken chords, flowering upwards in level semiquavers, are centred in the middle of the keyboard, and move very slowly. After a bar of tonic triad the C stays as pedal while the triad moves up a tone; the D is held in the tenor register while the bass moves down to B, making a first inversion of the dominant seventh of C, which then ascends, again to the tonic triad in root position. The next three bars repeat the left hand's progression, but the triadic arpeggios above are now A minor in first inversion, the dominant seventh of G in second inversion, and G major in first inversion; the chords glow as the sharpened Fs replace the F naturals. Still in G the left hand moves through dissonant suspensions to a full close in the dominant in bars 10–11. The steady flow of the music is now, however, disturbed by chromatics: a flattened B in the tenor and a sharp C on top of the right hand's arpeggio form a diminished seventh leading to a first inversion of the darker D minor triad:

Ex. 56

Again the inner left hand part is flattened, producing a diminished seventh return to a first inversion of the tonic triad. Tight suspensions occur in the left hand as the bass descends, plunging to a low G, which resonantly rings.

This dominant marks the eighteenth, not sixteenth, bar; but none the less sounds like the halfway house in a binary structure. And the next bar repeats the opening of the prelude, an octave lower, so the dominant modulation in the first half has been balanced by a gradual fall in pitch. The descent, moreover, continues, tonally; for in bar 20 a flat seventh creeps into the arpeggio, producing a subdominant modulation with suspended sevenths. From this darkness the chord sequence regathers power; the low F is sharpened, the top of the arpeggio flattened, to make a G minor diminished seventh:

Ex. 57

The bass moves pivotally from F sharp to A flat to G, on which dominant
pedal it remains immobile for eight bars. Over the pedal, the arpeggios move
with tortoise-like inexorability, from dominant seventh, to a 6–4, to suspended
dominant seventh, to chromatically altered G minor diminished seventh, and
so back to a 6–4 and suspended dominant seventh in C major. The bass falls,
at last, through a fifth to a low C which, ringing cavernously, is harmonized
with the tonic triad, but with a flat seventh added. This deeper darkness
effects, inevitably, a lyrical release; for the pattern of the arpeggios, lying under
the hand, is for the first time broken and extended, cadenza-like, through a
whole bar over a subdominant 6–4, no longer simply floating up, but flowing
up and down in a wave, the highest point of which occurs just after the second
beat. This asymmetrical wave is repeated in the next bar, a ninth higher,
embracing a dominant seventh arpeggio of C, still over the low C as a
dissonant pedal point:

Ex. 58

So out of an exercise in harmonic progression Bach has created another
minor miracle: a tonal drama that rises to luminosity, descends to darkness,
climbs slowly to a lyrical liberation the more remarkable because the texture,
over the dominant pedal, has become so claustrophobically enveloping. That
the figuration creates a 'theme' is explicit when the prelude is followed by the
fugue, the subject of which grows from the top notes of the prelude's arpeggios:

Ex. 59

An apparently unambiguous chordal texture reveals linear cross-currents, an
inversion of the habitual process whereby Bach's melodies contain harmonic
implications. This is essentially clavichord music, for an organ could not
make the chord sequences swell and 'glow', while a harpsichord couldn't
reveal the intimate nuances that suggest polyphony, usually in four parts. It is
this latent polyphony that conditions the tempo. The songlike lines within the

arpeggios cannot emerge if the piece is played rapidly, as an exercise in digital facility. The weighting and placing of the chords' components is all-important if the piece is to be revealed for what it is: a harmonic drama that is also a lyrical affirmation that has no need—notwithstanding what Gounod added quantitatively to Bach in his notorious *Ave Maria*—for overt statement in a 'tune'.

When he wishes Bach can, of course, create memorable tunes—which don't always need to be dignified with the appellation of 'melody'. None the less, listening to this unpretentious prelude, we can understand why he felt condescension towards the 'pretty little tunes' of the Dresden opera, which his fashion-conscious sons admired. Bach, as we've seen, was more than a man of his time; though aware of and expert in using current conventions, he transformed them in the light of the numinous. An attempt has been made by Friedrich Blume to play down the religious aspects of Bach's temperament, even to suggest that they were an invention of nineteenth-century sanctimoniousness. Such a swing of the pendulum was inevitable in a sceptical age, and even has value in so far as it deflates the image of Bach as a good churchman, a pious advocate of dogma. But no-one with ears to hear can doubt that Bach was at heart a religious composer, and that his religion springs from the depths of the human psyche, rather than from a topical and local creed. This is aurally implicit, as I've tried to demonstrate, even in the techniques of ostensibly non-religious works. It is now time to examine its explicit nature in two of his greatest, distinct yet complementary, achievements—the *St. John Passion* and the Mass in B minor.

THE SECOND ADAM

You see what sort of man I have grown into, but in order that you may be well informed about the times in which I lived, let me tell you that they were cruel.

HENRY VAUGHAN

God going out from Himself brings it about that we go into ourselves; and making Himself known to us, he makes us known to ourselves.

MARTIN LUTHER

Faith is, as Luther said, the readiness to enter confidently into the darkness of the future. . . . The Word of God addresses man in his insecurity and calls him into freedom, for man loses freedom in his very yearning for security. . . . Genuine freedom is not subjective arbitrariness, but freedom from the motivation of the moment. It is possible only when conduct is determined by a motive which transcends the present moment, that is, by law. Freedom is obedience to a law of which the validity is recognized and accepted, which man recognizes as the law of his own being. This can only be a law which has its origin and reason in the beyond. We may call it the law of spirit or, in Christian language, the law of God.

RUDOLF BULTMANN

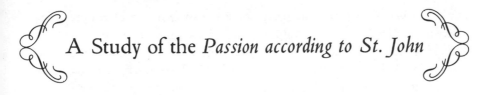

A Study of the *Passion according to St. John*

It is often said that Bach was born out of his time, a statement which would seem to conflict with the view that genius involves an ability to know the right time and place to be born. In fact there is no such conflict, for in Bach's case to be born out of his time was to be born in the time he needed, in a place that seemed to be relinquishing the values by which he lived. The rightness of time and place, if in this sense negative, was also positive in that the Bach family was the longest and most talented musical dynasty known to European history. The province of Thuringia, where Bachs were established as early as the fourteenth century, was propitious not merely because of the country's physical beauty, but also because its human community was small, self-subsistent and culturally vigorous. The Thuringians were sturdy, independent, devout, dedicated to music both for worship and pastime; at the same time they could not afford to be self-indulgently cosy since Germany was a network of petty princedoms distracted, throughout the fifteenth and sixteenth centuries, by religious and political dissension. Then, as ever, politics and religion were inseparable. A peasants' revolt was put down, in 1525, with the usual ruthlessness. Eventually, the cause of Luther, the new spiritual leader, became a rallying of the politically oppressed as well as a rediscovered faith. Culturally, especially musically, Luther's crusade was stimulating: education, by way of new schools with radically reformed curricula, was a weapon to be placed in the hands of the people; popular songs transformed into hymns could encourage nationalist fervour as well as a zeal for the reformed creed. In the seventeenth century, however, the Lutheran cause suffered many buffets. Acts of God or the Devil—storms, floods and plague—fanned the fires smouldering beneath the surface of religious and political life; and erupted into the Thirty Years' War, compared with which the earlier Peasants' War seemed trifling, because so soon extinguished. The religious motivation of the war was that the emperors Rudolf II (r. 1576–1612) and Ferdinand II (r. 1619–1637), both Catholics in close touch with the Jesuits, wished to extirpate the Lutheran heresy; their political objective was to contain Germany under the sway of the Habsburgs. The Swedes, under Gustavus Adolphus, were drawn into the conflict with the religious motive of defending Protestantism and the political motive of protecting their commercial interests in the Baltic. Later the French entered the war, with the usual dubious medley of motives. From the early 1620s Thuringia was occupied by foreign troops, which behaved with the destructive violence endemic to occupying forces.

The devastations, material and spiritual, occasioned by the Thirty Years' War were perhaps more appalling than those of any war before our presumptively civilized century. If a man is strong enough, belief may batten on distress; he may even feel the psychic realities of his nature the more deeply when the world seems to be passing them by. This was true of Heinrich Schütz, the greatest of Bach's seventeenth-century forebears, whose work offers evidence of the bifurcation which the war entailed. Culturally, this divisiveness was not all loss: it was to its enrichment that Schütz's music fused the Italianate flamboyance of the Catholic and autocratic south with the Teutonic abnegatory fervour of the Protestant, incipiently proletarian north. In musical terms the Italianate elements meant operatic lyricism and harmonic opulence, while the German elements involved old-fashioned contrapuntal science allied with a harmonic acerbity learned from the Italians, but rendered darker, more gloomy. Schütz himself went to study with the illustrious Monteverdi, whose sun-baked brilliance illuminated his early works and, through them, the chapels of German princelings. Yet Schütz's music preserves a mystical intensity that concentrates on Christ as man-God, equating his suffering with ours; and 'our' anguish was in Schütz's day patent enough, since after the war Teutonic oases of humanism flourished over an abyss. This was sometimes literally true. Esterházy, later the home of Haydn's patron, was a fairy-tale Versailles built by woefully oppressed serfs over a marshy morass, to prove that whatever a *roi soleil* could do they could do, if not better, at least in the teeth of more inimical circumstances. As the Electress Sophie put it: 'C'est la mode que les electeurs deviennent rois'. In the face of such desperate vainglory it is hardly surprising that Schütz, growing to old age, concentrated increasingly on Christ's passion, incarnate in musical styles that grew progressively more austere, ending in a vernacular version of plainsong monody, without even a continuo instrument, and with minimal choral interludes. Though this suited the penury of war-impoverished courts, the economic motive was less important than the spiritual.

By Bach's day the vainglory of a decadent humanism was to some degree in abeyance. The decline of central government and the warring multiplicity of petty tyrannies had led to a strong, if idealistic and unfulfilled, desire for order, reflected in the attempt of Karl Ludwig's Peace Church to reconcile Catholics, Lutherans and Calvinists; and in Leibniz's experiments towards a universal sign language. Similarly the 'harmonious' cosmology of Leibniz's philosophy was a pseudo-scientific refashioning of the medieval Chain of Being, wherein everything from inanimate stones to man had its place. Comparable notions lay behind the hierarchical fusion of the genres — German, Italian, French, Dutch — in the arts, though the Baroque attempt to canalize the luxuriance of the senses and the material world (with which Bach intuitively sympathized) was already being superseded by a subtler, quieter egotism (with which his temperament was not in tune). This was the Enlightenment's belief that man might play God not by admitting to and disciplining the extravagances of passion, but rather through Reason and Science. Enlightenment would come not through spiritual grace, but through the ability to *know how*, and therefore intellectually to control. This directly affected even religious teaching, for Christian Wolff attempted a compromise between the Lutheran justification by faith alone and rational comprehension. In his Weimar days Bach found himself in trouble because the rector Ernesti supported Wolff's progressive line as vigorously as Bach mistrusted it. At Leipzig Bach similarly came into conflict with the progressive sub-deacon Gottlieb Gaudlitz, who wished to abandon the old chorales in favour of new ones with fashionably rationalistic texts. For Bach the words of the old chorales were theologically crucial, matching the nobility of the tunes. We are apt to forget that Newton died a year *before* the *Matthew Passion* was completed; that Voltaire was Bach's contemporary; that Frederick the Great, who played the rationally refashioned flute, must have considered the *Musical Offering* which Bach made to him as archaistic, if technically impressive. Bach was content to be out of step. Except in the sense that his art became timeless and placeless, he was not cosmopolitan. Unlike Handel — who was as much Italian as German in taste and training and who became an anglicized European — Bach travelled infrequently and within a restricted range. True, as a young man, in the interests of his art, he walked a fair way to meet Reinken and a considerable distance to meet Buxtehude. Pilgrimages to seek fame and fortune did not, however, interest him. By the time he visited Frederick the Great he was as famous as he was ever likely to be, and at the end of his life's work. His enlightened sons, whose genuine respect for their father was tinged with condescension, were suns in the ascendant. Over them the Lutheran church was no longer dominant; one of them, indeed, became a Roman Catholic.

Eisenach, where several generations of Bachs lived and worked, epitomizes the cultural ambivalence into which the greatest of Bachs was born. It was a small walled town guarded by watchtowers, with a few thousand working-class Protestants for the most part serving an elaborately bureaucratic court. The art, architecture and culture of this court was French and Italian rather than German, and was in part aristocratic and Catholic, in part intellectually enlightened and deist. Given such conditions it is not surprising that the Lutheran church should, during Bach's youth, have cultivated a conservatism born of desperation; it had long been tuned to a fight for survival. At the same time it had the courage of conviction: Luther's church reforms had significant educational assets—especially when, with the dissolution of monastic establishments and the reduction of court chapel music he had founded the lay *Kantoreien*, municipal bodies of professional musicians and wealthy burghers who planned and financed civic and ecclesiastical music. The *Kantorei* tradition ensured that expert technical training in music was considered basic, not peripheral; and since music was essential to the health of the community, the *Kantor*'s position—at top of the hierarchy that began with *Spielmann* (strolling musician) and ascended through *Hausmann* (household musician) to *Stadtpfeifer* (court trumpeter)—was an honourable one. In two hundred years the Bachs had risen through these ranks. Johann Sebastian's respect for tradition must have been encouraged by the fact that he came from, and continued to propagate, so august a line of musicians. Loyalty to the family complemented loyalty to the faith; and this worked at a deeper level than subservience to church and state.

Bach's education, in 'backward' Germany, fostered his innate conservatism, as Jan Chiapusso's fascinating book *Bach's World* has demonstrated. The world view he inherited was still medieval, remote from rationalist deism. Though he seems to have been acquainted with the theories of Copernicus and Kepler his education was not only unscientific, but antiscientific. The distinction is problematic, since Copernicus and Kepler themselves believed in astrology, in the Pythagorean Harmony of the Spheres, in the Biblical story of the Creation, and at least in some aspects of alchemy and witchcraft. The difference is one of emphasis rather than of doctrine. For Bach as for Luther inner illumination, not the scientific attitude to fact, was the only approach to reality; and in apparent paradox the ultimate flowering of German music may be attributable to the survival of an obsolete educational system that stressed the light of faith at the expense of intellectual enquiry. In any case Luther had been consciously drawn to the Middle Ages in his attempt to restore what he believed to be the purity of Christian faith. He agreed with Melancthon that 'if theology is not the beginning, middle and end of life we cease being men and return to the animal state': so the basis of his educational system was theology supported, as means to an end, by the medieval trivium of grammar, rhetoric and dialectic. Physics, mathematics, astronomy, moral philosophy and history crept in by the back door, since they could be construed theologically as exemplars of divine law. The classics got in vicariously since everything was taught in Latin, a universal tongue, as well as German, and since Greek was the language of the New Testament. Later in the curriculum Hebrew was taught, as the Old Testament's tongue.

But the chief succour and support to theology was music, and Luther (in 'Table Talk') himself explains why, remarking that

I have always loved music. Those who have mastered this art are made of good stuff, they are fit for any task. It is indeed necessary that music be taught in schools. A teacher must be able to sing, otherwise I will not look at him. Also we must not ordain young men into the ministry unless they have become well acquainted with music in the schools. We should always make it a point to habituate youth to enjoy the art of music, for it produces fine and skilful people.

Of music's ethical value he further says:

Experience proves that next to the love of God only music deserves being extolled as the mistress and governess of the feelings of the human heart. . . . Even the Holy Spirit honours music as a tool of His work, since He testifies in the Holy Scriptures that through the medium of music His gifts have been put into the hands of the prophets (e.g. Elisha); again, through music the Devil has been driven away, as was the case with Saul. For this very reason the Fathers desired not in vain that nothing be more intimately linked up with the Word of God than music.

And of music's theological implications:

God has created man for the express purpose of praising and extolling Him. However, when man's natural musical ability is whetted and polished to the extent that it becomes art, then do we note with great surprise the great and perfect wisdom of God in music, which is after all his product and gift. ... St. Paul encouraged the use of music in order that through it the Word of God and Christian doctrine might be preached, taught, and put into practice. ... The whole purpose of harmony is the glory of God; all other use is but the idle juggling of Satan.

At the school which Bach attended in Ohrdruf the system of education was little changed from the old prescription. Music was second in importance only to theology, and was taught by the same master, who believed that music 'makes the heart ready and receptive to the divine Word and truth, just as Elisius confessed that by harping he found the Holy Spirit.' Such time as was not devoted to theology and music was somewhat grudgingly divided between history, arithmetic, physics and geography, taught from the classics, without reference to the new science of the Enlightenment. When Bach continued his education at the Ritterakademie in Lüneberg, the basis of instruction remained theology and music, taught by the same man. This institution also offered instruction in fencing, dancing, riding and modern languages, especially French. We have no evidence as to whether Bach availed himself of these politer pursuits; he certainly acquired a shaky familiarity with the French language and first-hand acquaintance with French music, especially that of Lully.

As a schoolboy Bach had been fairly precocious, two or three years in advance of his age-group. If he didn't continue his education to university level, that was due to no failure in ability, but to a conflict of interests. For his talents as a musical performer—first as a boy treble ('a fine penetrating voice of great range and high singing culture'), then as a player of stringed instruments and keyboards—were even more exceptional than his cerebral gifts; a young man thus endowed would naturally seek outlet in professional music-making. None the less he remained intellectually alert and, since the notion of 'pure' music would have been inconceivable to him, kept in touch with the manifold ranges of learning that were relevant to his art. In his library he possessed—in addition to several copies of Luther's works and many commentaries on and addenda to them—Buno's *Historia Universalis*, a mythological history of the world founded on the biblical story of creation but incorporating such snippets of classical and oriental lore as could be assimilated into Christian tradition. He knew some Roman history and law, mostly from Cicero; and acquired further knowledge of the pre-Christian world from Rufus's life of Alexander the Great, a legendary hero to humanists of the Baroque era. Bach's providential view of history helped him as a composer: since he had no doubts about music's destiny and purpose, changes in style or structure occasioned by the accidents of history could be no more than superficial.

Musical instruction for Bach began with history in a philosophical sense; first principles define music's nature and purpose, founded on Pythagoras. His friendship with his cousin Johann Walther was deeply influential, for Walther was an able composer who wrote extensively of music theory, speculating on the divine nature and spiritual import of the art. His textbook summarized music theory since Zarlino, mixing learned calculations of intervallic proportions with astronomical and alchemical information. Much of the latter was derived from Athanasius Kircher's immense neo-medieval *Musurgia universalis* of 1648. Kircher was an aftermath of the universal man of the Renaissance: he wrote on a vast range of topics, including acoustics, optics, magnetism and geography; invented the magic lantern; specialized in oriental languages. Kircher's science is—as Chiapusso puts it—highly suspect but sensational. Walther certainly knew the book and Bach at least knew of it through him. In any case he would have supported Kircher's derivation of music from the Hebrews; would have accepted Kircher's view that the Pythagorean proportions were primal and causal, a divine tool of the Creator; and would probably have sympathized with Kircher's charts of astrological analogies, which claimed that musical proportions governed some ninety varieties of 'entities', ranging from God downwards to stones.

More directly influential on Bach was the work of Andreas Werckmeister, who wrote a treatise on tuning. Though hardly more scientific than Kircher, he had wider experience as a practical musician. A modernist in that he hinted at, though he did not invent, equal temperament, he too justified technical theory on the authority of scripture, relating it to Pythagorean numerology, to astrology, and to Thomist and Taulerian philosophy. He frequently quotes from Kepler's *Harmonia mundi* of 1619 to support the notion that music is itself a metaphysical being, a creation of God, through which we may have a foretaste of the harmony of heaven: music as heard with the physical ear is an imperfect manifestation of true being within the Creator's mind. He discovers Pythagorean proportions not only in music but in Kepler's calculations about the distances between the planets—and in the structure of the Ark! Today's enquiries into supernature suggest that such speculations are not as fanciful as we used to think. It would be going far to claim that 'only wicked souls do not respect music'; but it is possible to produce some statistical evidence that Bach was right in his belief that the world's audible music is an ectype of an archetype; and that music may in some way affect the behaviour of humans, animals, birds, even plants.

We will return to the implications of Bach's philosophy of music at various points in our analysis of his Passion and Mass. For the moment we're concerned rather with the bases of his faith as inherited from Luther; and these were closer to Catholicism than they were to Calvinism, with its distrust of materiality and its connection of spirit with reason, of reason with science, and of science with commerce. The difference between Catholicism and Luther's (and Bach's) mystical humanism is that for Luther grace flows directly from God. Luther himself went through an identity crisis which has been brilliantly analyzed in psychiatric terms by Erik Erikson, and the crisis in European history which the Lutheran Reformation represents is Luther's personal pathology writ large. Or more accurately, Luther is a microcosm of the macrocosm: the conflict in him between obedience (to a demanding father, judging God and monolithic Church) and personal conscience (through which the Son may be discovered or rediscovered) parallels 'certain steps in maturation which every man must take'. Luther's religion, as manifest in Bach's music, speaks to us directly because it concerns a spiritual evolution which is our birthright. It internalizes the relationship of Father and Son, re-establishes identity through conscience, and reaffirms the trust of infancy. According to nominalist theory, on which Luther was nurtured, God could exercise *potentia dei absoluta*, acting as he wished in divine freedom. He could also exercise *potentia dei ordinata*, whereby he committed himself to reward a morally meritorious act on the part of man. But for Luther this *meritum de congruo* could not be an act of grace, since grace was not a bargain, and must be independent of the letter of the law. Luther's insistence that grace could come only through personal awareness of 'the sweet wounds of Christ' means that he was at heart both humanist and mystic. This bears directly on Bach's music, which is also simultaneously mystical and human, spiritual and material, sacred and profane. It was the mystical strain in Pietism that attracted Bach to texts which he repudiated morally, though he could not bring himself to tolerate the Pietists' emasculation of the austere old chorale tunes.

On the psychological significance of the Lutheran (and Bachian) insistence on the humanity of Christ Jung has written, notably in *Answer to Job*, with percipience. He sees Christ as an image of the Self in that through him God comes to consciousness. The traditional image that equates Jesus with a fish has many ramifications. He swims phallus-like through the unknowing waters, creating form from the inchoate void. In the patristic allegory of the capture of Leviathan, the Cross is the hook, the Crucified the bait. The fish that swallowed Jonah died, but revived after the traditional three days to spew him out, so that 'through the fish we find a medicament for the whole world'. In Matthew 12:39 and 16:4 Christ takes the sign of Jonah as a prefiguration of the Messianic age and of his own fate; so, *de profundis levantus*, as St. Augustine put it, the fish is a bridge between the historical Christ and the psychic nature of man, where the archetype of the Redeemer dwells.

The Old Testament God is a God of power, unconscious and therefore amoral, beyond good and evil. When Moses asked God to reveal his name, he replied 'I am that I am'; and henceforth was known as Yahveh (He Who, or That Which, Is). This evades any concept of ideas, even the idea of being itself. As Collingwood puts it, 'pure being would have a subject matter entirely devoid of peculiarities: a subject matter, therefore, containing nothing to differentiate it from anything else, or from nothing at all.' But when Yahveh torments Job merely to demonstrate his almightiness, something occurs, says Jung, 'that had never occurred before in the history of the world, the unheard-of fact that without knowing it or wanting it a mortal man is raised by his moral behaviour above the stars in heaven'. Job points out that although Yahveh may be 'king of all proud beasts', the beasts are neither blessed nor cursed with consciousness; which leaves Yahveh as no more than a phenomenon, *not a man*. Yahveh is changed through the failure of his attempt to destroy Job. *Ex perfecto nihil fit*; whereas the *imperfectus* of his 'fall' into marriage with the female principle of Sophia and Israel carries in it a germ of growth. For God to become man is a world-shaking transformation of his own nature. If at the time of creation he revealed himself in Nature, now he wants to become more specific. The revelation of God as Man is a millenial process.

The birth of Christ, Jung points out, is attended by the usual phenomena coincident with the birth of a hero. His appearance is preceded by an annunciation; he is lowly but miraculously born, of a virgin; he is persecuted, concealed, and flees on a dark journey through water, forest and cavern; struggles with a dragonish or serpentine adversary; is slain on a hill; is reborn after three days, at a time marking the beginning of a new astrological era. When Christ becomes a young Dying God his divine origin is attested by his association with a dove, the attribute of a love goddess. But he is demythologized in uttering his despairing cry from the Cross, 'My God, my God, why hast thou forsaken me?' In that moment his human nature attains to divinity, while God experiences what it means to be a mortal man and to drink to the dregs what he has made his servant Job suffer. This supreme moment is 'as divine as it is human, as eschatological as it is psychological.' Yahveh's intention to become man, which resulted from his collision with Job, is fulfilled in Christ's life and suffering. If we think of Christ as the perfect man it would seem that he cannot be total because, in Jungian terms, he omits the Shadow. 'If we call everything that God does or allows "good", then evil is good too and good becomes meaningless. But suffering, whether it be Christ's passion or the suffering of the world, remains the same as before. Stupidity, sin, sickness, old age and death continue to form the dark foil that sets off the joyful splendour of life.' In this sense Jesus is the *complexio oppositorum* which is the human psyche. He is the perfect man *who is crucified*, crucifixion being that 'acute state of unredeemedness which comes to an end only with the words "consummatum est" '. Only the complete person can know how unbearable man is to himself, and in psychological terms Christ saved the world because, if the individual does not become conscious of his inner opposite, there is no alternative but for that conflict to be acted out in violence. All opposites are of God; allowing God to take possession of him, Christ became 'a vessel filled with divine conflict'. In early Christianity Lucifer, the Shadow, was Christ's coeval, both being personified as the morning star or the planet Venus, embracing both spirituality and sexuality. 'We have also a more sure word of prophecy whereunto ye do well that ye take heed, as unto a light that shineth in a dark place, until the day dawn, and the day star arise in your hearts' (2 Pet. 1:19).

So it would seem to be a two-way process. God wants to become man in growing to consciousness; man wants to achieve Godhead in surrendering the I and entering into his true Self. This *complexio oppositorum* is symbolized in the central metaphor of the Christian faith, the Cross, upon which hangs the suffering figure of a redeemer, with on either side a thief, one of whom goes down to hell, the other up to heaven. There can be no up if there is no down, no good if there is no bad. Far from it being part of God's purpose to exempt men from conflict and evil, God's 'oppositeness' is the heart of his Cross. The conflict in his own nature is so great that the incarnation can be bought only by an expiatory self-sacrifice offered to God's dark side. There can be no bliss for God alone in his godliness; he has to be born in the human psyche. Jesus is the 'awakener' because the opposites were manifest in him through the Passion, and so became conscious. Jung expresses this meaning of the Cross as a *conjunctio oppositorum* in two diagrams:

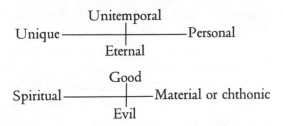

We have already observed the sense in which these horizontal-vertical polarities are manifest in Bach's musical technique. His music's linearity—its continually flowing melody and polyphony—suggests the 'spiritual' while its verticality—its periodic alternations of harmonic tension—stems from the physically 'humanistic'. Complementarily we have noticed in his work a horizontal-vertical cross between two concepts of time—the free rhythm of the individual parts, which tends to be or become airborne; and the metrical beat of the harmonic rhythm, which tends to be earthbound. Since God works in a mysterious way it isn't surprising that the metaphor also functions in the opposite direction: linear flow may be equated with the world's temporal progression, which is crossed at right angles by God's timeless present. Either way, the point of intersection is the Incarnation, which is simultaneously the point at which the Holy Ghost becomes incarnate in the flesh, and the point at which the human, through suffering, becomes divine. For us, at our stage in history, Bach must inevitably be the supreme religious composer precisely because these complementary aspects of Incarnation coexist in his art. Doctrinal verities and a human story are one.

It is in this matter of historicity that primitive and post-Christian myth are differentiated. In Eliade's phrase, 'primitive peoples do all they can to abolish Time, to conceive of life as a paradise of archetypes', wherein Time does not exist if we pay no attention to it. Suffering takes the place of history. *In illo tempore* patterns are repeated cyclically; dreams are fulfilled or calamities occur if divine laws are transgressed, but nothing can be done about it by individual volition. Monotheism, however, being based on a direct and personal revelation of divinity, necessarily entails the 'salvation of Time', of its value within the frame of history. The Old Testament king-God's victory over the forces of darkness no longer occurs seasonally every year but is projected into a future and messianic *illud tempus*. The New Testament Christ-king voluntarily lives out his *agon* and is, if in one sense eternally recurrent, in another sense fixed and final. 'Christ being raised from the dead dieth no more;

death hath no more dominion over him. For in that he died, he died unto sin once: but in that he liveth, he liveth unto God' (Rom. 6:9–10). So the legendary labyrinth becomes the winding streets and alleys of a provincial city; Jesus is murdered by reactionary philistines and an appeaser; the mythic search is not that of a goddess but of a fallibly human woman called Mary Magdalene. These are historical facts, which none the less reveal things no eye has seen. Christianity, according to Eliade, is thus the religion of modern and historical man who has simultaneously discovered personal freedom and continuous (in place of cyclical) time. The man who has left the horizon of archetypes and repetition can no longer defend himself against terror except through the idea of God. 'It is only by presupposing the existence of God that he conquers, on the one hand, freedom, and on the other hand achieves the certainty that historical tragedies may have a transhistorical meaning, even if that meaning is not always visible to humanity in its present condition. . . . In this respect Christianity incontestably proves to be the religion of fallen men; and this to the extent to which modern man is irremediably identified with history and progress, and to which history and progress are a fall.' Bach's Christianity, as manifest in his music, is thus both historical and true, or by an act of faith is believed in enough to seem to be so.

As a Lutheran Bach found the heart of his experience in the story of Christ's Passion and in the symbol of the Cross. He couldn't separate that story from the traditional doctrine of the Catholic Church, and wouldn't have wanted to since, as our quotations from Jung have revealed, story and dogma are identical in psychological terms. The emphasis between story and doctrine varies as between the *St. John Passion* (which we choose to analyse rather than the larger and perhaps still greater *St. Matthew Passion* because its humanistic passion is more direct) and the monumental ritual of the Mass in B minor. Archetypically, however, each work contains the other; if we start with the 'story' it is because what Protestantism protests against is precisely the substitution of ritual forms for revealed truth. This is idolatry which, Protestantism maintains, is recurrently a threat to the religious mind. This is why there is no answer to Christ's question 'To whom shall ye liken me that I am like?' except the story of his life. It's also why Bach tells the tale with all the dramatic force and musical cogency of which he is capable; and though no man has ever been capable of *more* force and cogency, Bach profited from being born at the right 'wrong' time. We have noted that the high Baroque was an age in which man dramatized himself in the mythological terms of opera; believing that man could not hope for a nobler task than an imitation of human actions, he evolved musical-theatrical techniques appropriate to the task. Bach never wrote an opera, or wanted to; none the less he used operatic techniques to tell man's ultimate story, which turns out also to be God's. The distinction is critical. Baroque opera, ostensibly recounting heroic man's triumph, proves to be concerned with a mythology of failure, or at most of wish-fulfilment, since man, however grandiose his aspiration, is in fact mortal. Bach's Passions, on the other hand, present a mythology of sublime success, however painful, since his hero is at once human and divine. In this insistence on the unfolding of a story—a birth, epiphany, humiliation, betrayal and martyrdom, leading to an apotheosis as bridegroom, monster-slayer and leader into a land restored—scriptural epistemology parallels most of the myths of classical antiquity, as well as those of primitive peoples. As Isak Dinesen has put it: 'All sorrows can be borne if you put them into a story, and tell about them.'

The meanings of the word *passion* are multiple, and are relevant to Bach's music. Its root is in passive suffering; but its association with *pathos* relates it also to pity and terror, and it also has overtones of enthusiasm, anger and sexual desire. We shall find evidence of all these in Bach's musical incarnation of the telling of the Passion story by St. John; and that so much of the complexity of a human psyche is thus manifest testifies to Bach's crucial position in history. This is the end of a process that began in the Middle Ages as a desire or need to humanize the mythological. Significantly the process was—long before the Reformation—a step towards popularization: the illiterate would more readily assimilate a lesson if it were presented narratively or dramatically. So medieval liturgical drama grew as the priest, still intoning monodically, assumed several voices to impersonate different roles in the Christian story; and obviously no aspect of the story lent itself more readily to dramatization, and was more 'crucial' in eschatological significance, than the Crucifixion itself. By the late Middle Ages and early Renaissance the monophonic liturgical Passion drama was a valued convention, the narration being told in plainchant by a priest-Evangelist, whilst Jesus and some of the minor characters were personified by other voices. The music itself—as exemplified in Davy's Passion—makes no claim to drama, since it remains monophonic and basically pentatonic, or at most modally heptatonic. Even when it includes a part for the crowd or *turba* it doesn't exploit the 'turbulence' of harmony; it remains ceremonial. None the less, this music had at least the potential of becoming dramatic, and it's not fortuitous that in war-racked

Germany Passion music gradually achieved an identity simultaneously dramatic and liturgical.

Schütz's teacher Monteverdi somewhat surprisingly said that recitative was the language of passion, and that there were three heroic passions, love, hate and prayer. Certainly this is evident in the Passions of Schütz's old age which, written for the denuded chapels of ravaged Germany, eschewed Italian orchestral opulence in favour of unaccompanied voices. The narrator tells the story in a 'German recitative' that is closer to plainchant than to Monteverdian arioso, and is unsupported by harmonic continuo. Yet drama is latent in the madrigalian writing for the chorus, personifying the crowd, and in the more pliant, even lyrically expansive, phrases given to the minor characters. Jesus himself is not usually characterized; his divine attributes are emphasized by setting his words for two or three voices, symbolizing the relationship of the Son to the Father and the Holy Ghost. None the less Schütz's Passions are simultaneously a drama and a sacrament, and in this offer a precedent for the wider-ranging musical-theatrical techniques of the Passions of Bach.

Since the passion in Bach's *St. John Passion* is the human joy and suffering in our pilgrimage on earth as well as Christ's sacrifice, it is logical that the heart of the experience should be in recitative. Any hint of plainsong intonation has vanished, for Bach's recitative is unambiguously operatic, growing from the spoken inflections of the German language, reinforced by the stabilities or tensions of the continuo's harmony. We live through the story with a physical and psychological immediacy which is no more than glimpsed in Schütz. The arias, on the other hand, though an operatic convention, are seldom operatic in effect, but rather lyrical reflections on what has occurred in the recitative and narrative or dramatic choruses. In secular Baroque opera the arias, even if wild or fierce, tend as we saw to be meditations after the event, the action having taken place during the recitatives, or even offstage; in Bach's reinterpretation this static quality of the da capo aria has greater relevance and justification, since *this* human story is *sub specie aeternitatis*, and to Bach's audience and in a sense to all audiences is literally 'a matter of life and death'. The same is true of the arioso sections which are a halfway house between secco recitative and the melodic fulfilment of aria. In secular Baroque opera, we observed, arioso usually occurs when people are 'beside' or 'out of' themselves with passion. In Bach's Passions arioso has similar functions, with the difference that unwonted passion tends towards transcendence. Arioso effects transitions between the mundane and the divine. Jesus habitually sings in arioso—speech heightened to lyricism and usually accompanied by instruments additional to the continuo; other characters do so when under stress that at least holds a promise of benediction (for instance Peter's weeping).

The threefold interrelationship of recitative, arioso and aria in the solo vocal music is roughly paralleled by the relationship between the three kinds of choral music which Bach employs. Just as recitative evokes the immediacy of the personal life, so short, naturalistic outbursts of the *turba* are the public life in immediate action: people's music, 'common' in being the utterance of men unredeemed. The large-scale polyphonic choruses, on the other hand, present the experience of mankind rather than that of men and women at a particular time and place. They usually start from physical gestures that are topical and local, but become arioso-like acts of transcendence, impersonal in their spacious polyphonic unfolding. The *turba* choruses are thus present action; the big polyphonic choruses are simultaneously action and reflection; while the third type of chorus—the originally congregational chorales—remains outside the historical context, being meditations here and now. Their function complements, in communal terms, that of the personalized arias: in the chorales you and I, as representative Faustian men, express our awareness of the story's relevance to us unredeemed, though not unredeemable, creatures. Allied to this is the fact that the chorale melodies are literally 'people's music', public property in the sense that Luther gathered them together for domestic use. Some were newly created by composers deliberately making sturdy tunes easy to sing and memorize; some were recomposed melodies from the liturgical monody of the old faith, or more regularly metrical transformations of composed melodies of the guild musicians or mastersingers; still more were adapted from secular folk songs more often erotic than pious, for Luther believed that the Devil didn't deserve to own all the good tunes. By way of his four-part harmonization Bach changes the character of the chorale melodies in rendering them expressive, even subjective, so that we sense the words' relevance to himself and to ourselves as worshippers. Yet despite this romantic introversion the popular and communal nature of the tunes—created not by Bach but by a people and a Church—is not relinquished; and this ability to function at once historically and mythologically suggests a parallel between a Bach Passion and a Greek tragedy. In both the audience is also a congregation which participates in story and action vicariously; both tell the tale of a Dying God in terms that are simultaneously dramatic and sacramental; both intensify speech to chant or song since human beings, in a cosmological context, may become 'larger than life'; both relate the hero's destiny to that of a people,

interrelating personal drama (dialogue, monologue, recitative-arioso-aria) with
public action and commentary (the varieties of choric writing).

The opening chorus of the *St. John Passion* is a superb example of the work's
fusion of immediate reality with universality. There are four slowly swinging
beats a bar, divided into continuously surging semiquavers. The present tense
is incarnate in the undulation of the stepwise moving semiquavers, often in
parallel thirds, enacting the sway of a vast crowd; in the acute dissonances of
the sustained semitonic suspensions for flutes and oboes, draped over the
semiquavers, prefiguring the pain of crucifixion; and in the slow thudding of
the bass which measures pulse, heart-beat and the turning earth:

Ex. 60

The physicality, the present reality, of this music does not, however, deny its cosmological implications; it suggests not so much a specific crowd at a given time and place as the nations of the earth gathering to attest to the divine mystery. The spacious proportions of the eighteen-bar orchestral prelude hint that the drama to be unfolded is vastly significant; yet the universal is always dependent on the particular. Thus after nine bars of tonic pedal (against which the dissonant suspensions grind) Bach moves to a dominant pedal, only to shift from the initial G minor to its subdominant and then, in declining sequences, to the subdominant's relative, E flat major. Though we cannot be aware of this at the moment, the relationship between G minor and its major flat submediant is to be a basic structural and allegorical polarity of the work. At this moment the major modulation is not, however, fulfilled. The last three bars of the prelude return to G minor by way of a falling chromaticized bass — an emotional heightening which prepares for the entry of the chorus.

This is unexpected and dramatic: for the voices at first ignore both the semiquaver figuration of the strings and the quasi-canonic suspensions of the wind instruments. Their entrance is as immediate as that of a *turba* chorus. In homophonic chords, separated by silences, they exclaim in awe and terror at the gathering of the multitudes, moving from a G minor triad, to E flat second inversion, to a 'horrendous' diminished seventh. These broken exclamations recurrently interrupt passages in which the voices double the strings in emulating the sway of the crowd. The reiterated tonic pedal in the bass is a rock against chaos, made the more necessary when the swirling moves, both vocally and instrumentally, in parallel 6–3 chords. This time there are twelve bars of tonic pedal instead of nine. The subdominant, but not the submediant, modulation sounds *through* the pedal; if the dissonance is more agonized, the stability is compensatorily greater. After four bars of tonic pedal, above which grind the 'crucified' suspensions and a drooping diminished seventh, the voices apostrophize the Lord in fugato entries, moving up from bass to soprano:

Ex. 61

Their theme—beginning with a noble descending octave, marching up the scale to leap in syncopation through a tensely diminished fourth—seems inevitable, the result of evolution; yet it is also new-born. The difference lies in its rhythmic and harmonic energy: man is no longer borne along on the flood of events, uttering cries of bewilderment, but becomes responsible for his actions. The surging crowd's semiquavers are relegated to low cellos and basses as the many-in-oneness of the counterpoint effects, within seven bars, modulations to the subdominant and relative, and back to G minor. In the sopranos' expansion of the semiquaver wriggle into oscillating thirds, high in their register, there is a hint of painful triumph:

Ex. 62

Herr, un - ser   Herr   .   .   scher, un - ser

which perhaps modifies our response to a transformed repetition of the initial eighteen-bar period. Through the first nine bars the tonic pedal is unbroken, beating in quavers. The choric entry, however, is intensified in being syncopated in exclamatory homophony, while the scalewise movement of the voices is augmented to deliberate quavers, then diminished in canonic inversion. With the change to the dominant pedal, presaging the modulations to C minor, B flat and E flat major, the vocal theme is again canonic, the semiquavers being introduced by rising fifth or fourth instead of descending octave. The chromaticized bass now consummates the music's momentum.

After what sounds like (and eventually is) a final minor cadence the music starts up again—and in E flat major, the flat submediant. Over rumbling semiquavers low in the bass, the fugato theme again opens with falling octave and rising fourth. Though these fourths are at first perfect, the diminished form returns (the lower note sharpened), as the music moves from E flat through A flat major, then its relative F minor, then B flat major, and so back to *its* relative, the original tonic, G minor. When the words speak of Christ's humiliation the orchestral texture thickens to murky chains of 6–3 chords, while the soprano line falls in a wide-flung arpeggio. The intensity increases because after only four bars of tonic pedal we have a dominant modulation in place of a dominant pedal. The voices' melismata are extended through this tonal sharpening which ends on the dominant of the dominant, A minor. The resolution, in the major, acts as a dominant of D minor. Though the canonic entries return over the growling bass, what looks like a return to G minor and the original pedal notes proves to be a springboard for renewed energy, even agitation. The sharpwards modulations to D and A minor (which do not occur in the first section) are repeated in rapid sequence, reinforced by undulating semiquavers in parallel 6–3s. The vocal parts have upward leaping octaves (balancing the motive of an octave descent), often phrased across the beat. The bass line shifts on each half bar, through rising fourths or falling fifths, and concludes with a chromatic undulation of B flat and G sharp around the dominant of D minor.

The final cadence has a *tierce de Picardie*, though this, of course, also proves to be no conclusion since it acts as a dominant of G minor to introduce a da capo of the whole of the first section. So the chorus has been not only an elaborately polyphonic movement on an ostinato bass but also an immense aria da capo in which the middle section offers not contrasted material but dramatic development of the original motives. That the chorus is a da capo aria has much to do with its monumental effect: not merely because the piece lasts so long chronometrically but also because its structure is cyclic. It involves, as we have seen, energy, pathos, excitation; it evokes a scene and prophesies a myth. Yet the form, in turning back on itself, denies temporal progression; the events referred to exist simultaneously in past, present and future—in both historical and mythological time.

This vast chorus calls on the full resources that Bach was to favour in his Leipzig days. According to a memorandum addressed to the church fathers in 1730 he was at the time employing a chorus of seventeen voices, somewhat curiously disposed, and heavily weighted to the bass. This is not necessarily opposed to the spirit of his music, though he makes it clear that he would have preferred a chorus more evenly balanced. His minimum requirements he set at three voices to a part; he would have preferred four concertists, presumably capable of taking solo parts, and at least eight ripienists, two to a part. If works for double chorus were performed these numbers must naturally be doubled. Orchestrally he needed two, or preferably three, first violins and an equal number of seconds; four violas; two cellos; one violone (double bass); two or preferably three oboes; one or two bassoons; three trumpets; and one timpanist. He doesn't mention flutes, not because he didn't use them but because they were played by amateurs or students or (if not used simultaneously) by the oboists. Horns and trombones he omits because they would be played by the trumpeters; there is only one festive instance in Bach's music wherein all the brass instruments play together. For the continuo instrument Bach specifies the organ, though he occasionally used the harpsichord too. Sometimes two chamber organs seem to have been employed, Bach directing from one of them. In the opening chorus of the *St. John Passion* the transverse flutes double at the unison either the oboes or the first violins and trebles, or double the violas and tenors at the octave. Indeed apart from two brief solo appearances the flutes function in this way throughout the Passion. The sonority is at once penetrative and mellow. What Bach aims for, and achieves, in this scoring is a homogeneous ensemble that supports the music's epic sweep. Expressive detail would be inappropriate and would, in this particular context, weaken the effect of the recitative that follows, in which we turn from cosmic events to one specific manifestation of them.

In the recitative the Evangelist begins to tell the Passion story. He is outside the action in being a narrator, within it in that his song-speech enacts experience. Secco recitative in Baroque opera tends to be intentionally perfunctory. Not far from speech, it tells stories through monologue or dialogue, without lyrical flair or harmonic potency, which are reserved occasionally for arioso, habitually for the reflective commentary of the arias. Bach's recitative, however, though starting from speech inflection, is always lyrically and harmonically expressive. This is not merely because he is a better composer than most creators of Baroque opera; it's also because the story he tells is of superhuman significance. And it is typical of the *St. John Passion* that Bach begins the tale *in medias res*, with the fact of betrayal. The opening chorus had been concerned with mankind's ultimate destiny; the Evangelist's first recitative transports us to a given time and place (a garden, by the brook Cedron) where man betrayed God incarnate. The tonality falls flatwards from C minor to F minor: for Bach tends to associate flat keys with a fall and with death, sharp tonalities with aspirations and transcendence, which may also involve pain since the sharp note may be a *Kreuz*, or cross; psychologically this ambiguity is profound. Though the line is wonderfully sensitive to the German language, it is musically self-sufficient. Its speech-like fragmentation doesn't preclude lyricism, which itself implies harmonic tension and energy. The continuo merely reinforces the harmonic momentum inherent in the vocal line, with the explosive diminished sevenths for the betrayal, and a fierce, upward-thrusting dominant seventh as the officers approach with torches and weapons:

Ex. 63

When Jesus answers his accusers the music relaxes into the flat submediant, E flat major, Jesus' key of benediction, as the opening chorus has already intimated.

Here the cadential appoggiaturas gently caress, rather than woefully sigh. But when Jesus asks the officers whom they seek there is an abrupt return to G minor and the first outburst of a *turba* chorus. The four bars of fast music have a bass of rocking thirds, chattering figuration in semiquavers for flutes and violins, and briskly metrical homophony for the voices, yapping for Christ's blood. The music, like most *turba* choruses which are the voice of a mob, is spiritually 'low' and a bit inane. Except for a few passing notes there is no dissonance, indeed no 'reality', in its savagery. The dissonance is intensified, however, when the Evangelist resumes his narration, telling us first of Jesus' admission of identity ('I am he'), then of Judas's shrinking from the fact of betrayal. Interestingly, having begun in C minor he 'falls to the ground' in its major flat submediant, A flat, which cadences into E flat major, Jesus' key of compassion, as though man's treachery were already divinely pardoned. But the *turba* of officers repeat their four bars of brutish babble, this time in C minor. Man with his herd instinct seems oblivious of redemption; yet not quite, since after Jesus has, in expansive arioso, handed himself over to the scribes and Pharisees and allowed the others to go their way (in the freedom of B flat major), the chorus —and by implication the congregation —sings the first chorale. The public is now we ourselves, in whatever church we happen to be. Bach doesn't suggest that we have not been, and will not be again, 'scribes and Pharisees' in a given historical situation; only that, since Christ's death, redemption could be within our reach. The nature of the chorale music bears on this. Unlike the big polyphonic choruses, the chorales use symmetrical hymn tunes, harmonized homophonically in four parts. If not 'low', like the *turba* choruses, they are 'popular', and are rendered profoundly human through their harmonic expressivity. Their harmonic richness is inseparable from the fact that the individual lines of the four-part texture are powerfully melodic, even lyrical. The elevation of the human towards the divine is implicit in this technicality, as one realizes —most potently in the act of singing them —if one compares Bach's chorale harmonizations with anyone else's, before or since. The tune of this chorale (dating from 1640) is by Johann Crüger, one of the finest of the Lutheran 'people's composers'. The melody begins with level repeated notes, then arches slowly up and down by step. The bass line, however, sings nobly, beginning with a falling fifth, cadencing with an octave leap and diminished seventh in the third bar. The music's feeling of resolution, after the tense recitative and nagging *turba* chorus, is achieved because the sturdy tunefulness and equable movement consummate, rather than deny, what has happened previously: this is evident when, in the sixth bar a modulation to the relative major is approached by a chromatically descending bass, creating a pain that is mysteriously healed in euphony. In microcosm this enacts the salvation of Christ's pilgrimage, to which the text refers; and the pattern is echoed in the answering five-bar clause. This time the modulation to the relative is approached by way of the dominant, with dissonant passing notes. A brief coda — the last two and a half bars —takes us back from B flat major to G minor by way of a diminished fourth and tritone in the bass. Again the bass line, rock-like, fuses melodic gesture with harmonic weight, after which the major resolution of the *tierce de Picardie* seems unanswerable:

Ex. 64

The scoring of this chorale, as of the others, is essential to its effect. The recitative, arioso and arias are operatically soloistic, with sharp differentiation between the strands; the *turba* choruses rely more on raucous sonority than on line or harmony; the polyphonic choruses render their complexities audible while achieving continuity. The heart of the chorales, however, is their homophony, however individually distinguished the lines may be. The tune, in the top voice, is doubled by two flutes, one oboe and first violins, the alto by only one oboe and second violins, the tenor by violas only. The already sonorous vocal bass is doubled by cellos, double bass and bassoon, descending to the lower octave in the cadential bars, thereby deepening their resonance.

The sonority is thus weighted towards the top and the bass, rich but never lush, since the oboes and flutes give an edge to the tone. The blended sound tells us that this is Everyman's music—and in particular ours, in this church, at this moment.

Bach's pacing of his material is both dramatically and musically effective. After the immensely long opening chorus, which seems to embrace time and eternity, we've been plunged into a whirlpool of events; indeed the recitative and the *turba* choruses move faster than life since they're dramatically selective and have the musical pith to transfer historical moments into present reality. Balance is restored by the first chorale which, compared with the opening chorus, is chronometrically brief, yet is once more outside time. Or rather it is simultaneously within and without time since it transports us from the historical moments which Bach has vividly evoked, but at the same time asserts the present reality of the building wherein we're sitting, resolving the (harmonic) pain of *our* passion in a (linear) act of prayer. Bach emphasizes this time-travelling effect by following the first chorale (apparently resolving the initial G minor into the major) with a recitative even more 'active' than the first one. In describing Peter's impetuous behaviour with his sword, it is the first intimation that this apostle is to be the most important character, after Jesus himself, in this telling of the Passion story. Bach's choice of Peter as the subsidiary hero bears on the Passion's immediate humanity. Of all the disciples Peter is the most fallible and, for that reason, the easiest to identify with. Though his fault, if venal, is not mortal like Judas's, he would not claim, even to Judas, to be 'holier than thou'.

Peter's sword recitative shifts abruptly, after the G minor chorale, to B flat major, then C minor, then sharpwards to G, D and A, all minor. This upward thrust in tonality supports a vocal line of savage energy, with tritonal and arpeggiated leaps to enact the lunging of Peter's sword at the High Priest's servant:

Ex. 65

The line, though fragmented, is compellingly lyrical, and this is inseparable from its fluctuating harmonies wherein dominant and diminished sevenths resolve only on to other dissonances. When Jesus advises Peter to put his sword back in the scabbard the key changes from D minor to F major, and the arioso line is more fluid. In the final two bars, however, the bass of the continuo acquires melodic identity from the arpeggiated gesture of Peter's sword. The half-close is on the dominant of D minor, in which key occurs the second chorale, admonishing Peter's (and our) rebellious flesh to accept God's will. Compared with the first chorale this one (based on Schumann's tune *Vater unser* of 1539 with its modality adapted to effect real modulations to dominant and relative) sounds restless, moving in brief clauses of two bars. The equilibrium between harmonic tension and lyricism is here both more potent and more dangerous, mostly because dissonances and passing notes are absorbed in the singing lines. In the first clause the bass moves by step but then unfolds in leaps to cadence on the dominant; the answering clause introduces chromatic passing notes in tenor and bass but cadences in the tonic *major*. This is immediately contradicted by an improbable shift to C major, which turns out to be an approach to A minor, with wide-spaced suspended sevenths between tenor and bass. The next clause briefly attains the C major modulation before moving flatwards again to F to restrain our recalcitrance. The final two and a half bars re-establish D minor, with hints of the major. Though the dissonant suspensions of the first bars return, the flowing bass line, answering a tritonal plunge with a scale that descends a fifth, affirms the 'perfection' of God's will:

Ex. 66

The next recitative, wherein Christ is cast into bonds, is more quietly narrative, for it simply describes an event, without stressing the emotions of the protagonists. Only at the end are the passional implications of the incident manifest in the music which, having moved conventionally from F to C major, cadences back in D minor as Caiaphas counsels that Jesus be made a scapegoat. The leaping sixths are arms outstretched, eyes uplifted; the 'death' is enacted in a Neapolitan sixth, stabbing from a first inversion of E flat major to a V–I close in D minor:

Ex. 67

Again, Bach turns an operatic cliché into a moment of reality. That the effect is unobtrusive, compared with the recitative about Peter's sword, is right, dramatically and structurally, for this recitative is followed by the first aria. The greater immediacy of the *St. John* as compared with the *St. Matthew Passion* is evident in its emphasis on action rather than reflection; when arias do occur, however, they are proportionally effective. Having given us that vast opening chorus followed by so much action in so short a space, Bach now offers in sequence two arias of complementary technique and intention. We have time to breathe; and to meditate on the implications of events wild enough to have been almost overwhelming.

The alto aria is not patently dramatic but rather a musical allegory of Christ's bondage. The metaphor is equivocal, since the bondage is both physical (a restriction of the limbs) and metaphysical (an acceptance of God's will); thus the aria tells us, in inherently musical terms, that submission is a condition of grace. The key is still D minor; and bondage is manifest in that the ritornello is a canon between two oboes over a bass that intersperses reiterated quavers with scalewise movement. The oboes are the normal ones that Bach has employed in the choruses and chorales. It would be a superficial judgement that maintained that the softer, more expressive oboes d'amore would have been more appropriate to an aria concerned with suffering; for the canonic rigour of the aria rather emphasizes the harsh inexorability of bondage. The theme opens with a godly perfect fifth, answered by a devilishly imperfect one. When the voice enters it doesn't directly participate in the canon, though it is a melismatically decorated version of the falling fifth; the arabesques create coils and chains. After eight bars there is a half-close on the dominant, and a ritornello incorporating another canon on a scale *rising* through a fifth. The melismata, in both voice and oboes, are diminished to semiquavers and demisemiquavers; emotional heat is generated in a Neapolitan progression wherein chains are forged:

Ex. 68

This injection of pathos into the hieratic style of the canons harks back to the anticipatory (Neapolitan) 'death' of Caiaphas's recitative (Ex. 67). It promotes a real modulation to the relative major, the falling fifths of the canonic theme being inverted to rising fourths. The passing modulations—through B flat and E flat major, C major and D minor, to A minor—become increasingly fluent, and the vocal phrases tend to flow over the bar-lines, as though both tonality and melody are seeking to escape bondage. This is why the ritualized impersonality of the aria doesn't deny Bach's (and Peter's) awareness of human fallibility.

Such humanization of the hieratic is stronger in the middle section, which has something of the feeling of a sonata development. The oboes' canon, with perfect fifth answered by tritone, is now in the dominant minor. But when the voice enters its line is more complex than in the original aria, both in rhythm and in ornamentation, and its tonality more agitated. This is prompted by the text's reference to the scourging of Christ: the lashes are heard in the twining of the semiquaver roulades, licking across the beat; in the syncopated phrases, suspended while the bass line pushes remorselessly in its ♩♪♪ rhythm; and in the acidly dissonant appoggiaturas, again tied across the bars. As the close texture moves through A, G and D minor the rising scale figure grows pervasive and climaxes, as the text refers to the purgative effect of Christ's wounds, in canonic sequences that establish a full close in G minor. This is not, however, merely an end to the middle section of an aria da capo, for it starts off again in the 'wrong' key (the subdominant minor instead of tonic), with a modified and intensified version of the canonic theme, the falling fifth being stretched to a sixth. There's a hint of a da capo when Bach returns to D minor, since the original version of the rising scale in parallel sixths is exactly repeated. None the less this preludes new developments: the melisma incarnating the 'chains' expands into *rising* sixths, which droop into appoggiaturas and, with a modulation from G minor to its relative major, the lyricism opens out, shedding the contortions. This melodic expansiveness creates the ultimate tonal climax: after the lyrical release sequences relax from B flat to E flat to A flat major; veer to F minor and major; and re-establish the upward-thrusting scale to return to the tonic D minor. The instrumental ritornello then repeats the first nine bars of the aria unchanged. This da capo, though brief, is deeply satisfying. During the aria we have lived through a drama wherein man's suffering since the Fall has been experienced, yet purged in being borne by Christ on our behalf; the 'bondage' is at once agony and relief. The recapitulation of the canon at the end again universalizes the passion; all is as it was and ever shall be.

This first aria is a 'Song of Experience', in Blake's sense. After a mere three bars of recitative telling us that Peter and 'another disciple' followed Jesus, Bach gives us a complementary 'Song of Innocence', also canonic. The 'Song of Experience' is scored for alto voice with obbligato oboes; the 'Song of Innocence' is for soprano voice, with obbligato flutes, the instruments being, however, in unison, not themselves canonic. Oboes had originally been martial instruments, penetratively at home in the open air. By Bach's day they had acquired their modern associations with pain and pathos but retained — as we've noted — something of their pristine raucousness. Flutes were originally magic and phallic instruments; Pan played the flute, which Orpheus' lyre disciplined. In medieval iconography Christ is often depicted as a flute player, both because he's a pied piper calling mankind to the cosmic dance or a shepherd wooing his flock, and also because a flautist emulates God in evoking *spiritus* — the breath of life and, indeed, the source of the word 'inspiration'. Bach seems to have associated the mystical aspects of the flute with the old-fashioned *flûte à bec*, or recorder, whereas his modern transverse flute equivocated between traditional magic and its eighteenth-century affinities with 'rational' purity. The transverse flute was his normal orchestral instrument since it blended better with other instruments and was audible in tutti. If the dulcet recorder seems more appropriate to this aria of innocence than the transverse flute that too may be a superficial judgement; for though youthful, even adolescent, the aria is not mystically transcendent. It is a secular love-chase, comparable with many in Baroque operas (for instance, Purcell's *Dido and Aeneas* and Handel's *Acis and Galatea*). The two disciples have 'followed' Christ in the recitative's rising scale which, transformed into the flutes' theme, makes Christ at once the girl singer's human lover and a superhuman fusion of Dionysos and Apollo. That would be a bit much for a frail recorder, which Bach, in any case, makes no use of in the Passion. The transverse flute as obbligato instrument here suggests, especially when doubled, the magic of youthful eroticism while implying experience *in potentia*.

Bach's recitative and arioso start from the personal and particular but give them universal application; the arias, on the other hand, deal in absolutes while rendering them specific. Thus the first aria is 'about' bondage and suffering and is simultaneously the song of a man-woman bound. This second aria is 'about' the innocence of acceptance, and is simultaneously the song of an adolescent girl in love; again it's impossible to segregate the sacred from the profane. (The sexual implications of both arias are not denied by the fact that in Bach's day they would have been androgynously sung by boys.) The innocence of the theme itself, as presented in the opening ritornello by the flutes, lies in its gentle stepwise movement in a pastoral 3/8, floating up through a fifth (and thereby inverting the previous aria's descent); in the symmetrical repetition of the first bar; in the graceful 6–4 cadence; and in the balanced sequences that flow from the B flat major tonic to the subdominant and back. There are vestiges of canonic dialogue between the flute melody and the bass; the canon becomes explicit when the voice enters with the same phrase (leaping fourth, scalewise rise through a fifth, descent through a third). The chase — as the girl follows her lover or as the soul seeks Christ — is at first quietly ecstatic, the flute delicately echoing the voice at one beat's distance. This gives a lift to the music, which is at this point free of rhythmic complexity or harmonic strife. The happiness is uncompromised, except perhaps by the sheer continuity of the flute's line, which never lets up and so is apt to sound breathless or breathy. One can construe this as evidence of Bach's 'divine' oblivion to human imperfection, yet can at the same time accept it as humanly realistic, apposite to a girl 'in love'! Certainly a tremulous agitation is suggested by the chromatic passing notes in the second eight bars, provoking momentary modulations to the relative, G minor, and to its subdominant. The first sixteen-bar clause ends, however, positively, with a firm cadence in the dominant.

A ritornello repeating the original theme in the new key leads to a middle section which is also development; the music's innocence proves, after all, to have the potential of experience within it. The voice enters with a free inversion of the original motive, entreating Christ to pursue *her*! A brief return to the tonic induces modulations to C and G minor, the flute's scales extended, the vocal line riddled with appoggiaturas. As the text speaks explicitly of pursuit, the voice's scales change into upward-pushing semiquavers phrased in pairs; this transforms the initial 'breathlessness' into excitation, which in the cadential melisma is chromaticized, tenderly erotic:

Ex. 69

blt - ten, selbat an   mir   zu   zie - hen, zu   schie - - - ben,   zu bit -

The catch in the breath, at the cadence, is touchingly naturalistic; and the ensuing ritornello, still in G minor, cannot be a simple return to the opening theme, for the semiquavers cannot forget what has happened to them. They flow in continuous, almost seductive, curves, and their continuity makes their lyricism more difficult for the player to project. We are not surprised when, as the voice re-enters, the music is more agitated. The vocal line, beginning with the inverted form of the theme, becomes wider in range, modulating from G minor to F major, to B flat and E flat major and so to its relative C minor. The tessitura is high, slightly straining; and the pursuit is enacted by gradually expanding leaps (second, third, fourth, fifth, sixth, seventh) in the bass. The line loses its symmetry, is stressed off the beat, tied across the bars. Having modulated from C minor to a relatively remote D minor it pants in paired semiquavers, at first diatonic, then chromatic. The cadential catch in the breath is repeated — more piquantly, after the virginally emotive music we've been listening to.

What follows is a conventional da capo, though it is not strict. Bach writes out additional ornamentation, such as would have been improvised by operatic singers, and thereby enhances the airborne gaiety. He also extends the roulades that symbolize the concepts of pursuit and of light. The phrases sound fulfilled because the chromaticism has evaporated; they wing in lucent diatonicism, the canonic two-in-oneness fusing the sensual with the spiritual. If the final cadential appoggiatura is a sigh, it's a sigh of contentment. The concluding ritornello, which exactly repeats the opening except that the line is filled in with unbroken semiquavers, remains virginal, yet offers a promise of married bliss. This is true whether one considers it as the marriage of the (or a) girl and her lover, of Christ and his spouse, the Church, or as the marriage of the human soul to God. Bach, like Blake, always deals in 'particularities'. The universal verities of this apparently simple song would not strike so deep were not its experience also specific. Its character-portrayal is religious insight.

Action has been delayed during the two complementary canonic arias, in which contrapuntal device is a spiritual metaphor—of bondage and of pursuit. Bach now returns to Peter's story in a long passage of recitative, equally eventful in dramatic and musical terms. While Jesus is being questioned by Annas, Peter skulks outside the door, is brought in, questioned by an anonymous 'damsel', and denies Christ—the beginning of *his* act of betrayal, which less venally parallels that of Judas. The Evangelist narrates the events, but the girl, Peter and Jesus are personified, so we have a miniature operatic *scena* of intense concision. Even the narrative stretches of the recitative have strong lyric and harmonic implications; Peter outside (alone on a high A and diminished seventh) is dragged in with a disturbing modulation to A minor. The damsel's question is direct, mounting to another high A, whereas Peter's denial is laconic, rising a sixth only to decline in a conventional appoggiatura. When the officers make a fire to offset the cold the continuo part glows like the coals, with a strange modulation from G major to B minor. They and Peter warm themselves in a melisma that manages simultaneously to suggest a flicker of flame and a shiver:

Ex. 70

The High Priest questions Jesus about his disciples in more sober narrative, centred around D minor. Jesus answers, as usual, in lyrical arioso, as he speaks openly to the world. The tonality tends, as is habitual with Jesus' utterances, to relaxation, moving flatwards to F major, but ends in a sudden E minor tension that explodes in violence as an officer strikes him in rebuke for insubordination. From this point a plethora of sharp keys anticipates the *Kreuz* on which Christ will work out his and our destiny. E minor changes to major, which falls to A. Jesus' reply, denying that he has spoken subversively, starts in A major's relative F sharp minor, a key which is to be of crucial significance in the Passion. Christ's wide⁄flung line is pervaded by sevenths, diminished and straight. The last falling seventh makes with the continuo a luminous dominant ninth, which resolves on the paradisal triad of E major:

Ex. 71

In the chorale that follows the indignities inflicted on Christ are related to *our* faults, in the life we're 'living and partly living'. Following so much agitation in the recitative it can afford to be simpler than the earlier chorales, and to relax tonally from the hint of E major bliss to its subdominant, A major. The tune is *O Welt, ich muss dich lassen* (by Georg Forster, dated 1539); at first Bach stresses the sober simplicity of its falling third, rising scale and declining cadence by resonant parallel thirds in the harmony. Pain is latent, however, in a few lacerating suspensions and passing notes and perhaps in the veerings back to F sharp minor which, at the fourth cadence, changes glowingly to major. There is a beautiful melisma, with floating seventh, in the approach to the final cadence which, being a simple 6–4, envelopingly comforts.

The assurance is momentary, however, for the agony of Peter's renewed denial is soon upon us. The Evangelist's recitative opens again in F sharp minor, which moves to B minor at a repetition of the melisma as Peter, standing by the officer's fire which ironically suggests a welcoming hospitality, either warms himself or shivers. It could be both — even more pointedly than on the earlier occasion — if the fire is not very effectual and his shiver is the gooseflesh of shame. In any case Peter's self⁄communing is shattered by the *turba* of officers, who bandy their perfunctorily metrical, teasing questions — 'aren't you one of his men, weren't you in the garden with him?' — from part to part. The crotchet⁄quaver⁄quaver rhythm is even more remorseless than the quaver⁄semiquaver⁄semiquaver of bondage in the first aria, for we are all prisoners of the world's social shackles. That the chorus begins in A major, hankers after B and F sharp minor, and ends apparently in E major has ironic undercurrents. In any case the E major triad sounds more like a dominant half-close than a full close in the tonic; and it acts as such when, in the next recitative, Peter utters his second denial, to the same phrase as the first, but without the sighing appoggiatura, as he's trying to sound unabashed. Back in F sharp minor, Peter is challenged by another servant of the High Priest; his third denial, recounted by the Evangelist, leaps desperately up a minor ninth. This necessitates a shift in vocal register which can easily — and perhaps should be allowed to — make the cry sound stifled. It anticipates the hoarse and providential crowing of the cock, tritonally in B minor, F sharp minor's subdominant:

Ex. 72

which is echoed in the bass line. Peter's weeping is incarnate in the most extended chromatic melisma in Bach's music; the line extends itself through tonal and rhythmic disintegration as the bass rises chromatically from B to G sharp, then declines chromatically to C sharp. Each two beats effect a modulation which is never stabilized; yet the line, sobbing in broken appoggiaturas, intermittently yearns upwards through a tritone, a fourth, a diminished seventh:

Ex. 73

The music is immediately physical; anguish feeds on itself, and the sobs that break Peter (and us) create a passionate rebirth of pain, which has to leap to fall again. The final descent from the diminished seventh stills the agony, however, as the chromaticized bass resolves on to a dominant-tonic cadence in F sharp minor. The voice's final melisma on the word *bitterlich* recalls the fire-warming melisma from the previous recitative; and the point is not merely ironic.

It is sometimes said that this bitter weeping is self-indulgent as compared with the miraculously economic sobbing at the comparable point in the *Matthew Passion*. Perhaps so; but Peter's self-indulgence is part of the human fallibility with which Bach is here concerned. In the *John Passion* Peter is a central character, whereas in the *Matthew Passion* he is subsidiary. His chromatic arioso therefore serves as a precisely appropriate, rather than excessive, prelude to his aria of remorse, which forms the climax of the work up to this point, and concludes the first half. The aria might claim to be the most humanly passionate music Bach ever wrote; yet its agony, being formalized in a da capo aria, is sublimated, so that Peter's passion becomes inseparable from, even identified with, the Passion of Christ. The aria is concerned, in Jung's sense, with the process of individuation; in and through it Peter becomes conscious of the Self and aware of his guilt. Ultimately this guilt must be recognized as inherent in the human condition, not as a mere transgression against a superimposed law.

We have seen, in our analysis of preludes and fugues, that F sharp minor was for Bach often a key of transcendence through suffering. Here Peter's (and our) suffering is far from passive, and the aria is heroic in more senses than one. It has analogies with the ceremonial sarabande, in that it stresses the second beat of its 3/4 metre, and incorporates a proudly swinging dotted rhythm. The speed, however, is certainly faster, more urgent, than a sarabande; and the ceremonial elements, far from being conventionally pompous, are rather a steeling of the nerves to hold on, come what may. The bass begins with a chromatic descent taken over from the 'weeping' arioso, above which the ritornello melody, fiercely doubled by *'tutti li stromenti'*, springs not in outward ostentation but with inner frenzy. A bar's forward lunge is counteracted by abrupt cessation on a dotted minim, as though the anguish were too great to be sustained (Ex. 74).

But the dotted rhythm in the bass becomes energetic, thrusting up through sharp sevenths, while the melody breaks into chains of semiquavers that recall the 'weeping' arabesques. When the voice enters, Peter sings the same melody, interrupting its thrust with fragmented exclamations of sorrow and dismay. By the unconscious alchemy of genius, these exclamations are incomplete permutations, suspended in mid-air, of the 'shivering' melisma of the recitative (Ex. 70). After sixteen bars the chromatically descending bass appears in the dominant, which key controls the next sixteen bar period wherein the voice grows more distraught (consider the leaping sixths, left high and dry), while the dotted rhythm stabs with ferocity in the bass.

Ex. 74

A middle section starts in C sharp minor but soon veers to A major, the relative, with a hint too of E major, A's dominant. The more affirmative tonality reflects the pathos of Peter's remorse; the line, turning in on itself, undulates through a semitone, and gets locked on dotted minims (bar 49 et seq). The instrumental parts are also momentarily quieter, though the dotted rhythm of the bass (again stressing the sharp seventh) counteracts any sense of stasis. In the ritornello after the E major cadence the rising dotted rhythm of the bass is balanced against the falling semiquavers of the melody, until the original chromatic bass reappears, in the subdominant. The voice's Neapolitan G natural hurts, yet is perhaps also desired, like a lover's pinch, for it leads to a wild explosion of cantilena which, if desperate, sounds also liberated. The vocal phrases span across the bar-lines, effacing the sarabande pulse and the dotted rhythms' remorseless thrusts. In its wildness, indeed, the vocal melody may escape time's domination. The line is freed from the harmonically contorted bass, which now falls not chromatically but in embellished diatonicism. The whirling melismata with which the voice ends directly recall Peter's weeping arioso and the crowing cock; far from being a deliquescence, their frenzy is now divine afflatus:

Ex. 75

The melodic release combines with the reasserted tonic to effect consummation rather than recapitulation; a strict da capo is neither necessary nor possible.

The arabesques of the voice remind us of the ambiguous potency of the cock as a symbol, especially in a Christian context. His sexual connotations in association with the penis render him theologically dubious, and therefore a bird of betrayal; yet the life-force is not thus easily disposed of, so the cock reasserts himself as the herald of a new dawn. Not surprisingly Bach, whose search for the spiritual was so deeply rooted in the corporeal, creates cock-crows of singular power and achieves from this equivocal bird a resolution which is not the less positive for being painful. In the final brief ritornello, after the vocal outcry, the lines dissonantly grate, in the energetic dotted rhythm, over a tonic pedal, and resolve through a triple appoggiatura, from strong to weak beat, on a major triad. Despite the music's tough complexity, the major resolution cannot be gainsaid.

To complete Peter's story —or rather to underline the story's relevance to ourselves —there is a final chorale, the text of which deals with the release from sin that Christ offers us: a freedom that has been agonizingly attained in the aria. The tune, *Jesu Leiden, Pein und Tod* (by Melchior Vulpius, dating from 1602) is one of the most positively affirmative of chorale melodies. It moves in two-bar clauses, almost entirely by step, makes a decisive modulation to the dominant, and expands only in the final period, when a falling third is answered by a rising fourth. Bach's treatment of the melody undermines its sturdiness, yet in so doing deepens its affirmation. Thus the chorale opens not in A major, as the simple tune suggests, but in F sharp minor, the key of Peter's remorse; and although it seems to be moving to the relative in the second bar it in fact cadences irresolutely on a first inversion of the dominant seventh of D major. The balancing clause finds its way to the expected A major, though with disturbingly dissonant passing notes, only to return to F sharp minor, in the second four bar clause, for Peter's confession. Again the stepwise music is undemonstrative, as it had to be after that exhaustingly self-conscious aria; and again the cadence—on a first inversion of the dominant seventh of F sharp minor—is uncertain. The second half of the chorale, however, attains serenity from the acceptance of Peter's pain. The tenor's leap to the high A releases flowing passing notes that lead to an unambiguous A major cadence; and although the next two bars are richly chromaticized, with a stabbing minor ninth between tenor and bass and a leaping tritone, the cadence achieves the bliss of E major, the dominant. In the final clause, when the words speak of the bursting of fetters and the freeing of conscience, chromatics become themselves a release, for they induce strangely elliptical modulations:

Ex. 76

The false relations between E major, G major and B minor counteract the tune's expansiveness, but are ironed out in the last two bars, wherein the re-establishment of A major is decorated with brief melismata that promise a new birth. The fact that this hymn tune is intrinsically the simplest thus far relaxes an emotional pressure that, in Peter's aria, threatened to be overwhelming. None the less it convinces absolutely as coda to Part I because its simplicity can embrace the astonishing modulations of the last four bars. Peter's personal dark night of the soul is not evaded although, with the crowing of the cock, he has come through it. His agony is also ours, and is Christ's, too, since Peter, like Jesus, is a scapegoat. It is not surprising that Bach, in this most passionately humane of his religious works, finds Peter obsessively haunting.

Given the direct humanity of the *St. John Passion* one might expect that its structure would seem episodic, following the vagaries of human passion. Looking back on Part I as a whole, however, it is clear that its proportions are precisely calculated in terms of their dramatic and musical efficacy; and we shall see ultimately that the Passion as a totality has an extremely elaborate chiastic structure hardly less formalized than that of more patently doctrinal works, such as the B minor Mass. Bach's mind instinctively worked in analogical terms; drama and doctrine were for him no more opposed poles than were the physical and the metaphysical. Thus Part I opens with a vast polyphonic, yet also dramatic, chorus in G minor, a key of tragic conflict for Bach as for Mozart (though not for Beethoven, who favoured a darker level of flatness, C or F minor). The act of betrayal and the arraignment are then portrayed with trenchancy, in recitative that remains anchored to G and C minor. Reflection after the event occurs in two 'public' chorales, first in G, then in D minor; and in two canonic arias, one in D minor (the dominant of G minor), the other in B flat major (G minor's relative). Together, the two arias balance the opening chorus, but slow down the action. Bach counteracts this in the second 'scene', which turns from Judas's betrayal of Christ to Peter's self-betrayal. In recitative, arioso and *turba* intermissions Bach physiologically and psychologically re-enacts the story in sound; Peter's fallibility as human creature is equated with ours. We suffer, and survive, man's weakness and remorse, in music that grows from physical gestures that are the outflowing of nervous stress. This movement—of intervals, rhythms and tonality—is wild, arriving at the ultimate possible distance from the initial G minor when Jesus' arioso touches F sharp minor, the lutanists' *ton de la chèvre*. When the action stabilizes from recitative into reflective chorale, A major, F sharp minor's relative, becomes the tonal centre. Bach insists on this modulatory extravagance by repeating it in a more developed form; for Peter's climacteric arioso and aria of remorse are also in F sharp minor, and their emotional perturbation is so great that they serve as counterpoise to the tragic grandeur of the opening G minor chorus. The latter deals with the destiny of mankind; Peter's arioso and aria *incarnate* the agony of a particular man at a particular time and place, making us aware that the Particular (in Blake's sense) contains the General. There never was a more powerful defence of the dignity of man, however undignified his degradation may seem to be. The tragic chorus in G minor and the arioso and aria in F sharp minor weigh equally in the balance. When the final chorale offers the communal comment on Peter's personal destiny, the tonality returns to A major; unconsciously we feel its remoteness as an *elevation* to the whole tone *above*, as contrasted with the tightness of F sharp minor's semitone *below*, the original G minor tonic.

The effect is the more poignant because, as we observed, reminiscences of F sharp minor survive in the mysteriously unstable tonality of the chorale. So a pattern has been established, the implications of which will become fully apparent only when, in Part II, the Passion of Jesus is experience as a parallel to the smaller passion of Peter. For Peter is tempted to deny his God, and falls. Jesus labours under similar stresses and is also tempted—to employ superhuman power to destroy his adversaries, to free himself from physical suffering and mental humiliation. This makes him one with Peter (whose human weakness Jesus loved), though he is also more than Peter, and remains unfallen. Similarly Christ's story, as musically recounted by Bach, is simultaneously one with Peter's, but also more than that.

Part I, centred on Peter, a mortal sinner like ourselves, climaxes in his great aria of remorse, wherein an inner anguish finds outlet in physical movement. It is impossible to sing or play the aria without experiencing these gestures of arms, trunk, head, eyes as physical sensation, whether or no one allows oneself to act them out. No opera composer ever created music that more powerfully equates the outward manifestation of passion with its inner reality. That Peter's passion has been so overwhelming makes the aria's position, at the close of Part I, inevitable. Nothing could follow such an extremity of human suffering except that of Christ—who seems to be a man but turns out to be also God. So Part II launches immediately into the Crucifixion, prefaced by an initiatory chorale that tells us that his betrayal and suffering were for our good. The final chorale of Part I had been in A major; this one (by Michael Weisse, dating from 1531) is in A minor, beginning and ending on a modal dominant. The opening is firm, beneath the tune's repeated Es; but tritones in the bass line and dissonant passing notes in the alto depict the secrecy of Christ's being taken 'like a thief in the night'. The second clause cadences on the dominant of D minor, and moves with chromatic restlessness back to A minor, D minor and G minor-major. The chromatics dissipate when the words tell us that all is as was foretold; the final unresolved dominant cadence is approached by concordant diatonic triads in C major. Although this chorale is sometimes chromatic and frequently dissonant, it is affirmative as compared with the irresolute cadences and modulatory vacillations of the chorale that ends Part I. True, it ceases on the dominant, not tonic. In so doing, however, it fulfils its preludial function; and when the drama has been unfolded this chorale will return, a semitone higher, the cycle completed.

In taking up the tale the Evangelist's recitative, centred on D minor, moves quickly and energetically. Its range is wide, spurting between low D and the tenor's high A. Pilate asks the crowd what accusation they bring against Jesus. They reply in a lengthy *turba* chorus which resembles the earlier, brief outbursts in that the music is rigidly metrical, obsessive in repeated notes and driving figurations. At the same time this chorus is different from previous outbursts, both because it's long, and because it becomes highly chromatic. The D minor tonality is splintered as chromatics, pushing upwards from the bass, invade every part; every half bar modulates, between D, G, C and F, all minor. Contradiction between the tonal instability and the thumping regularity of the metre inculcates frenzy. The mob is no longer trivial but has become, in its collective neurosis, both brutish and terrifying — perhaps also terrified since people in the mass, driven by irrational hatreds, are indeed 'beside' themselves. Again Bach's art, functioning in inherently musical terms, is also superb drama and psychology; and it becomes yet more so when, after fourteen bars, the chromatics are intensified with semiquaver figuration and with dissonant suspensions tied across the beats. The bass line stumps in grossly inimical glee; vestigial hints of counterpoint in the inner parts turn out to be a breakdown of even this crude rhythmic continuity, induced by rage. Interspersed rests make the lines stutter in wrath; the chorus explodes in a series of homophonic barks on a negation:

Ex. 77

Faced with the physical immediacy of Bach's music we can appreciate that Pilate must be frightened too, and can understand why, after the *turba*'s trill-screeching cadence back in D minor, he meekly hands Jesus over (in a mere three bars of recitative) to be judged according to *their* law. Bach points the *a priori* nature of law by a little number symbolism, for when the crowd yells that it is not lawful for them to put any man to death, the theme on the word *töten*

consists of five rising chromatic notes, in reference to the fifth commandment, while the tenfold repetition of the phrase reminds us that there are ten commandments in all. The *turba*'s renewed yelling is centred on A minor. The chromatics, the obsessive pulse, the tied semiquaver figure all recur in the vocal parts, raucously doubled by violins and oboes. Flutes and first violins now add an obbligato of chattering arpeggiated semiquavers, similar to that in the brief *turba* choruses in Part I. The sickeningly rocking thirds also return in the bass; the fury, though not allayed, is again trivialized, and the effect of this is slightly to diminish the *turba*'s forcefulness, as the chorus approaches the cadence through a dominant A minor pedal. When Jesus replies to them he, unlike Pilate, is not frightened. By him their bestiality can be dismissed as trumpery.

The next recitative is extended, and psychologically and spiritually eventful. The Evangelist begins by reminding us that Jesus' death was a necessity. But the tonality, wavering between A, G and D minor, is tentative, very different from the preordained laws of the world; and the solo lines remain lyrical, in arioso style, during the dialogue between Pilate and Jesus. This explicitly contrasts sacred with secular law. Pilate's arioso with its rising sixths and falling sevenths, is warmly expansive, even humane; Jesus' arioso, as he tells Pilate that *his* kingdom is not of this world, floats through an arpeggio. When Jesus points out that if his law were of this world his servants would fight, he indulges in a parody of Baroque martial music:

Ex. 78

mei - ne Die-ner würden da - rob kam - - - pfen,

The line flows in semiquavers, then in demisemiquaver divisions, with a heroic trumpet arpeggio in C major, echoed by the bass. Though lyrical, the music is worldly and Handelian rather than Bachian: appropriately so since Jesus is describing what those of His kingdom would *not* do. Present reality is restored as the cadence returns by way of D minor to A minor. The line is still arioso-like, but broken, the harmonies intense.

The succeeding chorale repeats Crüger's tune *Herzliebster Jesu*, which had appeared as the first chorale in the Passion. Here, a tone higher, differently phrased, and with a bass flowing in regular quavers, the parts all take on a songful character, which is apposite since the words concern our compassion for Christ's Passion. The first six bars are concordant, with only a few dissonant passing notes, and a modulation to the relative major. Moving to E minor, then D minor, the dissonant suspensions become acute, but are annealed in the cadential bars which counteract false relations with a lyrically expansive bass. In recitative Pilate and Jesus conduct their dialogue about the nature of truth, moving sharpwards from C to G to D. A change to the relative, B minor, occurs when Jesus affirms that He is the truth, and it is not fortuitous that Bach's 'truthful' key should also be the dark B minor of suffering in which he wrote so much of his profoundest music. Pilate again parries secular against sacred law in asking, flatly, What is truth?, and offers to release Jesus in an arioso that is lyrical, yet not emotionally involved. The *turba* dismisses the offer and again yells that Barabbas be released instead of Jesus. This brief *turba* chorus returns to the socially savage music of the original outbursts, in D minor, with the familiar chittering semiquaver obbligato, and the thumping thirds in the bass. Such perfunctoriness provides an ironic contrast to the following recitative, wherein the Evangelist describes the scourging of Jesus. He begins with phrases high-powered both melodically and in harmonic implication: with a leaping octave, falling and rising sixth, falling tritone. Having reached G minor from D minor he depicts the scourging in furious melismata that drive a ♫♫ rhythm into lashing triplets. The continuo bass thrusts in a ferocious dotted rhythm that licks like the whip, moving to C minor and closing in a 6–4 back to G minor. This is the first unambiguous resolution in 'tragic' G minor since the monumental opening chorus. It probably registers subconsciously; what was then presaged is now fact:

Ex. 79

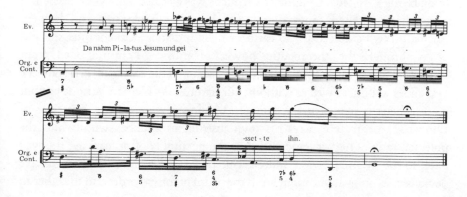

Thus the savagery of the *turba* has led into a recitative that briefly but shatteringly depicts the scourging of Christ; the melodic line physically creates the gesture of lashing, while the dissonances implicit in the line (as well as the continuo) incarnate Christ's and our pain. With scarcely a pause the music relaxes to the flat submediant, E flat major: a key relationship which had prophetically hinted at 'crucial' significance in the opening chorus. The dichotomy is between tragic intensity and balm-dispensing repose, which is what we are offered in the bass solo *Betrachte, meine Seel'*, explicitly described as 'arioso'. It is sung, like the arias, by an anonymous soloist; but the contours of the vocal line, as well as the key, encourage us to identify the soloist with Christ. The accompaniment has three obbligato instruments as well as continuo. A pair of viole d'amore (love viols) undulate in gently breathing quavers, their silvery, ethereal tones invoking the brooding wings of the dove—of God as benevolent Father and Holy Ghost. The dulcet other-worldliness of the viola d'amore's tone is usually attributed to its six sympathetic strings, although most instruments surviving from the eighteenth century don't have them. According to Curt Sachs, however, there are in existence viole d'amore, made in Bavaria in 1720, equipped with sympathetic strings. Vivaldi's concerto for lute and viola d'amore was certainly intended for such an instrument; Bach probably knew this concerto, and more than likely he intended these obbligato parts for the instrument with sympathetic strings. However this may be, their effect in context is indescribably beautiful, the more so since his third obbligato instrument is a solo lute, flowing in the middle register in semiquaver figuration, occasionally breaking into demisemiquaver scales.

It cannot be fortuitous that Bach introduced, for this one movement only, an obbligato lute, seeming to equate Christ as Man-God-Son with lyre- or lute-playing Orpheus. Originally Orpheus was a lapsed Dionysiac priest and poet who composed songs describing the creation of earth and heaven. Shaman-like, he descended to earth or hell, and sought to conquer sin and death through the therapeutic power of music. Transmogrified from Dionysiac frenzy into Apollonian order, he tamed the inchoate furies and the bestialities within, as well as without, our natures. As Herbert Whone has put it, 'Orpheus is man himself, son of Apollo's reason and yet possessor of Dionysiac energy. He plays his own instrument and has within him the potential ratio of higher logic and thus the possibility of unmasking the way back to the original power source. But he has fallen and has now to live deviously, existing at one moment in the realm of formal order and the other in the realm of free energy. His music expresses a yearning for the balance of the poles. His lyre is the laying down of the formal order and at the same time the possibility of a return out of it.' Small wonder that medieval theologians perceived analogies between Orpheus and Christ, for which there is evidence as early as the second century. Though the Church was equivocal about Orpheus' parleying with the creatures, which could be construed as submission to the sensual wiles of Satan, by the ninth century he is firmly established by Christian mystics, who trace a direct parallel between Orpheus' descent to the nether regions and Christ's harrowing of hell. They interpret his wooing of the creatures in terms of Christ the Saviour-Shepherd, whose 'sheep hear my voice, and I know them, and they follow me; and I give unto them eternal life, and they shall never perish' (John 10:27–28). Clement of Alexandria, in his *Exhortation to the Greeks*, makes the analogy explicit: 'Behold the might of the new song! It has made men out of stones, men out of beasts. Those that were as dead, not being partakers of the new life, have come to life again, simply by being listeners to this song.'

The instrument Orpheus plays is no less important than his voice. The lute is the post-Renaissance equivalent of the lyre, to the harmonies of which the soul responded instinctively — according to medieval Platonists — since its seven strings were tuned to the seven phases of the Music of the Spheres. As Macrobius puts it: 'Every soul in this world is allured by its musical sounds, for the soul carried with it the memory of the music which it knew in the sky, and is so captivated by its charm that there is no breast so cruel or savage as not to be gripped by the spell of such an appeal.' The New Song of Christ and the Neoplatonic Harmony of the Spheres are thus identified. Later authorities, such as Bersuire in his *Metamorphosis Ovidana*, turn myth into specific allegory:

Orpheus, child of the sun, is Christ the Song of God the Father [Sun = Son = Sonus or sound] who from the beginning led Eurydice, that is the human soul. And from the beginning Christ joined her to himself through his special prerogative. But the devil, a serpent, drew near the new bride while she collected flowers, that is, while she seized the forbidden apple, and bit her by temptation and killed her by sin, and finally she went to the world below. Seeing this, Christ-Orpheus himself descended to the lower world and thus he retook his wife, that is, human nature, ripping her from the hands of the ruler of Hell himself.

Christian apologists give the story a happy ending, which it does not have in the myth, except in wish-fulfilment. In psychological terms, however, that is what counts. Orpheus is at once healer and prophet. Animated by the creative energy of Dionysos, he is also, through his instrument, an apostle of Apollo's reason and spirit. He seeks to exist within the realms both of liberated energy and of formal containment; and the controlling of inchoate passion, followed by its resurrection, is human life.

The truth of this is profoundly manifest in the arioso, since the repose it induces is deceptive. Although it opens over low tonic pedal notes and preserves absolute regularity throughout its quaver and semiquaver movement, its harmony is complex, as is hardly surprising since it immediately follows that projection of mob violence and bestiality. After two and a half bars of E flat tonic, the bass undulates chromatically up and down, approaching if not consummating modulations to F minor and B flat major, only to fall to a dominant pedal of C minor. This again shifts chromatically to effect modulations, every half bar, to F, G, A and D minor, then back to G and C minor. Meanwhile the bass soloist's melody, harmonically earthed on the pedal notes and drooping chromatics, generates from spread chords, arching upwards through minor sevenths, a marvellously lyrical release. Despite the incidental dissonances and tonal instability, the expansive line, floated across the beats, is an act of benediction, as the text speaks of the redemptive significance of Christ's pain. Human suffering is still manifest in the melody itself—consider the rising C major triad immediately contradicted by the high E flat in false relation (bars 5-6)—and in this the voice part resembles the arioso lines that Jesus sings in dialogue with the Passion's real-life characters. But the lyricism of the line is now also sublimating in effect and tension is gradually released. After ten bars the majestic arioso, still pervaded by rising sevenths and falling sixths and fifths, returns to E flat, and for the remaining nine bars balances between this tonic and its subdominant, A flat. The spaciousness of the melody reflects the awe with which, then as now, the multitudes gaze on the figure of the wounded Christ. There is a reminiscence of agony when the final cadence is approached by a dark smear of B flat minor diminished seventh (bar 14); but this serves only to make the ultimate release, in a triadic arpeggio falling serenely through an eleventh, the more heart easing (Ex. 80).

In the postlude—after the voice's whole-tone appoggiatura, which sounds more like a caress than a sigh—the lute's demisemiquaver scales glide untrammelled over a tonic pedal.

That the melodic lines—for viols and lute—should be so calm while the harmony has such inner turbulence is the music's essence, for it sings of the

Ex. 80

auf Ihn,   drum sieh ohn' Un - ter - lass   auf Ihn, ohn' Un   ter lass,drum sieh'ohn'Unterlass auf Ihn.

joy that can be born only of purgatorial pain. As so often in Bach, symbolism
and musical appositeness are identified; and although he sanctioned the use
of harpsichord or of eight- and four-foot organ *gedackt* if no lute were
available, there is no real substitute for the lute's tone-colour, which is Christ-
like in being at once other-worldly and humanly expressive. Consummatory
though the postlude is, its final sound is the viols' double appoggiatura in
contrary motion: semitonic dissonances that tenderly hurt, yet resolve in
equilibrium. The silence that follows is of the kind sometimes described as
audible; it leads into an aria, *Erwäge, wie sein blutgefärbter Rücken* that translates
Christ's wounds into a paradisal vision. The key, C minor, is the dark relative
of the arioso's E flat major, and subdominant to the initial tragic-prophetic G
minor. This suggests how the aria embraces both the subjective and the
objective aspects of the story, which is again inherent in symbolism that is
simultaneously physical and doctrinal.

There's a Trinitarian concept in that the ritornello parts are for a trio of two
viole d'amore and string bass; there's physical immediacy in that the theme,
beginning as a doubling of the time values of the arioso's postlude, reveals itself
as *identical* with the scourging motive of the recitative. Yet Bach's music makes
a psychological and theological point in that these manifestations of pain are
transcended in the length and continuity of the lines, which flow across the
beats, spiralling eagerly upwards, drooping in weeping parallel thirds or

sixths. That Bach notates the aria in wide bars of 12/8 rather than in the more convenient 6/8 enhances this effect, for the players lose awareness of body accents. This is still more evident when the tenor enters, to poise his upward-yearning sixths, sevenths and octaves against the dialogue of the strings. Whereas the viols flow scalewise, the vocal line aspires brokenly. Intermittently the tenor holds on to long notes, around which the viols embroider arabesques. It's as though the tenor (who represents us, as we behold Christ scourged) is humanly fallible, whereas the divinely symbolic strings are not. A practical manifestation of this is that the singer, having virtually no time or place in which to breathe, has no choice but to aspire to the supernatural.

Tonally the opening ritornello echoes the first half of the arioso in veering between C, F and G minor. This pattern is repeated on the voice's entry, the high tessitura and the hemiola cross-rhythms audibly depicting Christ's wounds. The words contrast Christ's bleeding back with his heavenly face; the latter prompts a modulation to the compassionate key of E flat major. The respite is only momentary, however; the oscillations between C, F and G minor return as the vocal line grows distraught with chromatics as well as hemiola rhythms. The 'pleading' of the text becomes the physical gesture of upraised hands, the vocal phrases cut off in mid-air. To conclude the first section the opening ritornello, lengthy though it is, is repeated in full.

The middle section is not contrast but development, for the thematic material is intensified: partly because the tenor line now incorporates the scourging rhythm previously confined to the viols; partly because his melismata are vastly extended; partly because the modulations range wider. Though the vocal melody is still complex, and is even more difficult to sing, it becomes airborne; tied across the slow beats it melismatically 'weaves the garlands of repose', out of Christ's pain (Ex. 81).

Here the winging line describes the arch of the rainbow which, the text tells us, promises peace after storm. It seems relevant to recall Plato's image of the rainbow as a covenant between the absolute and the particular. Man is overspanned by the rainbow, which is beyond colour because it includes all colours, when his awareness of a finite moment (Christ's suffering and death) becomes infinite: 'in an instant light is kindled as from springing fire'. Bach emphasizes the point by repeating the rainbow melismata in extended and intensified form. After the first statement has relaxed from F minor to its relative major, there is a further ritornello, then increasingly contorted melismata in C and G minor, the leaps becoming more angular, ties and cross

Ex. 81

rhythms wilder. Even the continuo bass surges into arabesques on the scourging motive, so sustainedly lyrical that despite its earthbound nature it seems about to levitate. Again the painful difficulty of the music — there are especially acute breathing problems in the tenor's return, through a trill-embroidered, chromaticized D minor sequence, to G minor and a high A — reconciles agony with ecstasy; the rainbow is a pledge of forgiveness to which one must win through.

The middle section ends with a ritornello in G minor, with stabbing suspensions above the scourging motive. The cadence sounds final enough to remind us of the cadence which concludes the scourging recitative in the same key; that had in turn harked back to the opening chorus. Yet of course this G minor cadence is not the end; what is to come is a complete da capo of the first section, without even any truncation of the ritornello. The aria lasts about fifteen minutes which should sound, in no pejorative sense, like eternity; for its immense length, chronometrically considered, is part of the point. To cut the de capo, as was once customary, is musically nonsensical and theologically sacrilegious, for in the sequence of scourging recitative, arioso and aria we have assisted at a miracle; have lived through the process whereby the crown of thorns has been alchemized into a rainbow halo. Such a process of psychic and psychological metamorphosis is precisely what medieval alchemy was concerned with. That Bach had some acquaintance with alchemy is neither here nor there; what does matter is that, just as base metal is alchemically transmuted into gold in a spiritual rather than material sense, so in these winging melodies we are disembodied, even though melodic contours, harmonic textures and rhythms have all evolved from physical agonies and energies. The main phases of the Great Work of alchemy symbolize the spiritual evolution of man, copying the cycle of nature which moves from birth to decay to death to rebirth. Base metal is changed into first matter in order to release the life hidden within it: a process comparable with the release of the soul from the body's prison. When the alchemist says 'Whoever wants to make gold must begin with gold because a man cannot find truth unless he is true to himself, or God unless he has God within him', he's describing something very close to the psychic process that occurs in this arioso and aria. Despite the strict conventionality of its da capo form, this music is far removed from the Baroque opera house. The rigidity of the da capo structure, adhered to on so vast a scale, underlines the music's atemporal circularity; time ceases as we're reborn in a vision of Christ, rainbow-haloed, prophetically in heaven.

This arioso and aria, which with the scourging recitative form the emotional pivot of the entire Passion, were added only when the work was revived, to replace a shorter aria that emphasized intensity of physical pain. While the original aria followed naturally enough from the violence of the recitative, Bach's genius must have realized in retrospect that the work demanded its still centre. Without it, the *St. John Passion* would still be exceptional in its dramatic force, but would be less overwhelmingly transcendental. Something of this is immediately manifest when, from the arioso and aria's *musica mundana*, or music of the spheres, we brusquely return to a very mundane world. In brief recitative, moving from tragic G minor to B flat major, the Evangelist tells us that the soldiers bedecked Jesus in a crown of thorns and a purple robe. They yell a taunting chorus, mockingly addressing Jesus as King of the Jews, in conventional Baroque fugato, with a conventionally heroic theme beginning with a rising fifth, answered by a rising fourth. This is power music, public and social, yet in context equivocal. Though there are a few passing dissonances, the modulations to dominant and relative are likewise conventional; the swinging 6/4 pulse and the plodding quaver bass are as complacent as they are forceful. The music of a composer like Bach, who knows what he believes in, is seldom ironic, as is the music of Beethoven, who is in process of discovering belief. None the less in this *turba* chorus we certainly recognize 'other modes of experience that may be possible'. While Bach leaves us in no doubt as to where he stands (whereas Beethoven is often ambiguous), he's willing to give the Devil his due: an effect which often comes out as ironic, or even (as we shall see later) parodistic.

After this pompous public music Pilate, as the representative of social order, tells the people that he can find no fault with Jesus. Bach gives Pilate his due, too, for his recitative is arioso-like, with rising and falling sixths and diminished sevenths prominent in a fairly impassioned line. The music moves restlessly from G to D minor, back to G and F minor; according to his rather dim lights, Pilate is trying to be humane. But, back in G minor, the *turba* angrily silences Pilate with still more savage cries for Christ's crucifixion. After their initial outburst they sweep back to the power key of B flat major, again yelling Handelian public music in fugato. The chorus is remorseless in the consistency of its rhythmic figure, frenzied in the grindingly dissonant suspensions made by the fugal entries, usually on minor seconds or ninths, or on major sevenths. At the climax, back in G minor, the semitonic suspensions are in parallel thirds or sixths:

Ex. 82

When Pilate again insists, still in lyrical recitative, that he can find no fault with Jesus, the *turba* replies in another fugal chorus, substituting for the ferocity of their *kreuzige* fugato a pompously circumstantial, unambiguously diatonic, harmonically ordered fugue of a type more readily identifiable with Handel than with Bach. One may find it in context even more harrowing than the *kreuzige* chorus: that chorus unleashed the libido, and its nastiness was real, whereas this one is a form of self-deception. In F major, with conventional modulations to dominant and subdominant, it moves by step or leaps through syncopated fourths, metrically defining the secular law. A slight perturbation occurs in the tritonal progression of the bass, when the words tell us that punishment for transgression of this jog-trotting law is death. Again the effect is ironic since the crowd's music, accusing Jesus of presumption to divinity, betrays a mundane incomprehension of the numinous: how can they know?

The *turba*'s outcry scares Pilate afresh; and he's the more bemused when Jesus refuses to answer his questions. Eventually he asserts the distinction between earthly and heavenly power, the continuo's harmonies significantly moving from G major to B minor, from A major to F sharp minor, the key of transcendental suffering. A sharpwards progression to C sharp minor leads into its relative, E major, in which 'heavenly' key we as congregation participate in a chorale, thanking Christ for his self-sacrifice. The tune, *Mach's mit mir Gott, nach deiner Güt* (by J. H. Schein, dated 1640), is extremely simple, the first four bars moving in stepwise arches, effecting the conventional modulation to the dominant. The second four bars leap through a fourth to the high E, then decline by step. Bach's harmonization of the first two clauses is almost as simple as the tune, the dominant modulation being only slightly compromised by a touch of subdominant in the second bar. The second half, however, involving us with Christ as redeemer, strangely changes the music's temper. At first chains of suspensions grind against the widely separated bass; then all the parts, beneath the diatonic tune, are chromaticized, creating a rich deliquescence. This harmonization of the melodically and metrically austere hymn gives it a deeply subjective flavour. Although the chorale tune is communal and in that sense belongs to mankind, this harmonization makes it also ours, personally (Ex. 83).

One can understand why German (and other) Romantic composers found in rediscovering Bach not merely a revelation of forgotten values, but also an experience in which they could share. In this sense it may even be that our awareness of Bach as the greatest of religious composers is related to his awareness of human vulnerability; faith means most when one is most conscious of its frailty. If such a chorale harmonization is one of the primal stirrings of musical Romanticism, one can point to a parallel at Romanticism's twilight end: Delius's chromatic harmonizations of nearly pentatonic folklike tunes comparably, but more extremely, induce a sense of innocence lost and yearned for.

Ex. 83

This moment outside time, in the heavenly key of E major, is the central pivot of the entire work. It is swept aside, however, by the Evangelist's brief recitative wherein the Jews 'cry out' ferociously, through a rising minor ninth in B minor. The *turba* launches into another public chorus in fugato, asserting Caesar's law against God's. The theme moves by step, with syncopated leaping fourths; the texture is Handelian, the pulse obsessive. If the tonic, E major—taken over from the previous chorale—has its traditional associations with divinity it can only be ironically; Caesar's worldly is substituted for God's heavenly power, of which we've just had a humanly fallible intimation in the chromaticized chorale. Certainly in this *turba* chorus there's something monstrous about the chugging rhythm, especially when diatonicism is compromised by dissonant passing notes. Modulation is at first conventionally to dominant and subdominant, but finally to the relative minor, a more decisive event if only because, when the cadence has asserted Caesar's irrefutable kingship, the next recitative shifts to the crucial F sharp minor, as Pilate presents their self-styled king to the Jews. The *turba* resumes a permutation of its *kreuzige* chorus, starting in A major but moving through D, B minor, G major and so back to A. The original earthy thirds thump in the bass, the obsessive ♪♫ rhythm continues in the figuration, while the fugal entries occur on lacerating minor seconds or major sevenths. The music is at once savage and ritualized, as crowds often are. The latter part, with suspensions doubled to thirds or sixths, repeats the earlier crucifixion chorus exactly, but a semitone lower, in F sharp minor. The terror in the music is now beyond the range of irony, for it has engulfed the grandeur. Bach's dramatic pacing is again masterly, for when Pilate asks the mob whether they want him to crucify their king, they answer with a transposed and only slightly modified repetition of their first perfunctory utterance. We have *no* king but Caesar, they yell in tight homophony, while the bass reiterates the thudding thirds and the flutes chatter their inane semiquavers. The arpeggiated flourish at the end is the third appearance of this figure, now in B minor:

Ex. 84

It is instantly recognizable, like the threefold crowing of Peter's cock. The mob—in which we're included—has, like Peter, three times denied God. This is the psychological justification for Bach's repetition of the same music, which some commentators used to attribute to shortage of time, notwithstanding the fact that Bach substantially revised the work for the 1725 performance, and so had a year in which to produce some not very taxing new material. The point is surely that the crowd utters the same idiotic cries, over and over, because man-as-mob functions by reflex action. Peter, on the other hand, as an individual man, can experience remorse, and grow through it; as we saw, his aria evolves from, and dramatically and musically completes, his arioso.

The psychological reasons for the repetition of the *turba* choruses cannot of course be separated from the musical reasons, on which we shall be commenting later. In the present context one immediate purpose of the recapitulation of social man's triviality is to contrast it with the 'reality' of the Golgotha recitative, which is lyrically exalted, harmonically painful. It is also—as compared with the tub-thumping banality of the last *turba* outcry—unstable, for the diminished sevenths and Neapolitan progressions, moving from B minor to G minor, from D major to E minor, from A minor to D, and so back to G, minor, are so chromatic as to suggest atonality:

Ex. 85

The final Neapolitan close is, however, unambiguously and significantly in G minor, and leads to a bass aria which is the first full-scale movement in that key since the opening chorus. Since it's a piece of imposing dimensions, involving sopranos, altos and tenors of the chorus along with the soloist, and including ritornello parts for full strings, we sense its relationship to the Passion's monumental prelude. The scalewise rising theme again suggests a surging crowd, in a physically objective sense, while subjectively it expresses the individual soul's eager haste to find union with God. There's a further relationship to the second aria from Part I (no. 13). That was also in a lilting 3/8, being a canonic chase of girl and lover, of the human spirit and Christ: a love song of Innocence in a vernal B flat major. This climacteric number is a love song of Experience, the soprano voice deepened to bass, the B flat major tonality transformed into its dark relative G minor, the virginal-erotic flutes transmuted into humanly expressive strings. The sexual symbolism of stringed instruments is, as we saw in our introductory comments on the cello suites, adult; nor is there any barrier between this sexuality and an experience of the numinous.

The ritornello begins with a G minor scale rising grandly through an eleventh, with a tailpiece of falling third and lifting arpeggio. This is imitated at two bars' distance by the continuo bass, and interspersed with chordal leaps on the upper strings, agitated in cross-rhythm. The balancing clause inverts the scale but preserves the leaping arpeggio. The second eight-bar period groups the semiquavers in pairs over a stalking bass, then over a tonic pedal. The musical gestures here, like those of the opening chorus and of the B flat aria's love-chase, are at once physically descriptive—of raised arms, imploring hands—and psychologically revealing. The effect is enhanced when the bass soloist enters in dialogue with the strings' canon; although he starts with the surging semiquaver scale he continues in cross-rhythmed quavers that counteract the metres of the string parts:

Ex. 86

Barred according to its natural accents, the vocal part would consist metrically of 5/8 plus 3/4 plus 9/8 (or three bars of 3/8) plus 2/4. This musical-dramatic effect is prompted by the words, which concern the soul's struggle to be free of terrestrial bondage. Release seems promised in a modulation to the relative major, with a long melisma for the soloist. But after a precipitous inversion of the scale motive, the cross-accents return, with wider, more angular leaps, and with chromatic passing notes that provoke sequential modulations, one every two bars. By the time Bach reaches D minor, diminished seventh progressions have been absorbed into the cantilena; the exhorations to 'haste' are breathlessly broken by rests. At this point the chorus—which is both the crowd at a historical time and place and also mankind in eternity — enters with the leaping triads in cross-rhythm, gasping its question ('*wohin?*') while the bass solo urges them to hurry in the unbrokenly flowing scale:

Ex. 87

After that expectant pause on the dominant of D minor the bass provides the answer — to Golgotha — in a falling cadential phrase. A D minor ritornello is extended through F major and C minor. Weeping thirds emerge at the text's reference to the Cross.

Again the question is suspended in mid-air, on the second inversion of the dominant of C minor. After the pause, however, the music moves to E flat major and the vocal line, though still phrased across the beats, acquires the spaciousness of Christ's E flat major arioso (no. 31). This permutation is hardly surprising, since the words speak of the Cross's redemptive power; but although the original rising-scale theme appears in E flat, it teeters to C minor as the disturbed cross-accents reappear. The ultimate climax is distressfully chromaticized; and thrusts the music through F and C minor, B flat, E flat and A flat major, which functions as a Neapolitan cadence to the home tonic, G minor. A truncated recapitulation ensues, with the chorus's questioning interjections catapulted in close sequence. Again, these constitute physical action of an immediacy which few opera composers can rival, as do the soloist's hastening melismata and breathless tritonal suspensions on the word 'Golgotha'. The chorus has a last unresolved query on a dominant (not diminished) seventh; the soloist answers with a simple falling scale that anticipates Christ's *consummatum est*; we end with a literal repeat of the canonic opening ritornello. The climacteric effect of this aria with chorus, in relationship to the Passion as a whole, derives from its synthesis of immediacy with universality. The opening chorus depicts a crowd scene, and is also a statement about the destiny of man. This aria, in the same tragic G minor, vividly portrays the individual soul's yearning for God, in lines that complement nervous agitation with tensile strength, and in a form which, in its progressive evolution, has analogies with sonata. None the less this inwardly dramatic experience is distanced in being projected in theatrical terms, and in the symmetry with which the end recapitulates the beginning. We sense that the music is happening, with momentous excitement, in the present time, yet also know that it is timeless.

This immediate-universal, temporal-eternal dichotomy is preserved in the enactment of the Crucifixion itself: although it is related, following established precedent, by the Evangelist, this recitative is exceptionally wide-ranging and lyrical. Its arioso quality is apposite to the solemnity of the event, the cosmic implications of which are manifest in the text's reference to the *conjunctio oppositorum* of Christ and the two thieves, one light and heaven-aspiring, the other dark and hell-bent. Significantly the fact of the Crucifixion and the mention of the 'two others with him' evoke, tonally, the darkest music thus far; beginning in B flat minor, we move to F minor but, when Jesus is mentioned, unexpectedly cadence in his compassionate E flat major. The dark flatness is reinstated as Pilate affixes the 'title' to the Cross; but the recitative line, moving from F minor to D flat and A flat major, has a dignified grandeur and, for the moment, a minimum of implied dissonance. B flat minor and F minor return, with a tortured melisma on the word *gekreuziget*; the recitative finds not so much termination as dismissal. The significance of sacred events is briskly debunked by the uncomprehending rabble, who deny Jesus' right to the title of 'King of the Jews' in an almost literal repeat of the 6/4, B flat major fugato in which they had mockingly hailed him as that. The effect of the jaunty chorus, with its thumping quaver bass and emptily screeching semiquaver scales, is the more potent because it is slightly modified from fugato to brutal homophony. The irony of the repetition of material is here spine-chilling; and becomes more so when Pilate informs us, in a B flat major recitative cliché, that what he has written, he has written. A further, yet more devastating, irony is to come. For a moment we're allowed a vision outside time and the action as the chorus (representing the congregation and ourselves) sings a radiant version, in Jesus' benedictory E flat major, of the chorale *Valet will ich dir geben*. The grandeur of Teschner's bold tune (1613), with its initial rising fifth, is only slightly modified by the touch of relative minor in the first phrase; after the double bar the modulation to the dominant affirmatively rings on high Fs and Gs. Though the final clause darkens with chromatics, diminished sevenths and consequent false relation, and descends into 'lugubrious' F minor at the text's reference to Christ's affliction, the lines remain songful. And the frustrated cadence on C minor instead of the anticipated major leads back to E flat by way of its subdominant:

Ex. 88

The weight of the flattened seventh in the bass pulls like gravity, and prepares us for the upward, dominant thrust of the A natural in the final cadence. The false relation between this bass and the tenor's A flat dominant seventh heals as it hurts.

Immediately the Evangelist recounts the tale of the soldiers' lot-casting. The tonal movement is rapid —from B flat major to G minor and D minor, to F and C major. The calmly arpeggiated phrase that depicts Jesus' 'seamless' coat is a musical synonym for perfection; yet there's irony here too, since it is a C major arpeggio and it is in C major that the recitative ends, to be abruptly succeeded, in that key, by the soldiers' dicing chorus. This *turba* music is mundane enough, though not in the Baroque sense, for there is no hint of even worldly power or glory. Again, it contains a stroke of theatrical genius and psychological acumen. The soldiers yawp their nagging repeated notes, lurching into an inane syncopation and giggling semiquavers, for the division of the spoils:

Ex. 89

The principle of fugal oneness is employed parodistically, since the casting of lots is not communal but competitive; they shout their phrase against one another, its tailpiece of falling third followed by falling fifth growing horridly hilarious. The texture is thin, niggardly, the voices doubled by flutes, oboes and violins, the continuo bass low and detached, and in the middle register a footling Alberti figuration—such as was to become fashionable in the rococo society of Bach's younger sons—emulating the throwing of dice. Despite, or because of, its vacuousness the chorus is quite long, with modulations to the relative and back, then to E minor, with an almost comic, rhythmically dislocated full close; then to the dominant and subdominant; then to D minor with a repetition of the dislocated cadence. The fairly large scale of the trivial music suggests that there is no apparent end to human crassness. A kind of stretto repeats the modulations in telescoped form, attaining a climax of nasty farce, wherein the hammered repeated triads evoke the unholy glee—mixed with envy and desperation—of those who are blind and deaf to the meaning of the Cross. (It's impressive that a man of Bach's training and proclivities should thus be able to invoke mindless greed like that of a bingo session and violence like that of a rabble of soccer hooligans!) If we considered this *turba* chorus out of context we might be tempted to think that Bach took a depressingly low view of human nature. In context, of course, the horror of vacuity becomes part of Bach's Christian humility. These are the depths to which man, in his lapsed state, may fall; and man includes himself, and you and me. The heart of the Christian message is that there is another possibility, one to which we return in the sequence of numbers concerned with Christ's death.

That Bach was capable of so directly projecting the depths of human degradation is part of his greatness —and atopical 'universality'. As an opera composer he clearly would have been as totally honest and unafraid as Mozart. He never again, however, permitted himself a naturalistic outburst so *apparently* irreconcilable with his sacred task. The *St John Passion* remains the most uncompromisingly humanistic of his creations, though even here he evokes the depths —socially and spiritually —in order to set the heights in relief. After the dicing chorus, Jesus slowly expires. The recitatives, chorale and aria that describe his death complement the great central panel concerned with his scourging and his wounds.

The first recitative concerns the encounter between the dying Jesus and the two Marys —one light, one dark, like the two thieves —at the foot of the Cross. The lyrical vocal line is dominated by the interval of a rising sixth, as though the women were lifting arms and heart to their drooping God. The tonal movement is surprisingly energetic, from A minor to D minor, and then rising in sequential fifths through E, B and F sharp minor, each additional sharp being a *Kreuz* that intensifies pain. Yet anguish finally cadences in the relative, A major; and although the arioso grows more animated with the modulations, energy only enhances lyricism. Leaping sixths are transformed into diminished sevenths, octaves, minor ninths, balanced by falling tritones; the contours of the line, as well as the modulations, recall the similar passage at the end of Part I. This emphasizes the relationship between Jesus' Passion and Peter's; the effect is deepened because we're now aware of the divine connotations. Jesus' invocation of the Mother as he hangs from the Cross has profound psychological significance, for the boy Christ was presented as the traditional *puer aeternus* of myth who, at the age of twelve (the apotheosis of childhood before puberty) had been lost for the traditional three days, prefiguring his own death, three-day burial and rebirth. To deny the ties of family is an inevitable consequence of growing up: 'If any man come to me and hate not his father and mother and wife and children and brethren and sisters, yea and his own life also, he cannot be my disciple.' This apparently horrific doctrine doesn't in psychological terms mean that we must nurture hate in our hearts but rather that to follow the way of God we must be 'simply and wholly bereft of self'. Mary 'kept in her heart the memory of all this'; and after the finding in the Temple and the dismissive words at Cana ('Who *is* my mother?') came truly to find her son on the road to Calvary, when he'd been reborn on his dark journey. If in Jungian terms Christ as Man-God-Son equals evolving consciousness, in dying he makes his peace with the Eternal Mothers. Giving himself up to death is a feminine redemptive return to non-being and night, to the No-thing from which we came. As Alan Watts has put it, death is in a sense always a regression to the womb, which may be why the bone behind the uterus is known as the *os crucis*, or Holy Bone.

Though it would be fanciful to describe the lyrical contours of this arioso as feminine, it certainly adds a new dimension to the music; and the quality spills over into the next chorale. The tune (by Vulpius) is the same as that which concluded Part I, when the text had reference to Peter's anguish. Now the words are concerned with Christ as faithful son; God as son of woman is thus aligned with mortal man, as the stepwise moving lines smilingly cadence, in the second bar, in the dominant and, with the tune's descent, return to the tonic A major. Though a dissonant passing note leads, at the reference to the Mother, to a half-close in the relative minor, the affirmative A major is soon re-established. The first two bars of the second half are clear diatonic major; the second two again effect an uncompromising dominant modulation. In the fifth and sixth bars the reference to death prompts a momentary perturbation of passing notes; but since this death ends distress, the two final bars are diatonically serene. Only the bass's sharpened D in the cadence recalls the dominant aspiration of the opening. Though it's in false relation with the tenor's D natural, its cadential pull assuages; it embraces the *complexio oppositorum* which we have seen to be the essence of Bach's music no less than of his faith.

The next stretch of recitative, which describes Jesus's thirst, the offer of vinegar and hyssop, and his death, complements the previous recitative concerning the two Marys. The lyrical arioso manner is preserved, the line leaping through fifths, sixths and sevenths; only whereas the earlier recitative tends to upward aspiration, suggesting raised arms, this recitative falls more than it rises. After the Evangelist's expanding intervals as he tells of the fulfilment of the scriptures, Jesus thirsts in a simple falling fifth, counteracting an upward tonal progression from G to D major, and from E to B minor. The vinegar and hyssop promote falling sixths and tritones, in rhythmic fragmentation. The *consummatum est* is sung by Jesus —in fulfilment of the Golgotha aria's cadential phrase (Ex. 85) —to a scale drooping from D to F sharp, with the G sharp as implicit appoggiatura:

Ex. 90

Es ist voll - bracht!

Miraculously, the continuo's cadence changes the 'crucial' F sharp minor into major, which metamorphoses inanition into a ray of light. But this is prophetic, for the F sharp minor episode hasn't been a final departure from B minor, and the F sharp major triad functions as a B minor dominant, leading into the next aria. This tonal punning profoundly equivocates, like the Passion story, between death and life.

The alto aria, which reflects on the *consummatum est*, is in B minor, the dark key of suffering, subdominant to the transcendental F sharp minor. Its pathos is passive for it deals with the cessation of life in the spirit — with the dark night of the soul and the dark time of the year. Only in such darkness can the soul be 'stripped and poor and naked' and so 'born again of water and of the spirit'. Christ descends into earth-hell in order to ascend to heaven; so this aria balances the central rainbow aria which had metamorphosed the crown of thorns into a halo. Now Christ's surcease anticipates a world reborn. We can hardly miss the affinity with the rainbow aria since the obbligato instrument is a viola da gamba, darker brother to the love-viols that had woven the halo in the central aria. The gamba was the last survivor of the viol family, and even in Bach's day composers — including Bach himself — still wrote for it music of noble spirituality. With its top string tuned a fourth higher than the cello, it had wider range if slighter volume; it sang-spoke with infinite subtlety of nuance, at once humane and ethereal. Its tone is heroic yet melancholy, rich yet purged; nothing could be more appropriate to the drooping phrases of this aria, which so beautifully complement the aspiring lines of the rainbow aria. The ritornello theme starts from the simple falling scale, drooping under its own weight, to which Christ had expired. In the aria, however, the rhythm is dotted and this, at the immensely slow *adagio molto* prescribed by Bach, makes the music limp, almost halt, as the pulse falters and blood drains from the limbs:

Ex. 91

The effect is the more poignant because the dotted rhythm is a heroic convention of the Baroque age: a symbol of worldly pride has become a synonym for physical exhaustion and spiritual sacrifice—the death of a hero, indeed. Inevitably we recall not only the rainbow aria but also the dotted rhythm of Peter's aria of remorse at the end of Part I. That had transmuted heroic extraversion into inner strife. Peter's trauma is human, Jesus' is divine; and the one is implicit in the other.

An equation between the human and the divine is evident in the Golgotha myth itself, for Adam was said to have been born at the very spot—the earth's centre—where the Cross was to be erected. He was buried there too, at the foot of the Cross and the heart of the world; and the blood of the crucified Christ, dripping on his skull, redeemed him. St. John Chrysostom, quoted by Watts, speaks of the Cross as 'a Tree which rises from Earth to Heaven. A plant immortal, it stands at the centre of earth and heaven; strong pillar of the universe, bone of all things, support of all the inhabited earth, cosmic interlacement, composing in itself the whole medley of human nature'. So the Tree of Calvary has roots in the ancestral Tree of Life, Yggdrasil; in the Old Testament's wisdom that is 'a Tree of Life to those that lay hold of her', and in Nebuchadnezzar's dream wherein he beheld 'a tree in the midst of the earth, and the height thereof was great'. Not fortuitously was Jesus a carpenter, and was at Calvary simultaneously in torment and in bliss.

In the first section of this *consummatum est* aria the ritornello theme droops over a bass that slowly pulses, broken by rests, from tonic to dominant and back; modulates to the dominant minor; and returns to the tonic by way of a touch of relative major. The gamba melody, unlike the bass, is sustained, but moves in arches, each descent followed by an ascent—painful both because of the incidental dissonances and because of the creeping lassitude of the dotted rhythm. When the voice enters this arch is exaggerated; the voice is in dialogue with the gamba and each declining scale, garlanded with tremulous melismata, is separated by a silence. The duality between death and life is implicit in the contrast between the falling scales of the *consummatum est* and the broken but rising fifths and sixths that express the hope inherent in Christ's sacrifice. Meanwhile the gamba's song flows on. The voice falls through a seventh to balance its sixth; and the first section cadences, in the tenth long 4/4—or 8/8—bar, into the serenity of the relative major. The ritornello continues in D, relaxes to the subdominant, which turns into its relative, E minor, when the voice re-enters. As the music rises to the 'transcendent suffering' of F sharp minor, the vocal tessitura suggests the colour of night:

Ex. 92

Though the voice cadences in this key, the ritornello carries us back, by way of A major, to D, which unconventionally, but with allegorical appro-priateness, concludes the first section of what is apparently a (however metaphysically transfigured) aria da capo.

Only after his cry of loss on the Cross — 'My God, My God, why hast though forsaken me?' — does Jesus 'give up the ghost' and commend his spirit into God's hands. He recognizes, in the almost total inanition of this aria, that his sacrifice is not his physical death but his relinquishment of the I which alone can release us from the shackles of time. As Alan Watts puts it, 'the more we struggle to be free, to be just, good and useful and so on', the more we are trapped in temporality. 'Only God, who is the true Self, can perform self-sacrifice'; only Christ, escaping the entanglements of pride, can transform the Cross from an instrument of torture to 'the medicine of the world'. By the same alchemy the cruciform symbol of the earth, of conflict and opposition, is also a symbol of the sun: *Fulget crucis mysterium*. The superficially shocking Baroque worldliness of the aria's middle section is thus in context profoundly subtle. The clarity of the 'pure mind', emptied of all that clings to the past since it is a construct of memory, may be achieved by the individual soul, through God's grace. But mankind, as a totality, hasn't reached that point; and what happens in the middle section is the public face, rather than inner spirit, of a world reclaimed. The first section had revealed spiritual depths within the heroic cliché of dotted rhythm; the middle section accepts another Baroque cliché at its face value, for it banishes the solo gamba to the bass line and smothers it with violins brandishing D major trumpet arpeggios, resonant with open strings (Ex. 93).

The scales are exuberant, the motor rhythms corporeal; there is a minimum of dissonance; and only two conventionally manipulated modulations to relative and subdominant. Worldly power and glory are as manifest as they are in Handel's ceremonial choruses; though if we think of this section in

Ex. 93

comparison with the longer and grander stretches of similar music in the B minor Mass, we realize that its festal magnificence has elemental as well as mundane implications. For it is concerned with the *consequences*, for human beings, of Christ's sacrifice; not with the ecstasis that an individual may attain in union with God, but with the possibility of a world regenerated, as the earth itself is reborn, in spring, after the winter solstice.

The text refers to Christ as a lion who wins a battle over sin and death. Though the figurations are conventional Baroque battle music, the rhythmic energy is such as to evoke the lion as a natural force, equated with the sun that revitalizes the frozen earth. At the end of this section, however, the semiquaver roulades turn into falling scales followed by leaping sixths, the basic elements of the aria's first section. After tonal shifts from D major to E minor there's a sudden break on the diminished seventh of B minor; and an *adagio* repetition of the original *consummatum est* phrase, now drooping from G to B. There is no full da capo. The gamba merely repeats its initial ritornello, beginning halfway through a bar. This puts the final cadence on the first instead of the third immensely slow beat, above which the voice repeats '*est ist vollbracht*', the rhythm slightly altered, the appoggiatura long sustained, fading with the expiration of breath. After the lion-like middle we come back to the purgatorial Cross because it is the Cross that has laboured to achieve the Lion's birth. But we cannot murder God again; and the repetition of the mere four and a half bars of ritornello musically satisfies because its tempo, as compared with the middle, is so slow as to seem eternal. Nor is this an end to these inner relationships, for the two-bar recitative that carries us from B to F sharp minor is the prelude to another aria, this time in D major, a tonal relationship prefigured at the end of the *consummatum est*.

The bass aria is also a chorale-fantasia, which is significant in relation to the structure of the Passion as a whole, since the cosmological story is thereby linked to our own fate. The piece marks a stage in the work's spiritual pilgrimage in another sense also, for it fuses the contradictions of the first and middle sections of the previous aria. Its murky sonority—bass voice and a bass line that also serves as obbligato part—reminds us that we're still at the dark time of the year, celebrating a Dying God; but the D major theme itself is gently lion-like, swinging in a spacious 12/8, alternating falling sixths and leaping sixths, fourths and tenths. The leading notes at the top of the crests are garlanded with trills; as a whole the theme has an exalted serenity that is not quite repose. This is exactly apposite to the words, which are about crucifixion as a gateway to life, a point emphasized when the first six-bar period is repeated, as it modulates to dominant and subdominant and back, with melismatic arabesques. Against the aria the chorus intones the phrases of Vulpius's hymn, heard before the *consummatum est* aria, and earlier in association with Peter's remorse. The words are different, and so is the key—a fifth lower; moreover the first clause moves flatwards to the subdominant instead of sharpwards to the dominant. The metre is a regular 4/4, equated with the aria's 12/8, and modern performances often change the dotted figures into crotchet-quaver triplets, to fit with the aria. Though this is a Baroque convention its application seems in this case misguided. Conventions are not laws, and each case must be judged on its own merits. Here the cross-rhythms between the aria's triplets and the chorale's quavers and semiquavers separate us as congregation from the historical Lion-Christ and from the universal Godhead. What's happening concerns us but is not us; the effect can only be weakened by smoothing the chorale rhythm into conformity with the air (Ex. 94).

After a decisive cadence in the tonic the dialogue between voice and bass line becomes quasi-canonic, a duality in oneness. As the bass prances it grows more contorted, leaping not only through diminished sevenths but also through augmented sixths and minor ninths. The voice complements this perturbation with melismata syncopated across the beats, thereby reflecting the text's reference to Christ's afflictions. Lilting over the bars, the arabesques become a gateway to eternal life. The angularity of the bass's leaping tenths, with cadential trills, encourages rapid modulation through E, B and A minor

Ex. 94

and then, after the next interjection of the chorale phrase, through F sharp, E and A minor. The middle phrases of the chorale modulate to the relative and subdominant; the last phrase returns to the tonic by way of its subdominant. Again Christ's physical agony and spiritual ecstasy are contained in syncopated melismata, which prepare for, and contrast with, the simplicity of his yea-saying, bowed head. When he replies to our questions with silence the instrumental parts disappear. In the final ritornello the continuo bass has the voice's version of the lion-prancing theme:

Ex. 95

The effect of this aria-chorale is curiously equivocal since the heroic pride of its lilting theme is counteracted by its restless veering between high and low register, by the dark, earth-weighted sonority, and by the oscillating modulations. There is no hint of the transcendence of the rainbow aria, nor of the tragic sublimity of the first section of the *consummatum est* aria. Though it expresses a triumph — personal in its invocation of Christ as Lion, public in its introduction of the congregational chorale — it would seem to be a still uncertain victory. So when Bach abruptly follows the aria with the rending of the veil —

borrowing the incident from the Gospel according to St. Matthew —the effect is disturbingly ambiguous. The vocal line, whirling through sevenths dominant and diminished, carries us with shuddering scales and tremolandos from E minor to a B flat major chord that proves to be a Neapolitan approach to A minor, and back, through wide-flung arpeggios, to E minor. The brevity and discretion of the passage—which calls for no instruments beyond the continuo—seem only to intensify its horrendous quality. Such music might presage an end to mankind's redemptive hope; and though it does not do so, the lion-like mood is not recovered. What remains of the Passion is unequivocally purgatorial and tragic—in the Greek and Shakespearean senses.

The transition back to redemption occurs in a section, likewise explicitly termed *arioso*, which balances the 'Orphic' prelude to the rainbow aria (no. 31). Scored for tenor voice accompanied by strings as well as continuo, its vocal line opens with an arpeggiated G major triad, with repeated demisemiquavers on strings, emulating both the tremor of the earth and a fluttering of the heart. But although the arioso has a key signature of one sharp it isn't really in G major, since the sustained major triad acts as a dominant of C minor as the sun is shrouded, then quivers to D minor, with pulsing diminished sevenths, for the rending of the mountain. Demisemiquaver scales, derived from the previous recitative, become melodically ordered; two final *adagio* bars move from rocking 6–3 chords in D minor to a triple appoggiatura on a C major triad that proves to be a dominant of F minor:

Ex. 96

For it introduces the last aria, the only number in the Passion centred on this key of *chants lugubres*. It is a dark complement to the rainbow aria—in a slow 3/8, as contrasted with the rainbow aria's seraphically winging 12/8.

The obbligato parts again move in parallel thirds and sixths, but are scored for two flutes and two oboi da caccia, both in unison. This is the only movement in which Bach uses his alto oboe, which hasn't the romantic plangency of the modern cor anglais, though its tone, conditioned by its open bell, is mellower and more plaintive than that of the ordinary Baroque oboe. This makes it appropriate to this austerely tragic lament, which—for the first time since the flute-accompanied adolescent love-chase early in Part I—is entrusted to soprano solo. Subconsciously, we recognize the relationship: this 'Song of Experience' (also in 3/8) consummates that 'Song of Innocence', at a deeper level than the relationship between the 'love-chase' and the bondage aria (nos. 13 and 11), since Christ's Passion has intervened.

There are two main elements in the preludial ritornello: the undulation of demisemiquavers in parallel sixths recalling, less ecstatically, the viols' intertwinings in the rainbow aria; and the gentle pulsing of semiquavers in the bass, developed from the throbbing earth-beat or thudding heart of the previous arioso. A turning figure in demisemiquavers also derives from the arioso, becoming a bass to weeping parallel sixths and thirds, phrased in pairs:

Ex. 97

The ritornello moves flatwards to B flat minor—a key previously touched on only at the Crucifixion itself—and then back to the tonic. When the voice enters it repeats the ritornello theme, but answers the syncopated undulation with a simple falling arpeggio. The second two bars are exquisitely lyrical, yet tense in harmonic implications since they create melodically a dominant ninth of B flat minor. This music is thus more earthbound than the rainbow aria it patently resembles: appropriately, since the aria is not a joyous consummation but a threnody for the Dying God. The tone colour of flutes and oboi da caccia, plaintive yet bleak and bleating, as compared with the ripeness of normal oboes, enhances the aria's crepuscular atmosphere.

Yet despite its muted quality this lament for the slain Christ, being universal, is also blissful, generating transcendence from grief itself. When the opening phrase is repeated it stretches the dominant ninth through a scalewise progression that directly resembles the rainbow aria; and a second repeat takes us sequentially from subdominant to dominant minor. Meanwhile the trembling or pulsing semiquavers of the bass slowly rise and fall; and the obbligato's parallel sixths melt in the syncopated undulation or turning figure, and weep in falling thirds. The vocal line stands still at the reference to the Godhead of whom Christ is the son, recalling the long sustained notes in the tenor's rainbow. A 6–4 cadence in C minor is approached by weeping dissonances; the original theme, expanding its rising fourth to a fifth, extends and intensifies its melismata. A preponderance of the syncopated motive makes the vocal line more animated; the turning figure is in the bass, while the oboes have the repeated note pulsation. The first section ends with a cadential trill in C minor and a freely canonic ritornello wherein the rumbling turn, first in the bass, then in the upper parts, gains ascendancy over the weeping thirds.

The second section begins (bar 59) by moving simply from C minor to Christ's compassionate E flat major, the vocal line calmer, more restricted in compass. We are not, however, offered a contrasting middle section, for the aria returns abruptly to F minor, and to melodic fragmentation. The vocal phrases are separated by silences, in awed horror at the fact of God's murder; after a pause on a first inversion of the dominant seventh of D flat, the music cadences in A flat major. The obbligato instruments begin to repeat the preludial ritornello as though for a da capo; but another shock comes when the voice enters with a leap to the high G flat, and droops in weeping melismata through a Neapolitan C flat (Ex. 98).

With a chromatic rise in the pulsing bass this turns into a half-close on the dominant of B flat minor. After another pause and more fragmented appoggiaturas on the word *tot*, there is at last a full close in B flat minor. This time an orthodox da capo follows, with sonata-style modifications in that the sustained notes for the Godhead are now in the tonic instead of dominant. The

Ex. 98

aria ends with a coda that fuses the weeping semiquavers with the
demisemiquaver syncopations. In so doing the tears motive reveals affinities
with the scourging motive that, in the tenor's aria, had been metamorphosed
into a rainbow. This does not necessarily mean that Bach consciously
manipulated these relationships, though he may have done; certainly they are
audible to our ears and minds and senses.

This aria is sublime yet low-keyed emotionally, apposite to its placing as the
last aria of the Passion; the story 'runs down', is drained like the body of
Christ, yet the running down is a joyous fulfilment. Hence the next, fairly
extensive recitative makes the point that Jesus' destiny is the working out of
divine law. The Evangelist recounts the breaking of the legs of the crucified,
modulating from C minor to E flat major, and thence to G minor. The line
moves rapidly, being narrative; yet it is also lyrical, most potently so when it
reaches G minor. At the reference to the dead Christ there is a drooping
semiquaver scale that may — at least if the tempo is momentarily slowed — recall
his *consummatum est*. This doesn't, however, still the recitative's violence
which, at the piercing of Christ's side, explodes in half-bar modulations and a
tortuous line riddled with devilish tritones. All this eventfulness is then
distanced, in relatively static transitions, as a 'true record' of Scripture. Bach
brings in two quotations from the Old Testament as confirmation, setting
them in *adagio* arioso. The first quotation, in A flat, is heiratic in style — 'A bone
of Him shall not be broken'. The second quotation — 'they shall look on
Him whom they pierced' — remains incantatory, but is also physical in that it
depicts, in its slowly spread arpeggio, the wondering gaze of the onlookers
(Ex. 99).

This moment is indeed extraordinary. If Christ is an image of the Self, the
piercing of his side is self-laceration, the masochism that releases the more
appalling cruelties of the world. It should be noted here that throwing shafts or

Ex. 99

Ihr sol-let ihm kein Bein zer-bre-chen.   Und a-ber-mal spricht ci-ne an-de-re

darts at a Dying God predates Christianity. It's present in the Adonis-Orpheus myth, and in many northern permutations, such as the legend of Balder the Bleeding God, for whom all creation weeps, willing his resurrection. In Bach's Passion, creation has wept in the F minor aria; and it may be that this marvellous declining arpeggio moves us so deeply because unconsciously we relate it—despite its dissonant implications—to the consonantly falling arpeggio at the end of the Christ-Orpheus arioso (no. 31) that had first offered us promise of redemption. That concordant phrase was a prophecy, addressed by the Son of God Himself to men, who 'gaze' in awe. This more harmonically disturbed phrase enacts the bewilderment of the 'gazing' soldiers who intuitively, and to themselves unexpectedly, recognize that they 'know not what they do'. None the less the phrase recalls the grandeur of the earlier arpeggio. It enfolds the soldiers (and us) in a benediction, recalling the homely metaphor that tells us how Christ, whose own people 'received him not', yet gathered them to him, 'as a hen gathereth her chickens under her wings'. Calvary is consummated in Pentecost: 'I have a baptism to be baptized with; and how am I straitened till it be accomplished!' (Luke 12:50).

The benedictory conclusion to this recitative affects our response to the next chorale which, in context, is the most poignant in the Passion. Its melody is the same as that which opens Part II, a semitone higher. At first the harmonies are identical too; but since the cycle of the Passion is now completed, they become more disturbing in exploring the modal ambiguities of the tune. The tonality is a cross between F and B flat minor, synthesizing the 'weeping' aria with the 'gazing' arioso. The first eight bars divide into four groups of two, the first pair enclosed in F major triads, the latter pair in B flat major triads. Though passing dissonances and chromatics reflect the agony of the Passion, the fact that the harmony returns to its source affirms a certainty not manifest to the Golgotha or the Lion arias, but attained by way of the 'weeping' aria and arioso. The next four bars hesitate between D flat major and B flat minor;

while the last four equivocate between B flat and E flat minor, with false relations and diminished fourths. There's a strong tinge of G flat major in the cadence. Since the resolution is on an F major triad one might construe this as a Neapolitan approach to B flat minor; if so the tonic triad is evaded. Oddly enough, the effect of these modal ambiguities is at once to deepen and expand the sense of consummation. The chorale is self-enclosed in its circular harmonies and at the same time open-ended; so is the Christian story, in the sight of God and history.

And the story closes with the deposition from the Cross. At first the Evangelist recounts the incident of Joseph of Arimathea in narrative lyricism, the tonality moving from B flat to F to C minor. The anointing of Jesus' body continues the sharpening process to G and D minor, the vocal line being increasingly songful. For the burial in the secret garden—which recalls the garden wherein Jesus was taken at the close of day at the beginning of this Passion—a new dimension comes into the music, which changes from recitative to arioso. The vocal line is emotive, with leaping sixths and sevenths; modulation ranges widely. Again, Bach's pacing is masterly; the arioso allows the running down of the action to continue of its own momentum, yet is noble enough to preserve our new-found certainty, rather than hope, that Christ is God. This certainty becomes incarnate in the public act of the final chorus, which is in C minor, subdominant to the opening chorus's G minor, to which it stands in a passive relationship, using the adjective with multiple meanings.

This consummatory chorus is a mixture of aria da capo and rondo, incorporating fugato. It is physical in that it involves bodily gestures—an appeal to Jesus and to us his redeemed servants to lie down and sleep—and metaphysical in that corporeal movement leads to spiritual release. Like so much of Bach's music the chorus is thus simultaneously song and dance: a dance of God indeed, in fulfilling the vision of the early Christian mystics who saw the lyre- or viol- or flute-playing Christ as 'leader of the dance; he knows how to touch the strings, to lead from joy to joy, with cherubim and seraphim the soul dances in the round'. Christ as paraclete and heavenly musician leads us dancing to heaven, his relation to the soul being that of bridegroom to bride. It is thus significant that this choric dance resembles a sarabande which, as we've seen, was often a marriage dance, at once ceremonially erotic and sacral. True, it cannot be danced as a sarabande except by treating the upbeat as the first beat of a 3/4 metre, which leaves one with a beat too many in the third or fourth bar. None the less to think of the chorus as a sarabande is to approach it

in the right spirit and to secure an appropriate tempo: which must be fast
enough to suggest the physical presence of a multitude of worshippers, aware
of the storm from which they're now becalmed, yet not too fast to endanger the
music's grandeur.

The rhythmic ambiguity at the opening is crucial, for it gives forward
energy to what seems to be consistently declining music. The melody begins
with a drooping arpeggiated sixth and a seventh, followed by a falling scale
that, flowing from top to bottom of the orchestral texture, expands again to an
arpeggio:

Ex. 100

This musical image springs from the notion of deposition, perhaps even from
the drooping figurations of the *consummatum est* aria and the grand descent at
the end of the 'gazing' arioso. Yet the rhythmic ambiguity of the upbeat that
we hear as a first beat, allied with the upward thrust of the bass, transmutes
these descents into affirmation, so that musical facts render incarnate a
theological truth. This covers the first eight bars. The theme needs another four
for its completion and in these the balance between declension and forward
momentum becomes melodically explicit. The line undulates chromatically
between C, B natural and a Neapolitan D flat, lifts yearningly through a sixth
which is dissonantly tied across the beat, and resolves in falling arpeggios:

Ex. 101

Meanwhile the bass rises steadily but diatonically, without the chromatic interventions. Thus the music continues its affirmation without surrendering an inner agitation.

This ritornello is scored for strings with the first violins doubled by flutes and oboes—a rich sonority. The instrumental music is repeated as the chorus enters homophonically, substituting repeated notes that 'lie still' for the bowing motives of the strings. Despite the homophony, the vocal parts are pliantly lyrical, and become more so as the music, with vestigial canons, modulates to the flat submediant, A flat, and then expands, in hemiola rhythm, to the relative, E flat major. By this time the twelve bars of instrumental ritornello have been answered by seven plus seven bars of choral homophony; another six bars move back to C and G minor, and to another cadence in hemiola rhythm. The resolution is major instead of minor, and serves as dominant of C minor to effect a restatement of the original eight bars, the chorus now singing the 'bowing' instrumental theme. In an eight-bar codetta the declining arpeggios are balanced against rising scales, with a hint of imitative counterpoint. The Neapolitan D flat of the introduction here creates a climax as the sopranos leap to their high A flat, tied across the bar and then descending, in a mere two and a half bars, to the low C. The orchestra rounds off the first section with a strict repeat of the opening ritornello.

The next twelve bars, in the middle section, resemble a rondo episode. The text tells how the grave of Christ became a pathway of heaven; the texture is sparer, the tonality changes at first to B flat major, and the lines attain metrical freedom, flowing across the bars. The regular pulse of the bass's repeated notes recalls the F minor soprano aria (no. 63), for the chorus is a public restatement of what was, in the aria, individualized experience. Descending arpeggios intermittently reappear in the strings, now suggesting wings as well as deposition. The final cadence to this episode—after B flat has veered back to C minor—is in A flat major, again in hemiola rhythm. We don't however stay in the new key but proceed to a full-scale recapitulation of the first forty bars. Another rondo episode passes through sequential modulations to those crucial keys, F minor, G minor and E flat major. Here the bass falls in its pulsing crotchets, and the downward arpeggio appears twice. The vocal parts, on the other hand, are for the first time dominated by ascent, pushing upwards in parallel thirds or sixths, usually across the bar-line, to envisage heavenly release on the high A flat, again floated across the bar (Ex. 102).

The cadence into E flat major, though spatially a descent, is a spiritual release, especially if we keep in mind the significance of E flat major as a key of epiphany.

Ex. 102

None the less the episode *is* an episode. Bach appends a da capo sign, and the recapitulation covers the first forty-eight bars of the movement. The monumental scale of the chorus and its cyclical form indicate that it is not concerned with progression, but rather with something that happened in historical time but has become eternal. The miracle of Bach's music is that it evokes present action and transcends inner stress in a peace that is the ultimate *conjunctio oppositorum*. The aria-rondo-fugato is the peacock's tail wherein all the colours of the spectrum are one. So this chorus, which fulfils the prophecy of the tenor's central aria in the same key by offering the rainbow vision to us all, is the Passion's inevitable conclusion though not its absolute end. For having made its timeless statement Bach returns briefly to the present time and place—the church wherein we are gathered together—to sing a valedictory chorale. Its key is E flat major, Christ's key of benediction: the Passion story is essentially that of God's humanization. Furthermore, the second cadence of the irregular seven-bar clause has a false close on the triad of G minor, the tragic key which had initiated the story and which, along with E flat major, had been a point pivotal to C minor in the previous chorus. The cadence back to E flat major is stabilized by touches of subdominant and dominant. The next eight bars after the double bar alternate between tonic and dominant; in the final six bars the mysterious G minor chord leads back to E flat by way of an agile bass line:

Ex. 103

Throughout the parts are widely spaced, sturdy, resilient. Such affirmation is possible only after heights have been scaled, depths plumbed.

The finale chorale (the tune of which, *Herzlich lieb hab ich dich* by Reinigius, dates from 1587) did not exist in the original 1724 version, but was added for a revival to replace another concluding chorus. The C minor choral 'sarabande' is musically satisfying as a conclusion; yet it is fascinating to note how Bach, having decided to bring back the congregation in an epilogue, does so with regard for the total musical and dramatic structure by his choice of E flat major as tonic and by his unconventional reference to G minor and major as well as C minor. Repeatedly we find such relevance to the total structure in individual movements, such as this brief chorale or the monumental sarabande-chorus, improbable though this may seem, given the work's humanistic immediacy. Diagrammatically, we may plot Part I of the *St. John Passion* in these terms:

No. 1   Monumental chorus: aria da   G minor
             capo with fugato; tragic,
             impersonal, universal
             statement, yet also physically
             realistic (surging crowd)

Nos. 2–6	Dramatic action, alternating narrative recitative with *turba* choruses, the latter repeating the same music, with slight modifications, three times	veering between C minor, G minor and B flat major
Nos. 7–10	Reflective chorale, alternating with dramatic rather than narrative recitative (Peter's sword)	shifts sharpwards from G minor
Nos. 11–13	Two canonic arias, separated by brief recitative	D minor and B flat major
Nos. 14–20	Peter's story: long, eventful recitative and arioso	modulating sharpwards to F sharp minor
	Chorale	A major with hint of F sharp minor
	Peter's arioso and aria of remorse	freely chromatic, F sharp minor
	Chorale	A major with hints of F sharp

The large-scale movement in Part I is from G minor to the extreme (related) distance of F sharp minor and A major, with the two canonic arias (Experience and Innocence) as a midway point of repose. The music grows sharper as we approach the *Kreuz*.

Part II is more rigorously schematicized, perhaps because God ought to be more ordered than fallible man:

Nos. 21–29	Chorale	A minor (modal)
	Alternations of recitative with *turba* choruses (music adapted from Part I); dramatic, eventful	centred around D minor and A minor
Nos. 30–32	Scourging recitative	ending in G minor
	'Orpheus' arioso	E flat major
	'Rainbow' aria	C minor (The flatwards modulations are death-tending)

Nos. 33–45	Dramatic recitative alternating with *turba* choruses and chorales	Tonally wide-ranging, from B flat major and G minor, sharpwards again for the Crucifixion, landing in F sharp minor, A major, E major (No. 42 adapts material of no. 38, no. 44 adapts material of no. 36)
Nos. 46–50	*Turba* chorus (adapted repeat of nos. 5 and 29)	B minor
	Golgotha arioso and aria with chorus (related to nos. 1 and 13)	G minor
	Crucifixion and *turba* response (This group balances the scourging recitative, arioso and aria, nos. 29–32)	B flat minor and major (Sharps change to flats again from no. 48)
Nos. 51–54	Chorale, recitative and *turba* choruses, including the dicing episode	from E flat major to C major
Nos. 55–60	Arioso: the two Marys	free tonality
	Chorale	A major
	Consummatum est, arioso and aria (related to nos. 31 and 32)	B minor
	Aria with chorale fantasia (same tune as nos. 20 and 56)	D major
Nos. 61–63	Arioso: the rending of the veil	free tonality
	'Tears' aria (related to nos. 32 and 13)	F minor
Nos. 64–68	Arioso (Christ's pierced side)	free, ending in B flat minor
	Chorale (same tune as no. 21)	F minor
	The Deposition: arioso	free

| Choral sarabande-rondo-aria | C minor |
| Chorale | E flat major |

It will be observed that the central panel of Part II, nos 27–52, forms a chiastic structure A B C D E D C B A (first pointed out by Smend in 1926): in general terms, with the disposition of kinds of material and keys; in particular terms, with literal repetitions or adaptations. As Geiringer has written, 'the deeply religious composer may have found satisfaction in the thought that works in chiastic form have their visual equivalents in the structure of a cross, with two corresponding side-arms emerging from a middle beam, or in that of a church with wide transepts flanking a central nave. Such correlations seemed quite natural to Baroque artists and Bach was in this respect a true son of his time'. Even in the humanly mutable Part I repetitions of material serve a comparable function. Here is the chiastic structure of Part II:

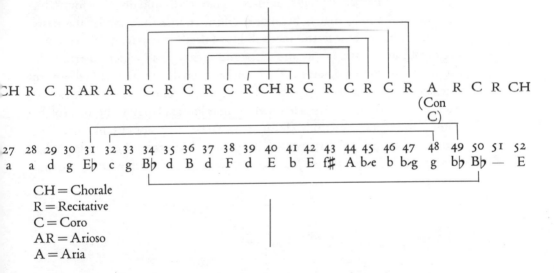

| CH | R | C | R | AR | A | R | C | R | C | R | C | R | CH | R | C | R | C | R | C | R | A | R | C | R | CH |

(Con C)

| 27 | 28 | 29 | 30 | 31 | 32 | 33 | 34 | 35 | 36 | 37 | 38 | 39 | 40 | 41 | 42 | 43 | 44 | 45 | 46 | 47 | 48 | 49 | 50 | 51 | 52 |
| a | a | d | g | E♭ | c | g | B♭ | d | B | d | F | d | E | b | E | f♯ | A | b-e | b | b-g | g | b♭ | B♭ | — | E |

CH = Chorale
R = Recitative
C = Coro
AR = Arioso
A = Aria

Such a schematic disposition of material cannot possibly have been fortuitous. What is more important is the manner in which conscious contrivance cooperates with thematic interrelationships and with affinities of figuration, texture and timbre which for the most part functioned unconsciously. Bach's genius cannot be separated from his craftsmanship, and both are related to the tenets of his church. He composed the *St. John Passion* by 1724 when, at the age of thirty-nine, he was entering into the plenitude of his powers. Geiringer tells us that during Bach's Leipzig years *young* musicians and churchmen seem to have been his most ardent supporters; presumably they were able to see or hear beyond fashion, recognizing that the rich complexity of Bach's art, if apparently archaistic, was in human and musical terms progressive rather than regressive. Middle-aged and old councillors and congregations had been bewildered, during Bach's youthful period at Arnstadt, by what they considered the extravagance and licence of his chorale improvisations; that the city fathers at Leipzig should have been disturbed by the dramatic vehemence of the *St. John Passion* is hardly surprising. We're apt to forget, because we justifiably think of Bach as in some senses a backward-looking composer, how startlingly modern and even, by eighteenth-century standards, how indecorous the work is. Yet despite Councillor Platz's notorious gaffe ('Since we cannot get the best man, we must make do with a mediocre one'), we shouldn't be too severe on the burghers. Bach — whose acute intellect never suffered fools gladly — was to give them as much as he got during their rebarbative years of non-cooperation; if, initially, they found his Passion hard-going, that is because it affirms rather than evades the nasty brutality of life and the fearful inevitability of death. Yet it *is* an affirmation: a cycle of life and death, of pity and terror and ecstasy, from which we return, in the gradually sloping descent to the ceremonial finale, purified and reborn. In listening to the Passion we re-experience how 'the Word was made flesh, and dwelt among us, (and we beheld his glory, the glory as of the only begotten of the Father,) full of grace and truth' (John 1 : 14). So Bach's historicity, like that of the Cross, is identical with his reality in the present. 'After such knowledge, what forgiveness?' Hearing the *St. John Passion*, we acquire the knowledge, and find forgiveness.

III

THE RESURRECTION
AND THE LIFE

Unless the man cries out of an utter and real destitution, deserted by reality, by truth, by the promise of the very Law he comes to fulfil, out of what that is not too trivial for the event does he cry—Why hast thou forsaken me?

God died from and into the extension of Its Self, so that the Resurrection and Revelation is a new identity of all persons and intentions. 'If you have not entered the dance', the Christ says to John in the Gnostic Gospel of John at Ephesus, 'you misunderstand the event.' But this *dance* is exactly the extremity out of which the ultimate cry of anguish comes. Each child, taking breath, leaps into life with such an anguish. At the heart of the Universe, the cosmic order that is a music in which the harmony of all things is established in the fiat that it is Good, we remember there is also just this risk, this leaping into life or dying into life, that only mortal things know. So, the poet understands the truth of the anguish of Christ's Passion as a truth of poetic form. The fullness of the creative imagination demands that rigour and painful knowledge be the condition of harmony; that death be the condition of eternal forms.

ROBERT DUNCAN: *The Truth and Life of Myth*

Now the Supreme, because within are no differences, is eternally present; but we achieve such presence only when our differences are lost. We have at all times our centre There, though we do not at all times look Thither. We are like a company of singing dancers, who may turn their gaze outward and away, notwithstanding they have the choirmaster for centre; but when they are turned towards him, then they sing true and are truly centred upon him. Even so we encircle the Supreme Being always, and when we break the circle, it shall be our utter dissolution and cessation of being; but our eyes are not at all times fixed upon the Centre. Yet in our vision thereof is our attainment and our repose and the end of all discord, God in his dancers, and God the true Centre of the dance.

PLOTINUS: *Enneads*, vi (trans. Dodds)

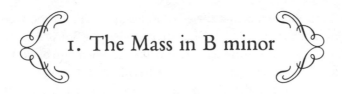

1. The Mass in B minor

The *St. John Passion* is Bach's most 'modern' work in that, dealing with the phenomenon of Incarnation, it is humanistically oriented: in Jungian terminology, it concerns God's need to become Man. The so-called B minor Mass, like any liturgical mass, is also about Incarnation, but approached from the opposite angle in that it concerns fallen man's need to attain to Godhead. The doctrine of the Fall does not refer merely or mainly to the biological origin of the bifurcation of sex. In mythological terms male and female, Yang and Yin, signify not so much sexuality as the duality to which the Fall submits us. Dualities of male and female, light and dark, pleasure and pain, good and evil, life and death are man's birthright ever since, in attaining to consciousness, he separated subject from object. He has a chance to transcend them because, although 'dis-ease' and 'Eve-il' stole into the heart of the First Adam through the agency of the Serpent on the Tree, redemption may come through the Second Adam—Christ crucified on the Tree-become-Cross. Medieval iconography often relates this Tree-Cross to the brazen phallic serpent that Moses lifted up 'in the wilderness, even [as] the Son of Man [must] be lifted up' in the New Testament era. St. Ambrose makes the same point: 'Imago enim crucis aereus serpens est: quod proprius erat typus corporis Christi: ut quicunque in eum asperet, non periret'. Relevant too is the riddle of the compass which God 'set upon the face of the deep': since it is two at the points, one at the pivot, he who holds it is above and beyond dualities, Being and Non-being, Father and Mother.

Man came to consciousness because God willed and needed it; through the Word—God of God, Light of Light, begotten not made—he attained the recognition of name and number, revealing the distinction between *thought* and *thing*. Yet as soon as man is conscious he yearns for an eternal return to the one source, in which sense incarnation is not the metamorphosis of God into man, but of man into God—the awakening of his divine self as distinct from his humanly conscious ego. So long as the soul is captivated by the constructs of memory it can—as Alan Watts has put it—do nothing to save itself. The

'I' must learn to confess that there is 'no health in it'. In the words of St. Luke's gospel: 'Even thus shall it be in the day when the Son of Man is revealed. In that day . . . he that is in the field, let him likewise not return back. Remember Lot's wife. Whosoever shall seek to save his life shall lose it.'

Lot's wife, rooted in the 'I' of memory, turned into a pillar of salt; but the day when the Son of Man is revealed is the Last Day which is also the first — Dante's *punto a cui tutti li tempi son presenti* —wherein we are reborn. Repentance, as Watts points out, is dust and ashes because everything the 'I' remembers is past and dead. Hence the New Testament admonition: 'Be not anxious for the morrow'; and the reproof of the anonymous man to the women at the sepulchre: 'Why seek ye the living among the dead? He is not here'. When St. Paul advises 'thou that sleepest' to 'arise from the dead, and Christ shall give thee life', he refers as much to the resurrections we may achieve here and now, through identity with Christ, as to a millennial resurrection. 'See then that ye walk circumspectly, not as fools but as wise, redeeming the time, because the days are evil' is on one level an exhortation to morally 'good' behaviour; on another level it is an invitation to 'redeem' Time by ceasing to identify the Self with the past. In being reborn in the Now, man momentarily becomes God: 'before Abraham was, I AM'. This is the moment which Christians perennially re-enact when they partake of the blood and body of Christ during the ceremony of the Eucharist. The representation of Dionysos' death and resurrection in the Eleusinian mysteries, the representation of Persephone's descent to the underworld and back, began as vegetation magic; similarly, the primitive version of Christian communion was probably a commemorative meal at which Christ's death and rebirth were realized afresh. These phenomena bring absolution from spiritual benightedness. In eating and drinking Christ the congregation shares in his power. We ourselves, in St. Peter's phrase 'die along with our Lord', and what lives afterwards is I 'yet not I, but Christ liveth in me'. It is in this sense that Christ is 'the resurrection, and the life: he that believeth in me, though he were dead, yet shall he live'.

That Bach, a committed Lutheran, should have composed a Roman High Mass is only superficially odd. As the greatest of religious composers, he was preoccupied with the heart of the Christian mystery, which is beyond denomination. Luther himself, who admired the music of Josquin, had admitted the Kyrie and Gloria as part of Protestant ritual, and Bach produced four short masses, consisting of Kyrie and Gloria only, for liturgical use. In also completing a full setting of the Ordinary on a scale so immense that he can hardly have expected that it would be presented liturgically, his unconscious motivation may have been to create an absolute statement of faith comparable in grandeur to his 'humanistic' Passions. The Passions tell a story in dramatically operatic terms, but reveal that that history is transhistorical; the B minor Mass enacts a rite in the ceremonial terms of the Baroque, while revealing that that rite incorporates —gives body to—a human story that is also divine.

The chronology of the sections of the mass is obscure. We know that the Sanctus was composed in 1724, for a different occasion, and that the Kyrie and Gloria were composed in 1733 as homage to mundane masters: the Kyrie as a funeral lament for the deceased Elector Augustus the Strong, the Gloria as a paean to celebrate the ascension of his successor. Smend suggested, on more tentative evidence, that the Credo may have been written in 1732, for the dedication of the rebuilt St. Thomas's School; more likely it was composed a good deal later. The Gloria and Kyrie were performed in 1733, though not in the presence of their Catholic dedicatees. And in any event, all the music, apart from the Sanctus, must have been completed between 1732 and 1747 or 1748, when Bach copied out, in noble calligraphy, a full score. If Bach set about completing the Ordinary in the hope that it might be performed at the coronation of Augustus III as King of Poland he was disappointed; and he certainly took his time over the task, garnering material composed at various times of his life, refashioning it, fusing it with newly composed music. Thus in the Gloria the 'Gratias agimus' is translated, in more than one sense, from Cantata no. 29, *Wir danken dir Gott*, which, composed in 1731, has the same words in the vernacular. The 'Qui tollis' is substantially remodelled from the opening chorus of Cantata no. 46, *Schauet doch und sehet*, which has a related text. In the Credo the four-part chorus after the plainsong intonation is lifted from the first chorus of Cantata no. 171, *Gott, wie dein Name*, dating from 1729; the 'Crucifixus' is adapted from the passacaglia that opens the early Cantata no. 12, *Weinen, Klagen* (1714); the 'Et expecto' uses material from Cantata no. 120, *Gott, man lobet dich*. The 'Osanna' comes from a secular cantata *Preis dein Glücke*, the Agnus Dei from an aria in the cantata *Lobet Gott in seinen Reichen*, dated 1735.

It is clear, however, that Bach's self-borrowings were not in this case prompted, as often in his day they were, by lack of time consequent on a harried professional life. We shall see that the interrelation of the sections, thematically, rhythmically and tonally, is of extreme complexity both in musical and in theological terms. He chose from his prolific output precisely those pieces which were most appropriate to his purposes, and rewrote them so subtly and extensively that they often became new music. One might even say, since his musical language had always been consistent, that the remoulding of earlier sources worked towards, rather than against, integration; thus the mass became a summation of Bach's life-work, and the most central manifestation of Christian faith and dogma. That it wasn't performed as a totality during Bach's life isn't surprising. By the time he copied the score, he was composing for no master but for himself and God, as a servant of the church universal. For his employers at Leipzig, however, he was the servant of their community. Although they were the establishment and Bach didn't often grudge them his support, he knew that his mass could not be confined to any established church, nor to a specific time and place. This is why the mass, though it may sound even more impressive when performed with some historical sense, works magnificently in any performance that is musically and spiritually dedicated.

There are four basic liturgical elements in the mass as celebrated by the Catholic Church. The first concerns the consciousness of sin in man (Kyrie); the second, the atonement through Christ (Gloria); the third, the Christian Church as a humanly operating institution proceeding from God (Credo); and the fourth, the memorial supper wherein the Church celebrates its union with and in the founder (Sanctus, Benedictus and Agnus Dei). We begin, therefore, where we are, with the confession of our humanly fallible sinfulness. Yet the appeal to God for succour is a cry of hope as well as of lamentation. And we must remember the physical circumstances: to enter the church we have mounted steps to a 'place of vision' comparable with the mountains on which many divine annunciations have occurred, not to mention Calvary itself. As we look up to the heights of this awful building, we admit that *terribilis est locus iste*, yet can also say, looking towards the altar: 'I will lift up mine eyes unto the hills, *from whence cometh my help*'. All this is manifest in Bach's marvellous opening apostrophe (Ex. 104).

Corporeally, this enacts the gestures of imploring multitudes. The soprano line aspires slowly upwards from the minor third through the interval of a fourth, while the bass line thrusts upwards from the tonic B minor to a major third. The gesture of prayer thus starts from a false relation—the *mea culpa* of our sinfulness—between minor and major third; and the bass's sharp third also effects a modulation to the subdominant E minor, which later we shall recognize as the key of crucifixion. This massive homophony has involved us in a gesture of aspiration which is also anguish; after a tritone leap to take us back to the tonic, the bass declines diatonically in an act of acceptance. From anguish, aspiration and acceptance prayer may begin; and although this opening is a public utterance, it's also a concourse of praying individuals.

Ex. 104

Each part is dramatically particularized. The aspiring scale in the top voice is agitated by the tritonal arpeggios in second soprano and tenor, which we 'feel' almost as though they were movements of our own outstretched arms. The physical sensation is intensified by the fact that the rising arpeggios cadence orchestrally in dissonantly drooping suspensions, often on diminished sevenths. So this initial seemingly vast—though only four-bar—paragraph is a public statement in which each of us is involved. Both personal and communal aspiration are suggested by the rising treble and thrusting bass, and by the upcoiling arpeggios; agony is inherent in the suspended minor seconds and diminished sevenths, and perhaps in the rests that sound like catches in the breath. Such aspiration and agony are opposite but inseparable poles of the same experience; they are reconciled as the violins float down the diminished (semiquaver) scale, over the dissonant suspension, to stabilize on, not in, the dominant.

The key is B minor which, as we've observed in reference to the *consummatum est* aria of the *St. John Passion*, is a key of passive suffering, as compared with the lacerations of F sharp minor. Yet although the mass is usually described as being in B minor, the terminology is misleading since the relatives B minor and D major act as equally weighted cornerstones. We'll see later that other keys related to these two are deployed by Bach with hieratic schematization, the tonal dispositions being at once musical and allegoric. All these relationships, with one crucial exception, are touched on in the Kyrie, which is none the less so long and so unremittent in rhythm that the noble suffering of B minor seems to be established as irremediably the human condition. The gigantic movement is a fugue wherein the theme is submitted to no metamorphoses—no diminutions, augmentations or stretti—so that its unified recurrences seem as inevitable as fate. But the fugue embraces rondo-like episodes in which the unity is tonal and harmonic rather than linear: again there is a synthesis between the pre-ordained, godlike order of counterpoint and the temporal and worldly order imposed by harmony and tonality. The corporeal and spiritual meet since we human creatures are 'gathered together' in an act of solidarity which is also an appeal to God.

The nature of the fugal theme, which is first presented in an orchestral ritornello, emphasizes this ambivalent quality. It's a formalized version of the introduction's dramatic ascent and descent:

Ex. 105

Moving in slow 4/4 pulse through a wide arch, it feels its way up chromatically from B to E and then to F sharp and G, from which high point it descends diatonically to B. The agony is now disciplined, however, for the theme begins with four repeated tonics in dotted rhythm, as though affirming the Rock we might cling to. Repeated notes in this rhythm seem to have a similar significance throughout European music. There are countless examples, often glossed by a verbal text, in sixteenth-century polyphony and in the work of the Baroque masters; the figure crops up repeatedly in Beethoven (first movement of the 'Moonlight' Sonata), in Chopin (Preludes in A minor and E minor) and in Wagner. The repeated notes, in dotted rhythm, are like a gesture of courage in the face of threat; in this case the threat is potent and palpable. For after the repeated notes have moved up from B to C sharp the theme proceeds in wedge or 'cross' formation: the C sharp plunges through a tritone to G; the succeeding F sharp rising through a perfect fifth to

C sharp, balanced with a falling fifth from D, expanded upwards from F sharp by a sixth, and climaxing in a descent from E to the Neapolitan flat C. The final upward leap is stretched to a diminished seventh from A sharp to G natural; the theme cadences in a three-note scale to the dominant. The melody itself thus contains, even in its linear structure, tremendous harmonic momentum, the interior agitation of the ills that flesh is heir to. At the same time the continuity of the quavers, the solidity of the texture and the regularity of the entries become themselves affirmative. The ravages of our suffering — seen in the light of the *mysterium* of the crucified God which we are about to celebrate — become an impetus to worship and a source of strength. The harmonic potency of the theme naturally generates richness of texture, even in the initial fugal statement in which the rising and falling bass line diatonically echoes the more acute chromatic progression of the bass in the introduction. The relatively thick scoring, with oboes and flutes doubling the upper strings and bassoons reinforcing the cellos and basses, contributes to this effect.

The alto entry of the repeated notes on the dominant turns into a modulation *to* the dominant — the crucial key of F sharp minor. We stay there for eight long bars. Although the strict fugal theme disappears, the texture remains polyphonic, weaving patterns from the scale motive, rising and falling, that concludes the theme. Sometimes the falling scale is preceded by a rising fourth: a conventional tag of ecclesiastical counterpoint which is to undergo many sublime permutations during the course of the mass:

Ex. 106

Painfully dissonant suspended seconds still occur in the inner parts, especially when the music moves from dominant to subdominant minor, and then back sequentially to the tonic. The contrapuntal texture disperses in favour of ripe harmonic sequences supported by a declining bass in dotted rhythm — a relaxed inversion of the bass to the introduction. The sequential sevenths in the upper strings and the falling dominant-tonic cadences in the bass produce an effect of ceremonial grace:

Ex. 107

It's as though the act of worship has brought the congregation into a concord capable of alleviating the distress inherent in human existence. Physically — and we must never forget how physical Bach's music always is — it's a gesture of *bowing*: common men may act like regal lords when they're paying homage to their God as well as to one another. The sequential bows lead inevitably to a return of the fugal theme again in the tonic, and in the bass, with low strings doubled by bassoon, so that we do indeed experience the theme, for all its implicit harmonic anguish, as the Rock on which we are founded. The orchestral fugue resolves on to a dominant cadence; and the voices embark on their fugue with the tonic entry of the tenors.

Four entries of the theme — tenor, alto, first soprano and second soprano — extend through an immense paragraph unbroken by the homophonic episode; the modulatory pattern — tonic, dominant (via subdominant), tonic, dominant, subdominant (via relative), tonic — repeats that of the introductory ritornello. In their vocal form the lines have greater freedom and a more tensile strength; from the deliberate repeated notes the wedge-shaped theme uncoils like a spring, the tension increasing as the leaps stretch wider. The Neapolitan cadence to the dominant, with its diminished third from G natural to E sharp, stabs into a dominant minor ninth in the orchestra; in the subdominant modulation passing notes create the sob of an augmented fifth. Gradually the leaping fourths and tritones of the theme are fragmented as the phrases, broken by rests, override the bar-lines:

Ex. 108

The leaps stretch to sixths, which traditionally promote animation; they do so here, yet, given the complex texture, the effect is also one of agitation. At the same time the leaping sixths are stabilized by the sturdy line of the instrumental bass and, at the touch of relative major (bars 43–44), seem to reach towards the light. The magnificently delayed entry of the theme in the vocal bass reinforces the music's passionate (in every sense) inexorability.

This time the fugal entry is in the tonic, and is followed by the two sopranos, both in the dominant. The texture is no longer strictly contrapuntal. Countermotives derived from the rising fourth and falling scale of the theme's tail are expanded in the other parts, while the orchestra gradually introduces the 'bowing' motive of the ritornello. The level quaver movement and the dominant⁄tonic cadences of the bass create a majestic stability, which is counteracted by chromatic sequences moving sharpwards to C sharp minor; by acute suspensions of major seventh and minor second; and by the angularity of the second soprano line, in which the leaping sixths tease one another in inversion. In the section beginning at bar 58 the bass line asserts a sequence of dominant⁄tonic cadences in E, F sharp and C sharp minor, with proud and courtly fourths and fifths, while in the other parts are entwined fragments of the theme, anguished in being both tritonal and syncopated. There cannot, it seems, be any final resolution of human suffering in the worldly, if heroic, glory which the dominant⁄tonic sequences imply. So once more the inexorable return of the fugal theme in the bass, and in a dominant that seems more than usually dominating, is as welcome as it is inevitable. This time, moreover, it leads to an unequivocal full close, prefaced by a dominant pedal.

At this architectural midpoint there comes again the original ritornello, but in encapsulated form, with only two entries of the theme, and without fugal extension, intensified because the sequential modulations in the homophonic 'bowing' are more rapid. The sequential sevenths here dissolve in an emotive chromaticism such as Chopin was to transfer to the nineteenth-century keyboard. The parallel is not fortuitous, for in such a passage Bach's chromatic harmony hints at the deliquescence of worldly glory, of socially sanctioned absolutes, which was to become the mainspring of early Romanticism. Only whereas Chopin was to accept the moment of sensation as an end in itself, for Bach such moments are temporary, and perhaps also illusory. In any case when the sequential fifths have declined from E to A to D to G major, the last key serves as a Neapolitan approach to F sharp minor, which becomes a dominant to the tonic B minor; and four fugal entries build up cumulatively from the bass. These alternate tonic with dominant, the conventionality reasserting order after the emotive threat of the chromatics. There's still a reminiscence of this chromaticism in the bass, however; and the progression from F sharp minor to A, D and G major leads at bar 97 to a fugal entry for the first (and only) time in E minor, B minor's subdominant. We hear this as both climax and resolution, though only much later can we apprehend its significance in relation to the tonal scheme of the entire mass, and to the association of E minor with crucifixion. As the sequences climb back from E minor to A major and B minor the fugal texture spaciously opens. The wedge form of the subject merges into figures growing from the rising-fourth-falling-scale motive; the bass both marches and sings, in regular quavers. At bar 112 the dominant cadence is again prefaced by a long pedal note; and the next episode repeats that, but beginning in the dominant instead of the tonic. This means that the chromatically dissolving sequences work the other way round, re-establishing the tonic as the fugal theme is chanted sonorously by the vocal basses, reinforced by low strings and bassoon. The opening Kyrie is thus rounded off. Recognizing that this theme is the Rock on which we and the Church are built, we can respond to its harmonic tensions as representing not only the human lot, but also as the suffering which God-become-man endured for our sake. For that reason the theme is unchanging, without diminution, augmentation or stretto; and the upper parts can in this final peroration songfully unfurl the rising-fourth-falling-scale motive, that age-old cliché of ecclesiastical polyphony, in canon:

Ex. 109

Though agony is still present in the suspended minor seconds and, later, in the alto's lurching minor ninth, the agitation now flows into stability. The ultimate resolution of the major *tierce de Picardie* is the only possible end to the planetary movement of this passionately human music.

The first Kyrie can last (as in Klemperer's recording) a full fifteen minutes. Even at quicker and historically more authentic tempi the dimensions are vast, and must seem so since the music concerns the human condition *in essentia*. The right tempo must be unhurried to allow the sensuality and anguish of the harmony to tell; yet not so slow that the remorseless unfolding of the counterpoint should seem to falter. Related to this is the fact that the Kyrie is spatial as well as temporal. Its four-bar introduction generates a fugue on a wedge-shaped theme, first presented in twenty-four bars of orchestral ritornello, incorporating a homophonic episode. The fugue is extended in five vocal parts, absorbs the homophonic episode into its texture, and reaches a full close in the dominant after twenty-eight bars. The second half repeats this pattern, with the homophonic episode recapitulated at the same point but in the modified key, so that the final fugal statement can return to the tonic. The fusion in the opening Kyrie of linear with harmonic-tonal order again suggests a combination of the celestial and terrestrial. The symmetrical periods of the homophonic episode seem grounded in the earth as proudly as does a Baroque palace, yet prove as vulnerable (chromatically) as any such symbol of human pride. The only certainty is the linear order of the fugue, which survives unalterably, whatever the inner tension. Significantly the keys of suffering, B minor and F sharp minor — reinforced by a transition to the dominant of the dominant — *dominate* the movement (the pun is not merely technical). In total effect this fugal chorus is humanly oriented, being man's cry *de profundis* to God. None the less its harmonic sensualities and intensities, its spatial as well as spacious architecture, have a grandeur one can only call superhuman. Praying to God, given this level of conviction, is to have already half attained to Godhead.

The perfect fitting together of contrapuntal parts in the Kyrie also creates a human resonance and warmth manifest in the solidity of the scoring. The vocal basses are always doubled by strings and bassoon; the upper voices by flutes and oboes in unison or by strings or, at climactic points, by woodwind and strings together. With Baroque wind and strings the effect is rich yet incisive. Modern instruments blend less well, though the doublings are essential, especially if the work is performed with a large chorus. Since the Kyrie's range is so monumental and its duration so long it needs to be succeeded by a marked period of silence, though not of course one so long as to suggest that the work is complete, both because we know it isn't and also because the Christe that follows is the Kyrie's complement.

After the Kyrie's public utterance, in which we have called on God as Father and as Spirit, the Christe invokes God as Man-Christ, changing the idiom from monumental polyphony to the intimacy of aria. It isn't, however, an aria da capo but rather one involving contrapuntal organization. There's a secular prototype in the duo cantatas of Steffani, which Bach admired. The textures are gracious and sensuous, which is appropriate, since we speak to God-become-man in our own, inevitably sensuous, terms. At the same time the contrapuntal organization introduces another dimension which is not sensuous but explicitly theological, since the aria is scored for two equal soprano voices that function both in harmonic concordance and intermittently as a canon 'two in one'. The inevitability of the counterpoint distances the sensuousness, even as the physical movement of the dance floats and flows. Christ and the Father are co-existent.

The key is D major, which steals upon us, giving little intimation of the Power and Glory which this relative is to represent in the whole mass as the opposite pole to B minor's suffering. None the less, the effect of the key change is profound, especially since it occurs in false relation with the B major triad on which the opening Kyrie had ended. (The effect is weakened if the pause between the movements is too long.) The Christe opens with an instrumental ritornello that establishes a consistent movement of quaver bass and semiquaver figuration, unhurried, in quietly confident expectancy. The obbligato part is played by the violin, or rather two violins in unison, symbolizing the identity of the Son and Father, with this instrument's appropriately seraphic songfulness and human expressivity. The theme opens with a literal inversion of the 'ecclesiastical polyphony' tag that had pervaded the final pages of the first Kyrie. Moreover as the melody moves up the scale after falling through a fourth it lands not on the leading note, C sharp, but on C natural, thereby effecting a momentary modulation to the subdominant, G:

Ex. 110

Though it's immediately contradicted by the semiquaver figuration and by the dominant⁄tonic cadence of the bass, the plagally relaxed feeling of this C natural is both unexpected and potent; we can appreciate why only in the context of the large tonal scheme of the mass, which recurrently leans towards G major as a point of equilibrium between the splendour of D major and the sorrow of B minor. The rising fourth and falling octave of the bass recall the ceremonial bowing of the opening Kyrie, especially since they move sequentially from D major to B minor. Deeply and delicately they support the obbligato line, which balances the upward movement of the original motive against falling semiquaver scales. The effect is relaxed and radiant: smiling because we now appeal in a personal rather than public act of faith to Christ the Man⁄God, yet far from complacent because the harmony is faintly disturbed by false relations between the rising leading notes and the flattened falling scales. The modulation to the dominant in the fifth bar is, for instance, immediately cancelled by the bass's arpeggiated rise to the flat seventh. The effect is sequentially repeated in the next bar, achieving a real modulation to the subdominant. Two more bars complete the ritornello, covering nine bars in all. D major is re⁄established in the bass's regular quavers, and in the unbroken semiquavers of the violin melody, now sometimes phrased in pairs rather than fours.

The two solo voices enter not in canon, but in a luminous chain of parallel thirds. The string bass has the falling-fourth-rising-scale motive, which the voices' flat seventh and fifth sensuously embellish. There is pathos beneath the radiance since the drooping thirds on the word 'Christe' create sighing appoggiaturas that conflict, moreover, with the C sharp in the bass:

Ex. III

The double appoggiatura is repeated in the next bar, further disturbed by syncopation, by a triplet arabesque, and by an extension of the flowing scales across the beat, culminating in the momentary intrusion of a B flat in the approach to the major cadence. The two voices get slightly out of step here, in preparation for their canonic dialogue in the next bar. They start in the dominant, a fifth apart, with crotchet tied across the bar, followed by a semiquaver descent. The semiquavers are phrased in pairs, but if there's a hint of weeping in this it is remote: just sufficient, along with the fleeting false relations and the double appoggiaturas, to deepen the music's serenity. After the first Kyrie, this Christe could not come as child-like euphoria. It's significant that just before the voices move together again (in parallel sixths, richer than the original thirds), the cadence is approached by way of the *minor* dominant. Though the main tonal movement is upwards, towards the dominant of the dominant (E major), minor flattenings intermittently recur during the re-established vocal canon, this time at the fourth. The ceremonially falling arpeggios of the bass even cadence on a momentary touch of E minor, the Crucifixion key; and false relations still flicker through the vocal lines as enhanced dominants establish a full close in A major. This ends the first section after twenty-three bars of vocal aria alternating parallel movement with canonic duet. If one considers the obbligato part as a third solo voice it might be construed as a Dove-Ghost to complete the Trinitarian analogy.

The instrumental ritornello at bar 33 is a literal repetition of the first nine-bar period, centred on the dominant instead of the tonic. At bar 92 the voices enter in parallel sixths, not thirds; and develop a more independent melodic movement which in turn creates a more intense harmonic pathos. The canonic dialogue contains painful suspended seconds; and the traditional association of drooping parallel thirds with weeping can hardly be evaded when the voices chant 'eleison' in quavers, modulating to E and B minor:

Ex. 112

After eleven bars (instead of twenty-three this time) there's another ritornello, now in B minor, veering intermittently to D major. The radiance has gone; and the more strenuous, if not exactly painful, flavour of the music in its B minor presentation is emphasized by the instrumental bass, which insists on its arpeggiated flat sevenths. The voices enter canonically, with the original motive of falling fourth and scale rising to the flat seventh. The ornamentation is more elaborate; and for the first time the continuo's level quavers are sundered by rests. The canon begins in E minor, moves to B minor, resolves in G major, with touches of D. By the time the voices meet again in parallel sixths the radiance has returned, and is enhanced. The final cadential approach of the voices, at bar 71, resolves the similar passage that appeared at the midway cadence to the dominant, with the voices now inverted, soprano 1 having the dotted figure, soprano 2 the tied figuration. The bass expands its flat seventh arpeggios into open octaves, though touches of plagal subdominant survive in the voices' cadence. To speak of an 'enhanced subdominant' may seem a contradiction in terms. None the less the subdominant here functions, in relation to the dominant-tonic cadence, in a manner complementary to Tovey's enhanced dominant.

In the cadential bar the voices merge on a unison, perhaps with some (conscious or unconscious) doctrinal significance. The Christe concludes with a repetition of the original ritornello, unchanged except for the fact that it begins, and therefore ends, halfway through a bar instead of on the beat; this adds to the sense that the Christe requires completion by the second Kyrie, which fuses characteristics of both the previous movements. The first Kyrie is a fugue with certain features of a binary aria or concerto grosso, polarized on B minor and its dominant. The Christe is a duet aria in extended binary form, also involving counterpoint, polarized on D major and its dominant *and* subdominant. The second Kyrie is a strict fugue of archaistic type, which is why Bach notates it *alla breve* in 2/2 time. The key, F sharp minor, is a transcendent intensification of B minor's passive suffering; despite or because of this identification the music attains ecstasis. Though it hasn't the serenity of the Christe, this Kyrie theme also moves almost entirely by step, though at a faster tempo, if we think of the Kyrie's crotchet as equatable with the Christe's quaver. At the same time the stepwise-moving theme creates, in its first bar, tremendous harmonic energy since the second step is not strictly speaking a step but a diminished third. Of course in equal temperament it sounds identical to a second; but we don't sing, play or hear it as such. Significantly, this interval appears at the end of the 'wedge' in the first Kyrie theme. (Beethoven, in his C sharp minor Quartet op. 131, exploits the same tension of a diminished third in the stepwise-moving texture of a ricercar-like fugue.) In the second Kyrie Bach starts from the first Kyrie theme's point of maximum tension, and allows it to flow into song, moving by step in narrow compass, up and down through a fourth (Ex. 113).

The harmonic implications of the movement from G natural to E sharp are Neapolitan, as they are in the comparable passage in the first Kyrie. Bach makes this patent since the bass entry is reinforced by a sonorous three-part orchestral texture. The second (tenor) entry is conventionally in the dominant. Returning by way of F sharp and B minor to the relative, A major, Bach

Ex. 113

repeats the pattern of tonic and dominant entries with the appearance of alto and soprano. After the dominant close at bar 14 the bass drops out, and the three upper voices introduce a countersubject that breaks the stepwise movement with falling third and rising fourth, enlivened with syncopations and rising chromatics. Dissonant suspensions, single and double, create pain that enhances, rather than stanches, the flow. The modulations, though more complex than those of seventeenth-century polyphony, have a seventeenth-century flexibility, undulating between C sharp, F sharp, B and E minor until, at bar 25, the fugal theme sings grandly in the dominant, in the bass, and is extended to embrace the rising chromatic scale. The effect of this delayed bass entry is, in the strict sense, superb. It coincides with the sob of an augmented fifth; and although the flow is momentarily stabilized by an internal pedal in the alto, the music climaxes in a thrilling interfusion of subject and countersubject. Double suspensions on dominant ninths again give impetus to the music's spate, instead of damming it; the only hint of a pause is at the 6–4 cadence into B minor, approached by way of sequential modulations from E to A to D. But the fifth of the tonic B minor chord acts as an F sharp minor tonic for a new fugal statement. The counterpoint is now in stretto, more animated; at bar 25 the countersubject appears in stretto also, the crotchets surging onwards, the tonality in oscillation. At bar 51 we seem to have reached a climax in the relative major. The triad is, however, in first inversion, not root position; and the four voices descend chromatically in wild stretto from the high A, passing through G sharp to C sharp minor, and so back to the original tonic:

Ex. 114

The first fugal theme sings in stretto, oscillating to the dominant and subdominant. The final 6–4 cadence is resonant in the middle register, resolving on to an obligatory *tierce de Picardie*.

The total effect of this fugue — it may be more apt to use the old-fashioned term ricercar, which means a seeking out — is intrinsically extraordinary, and the more so in its context as sequel to the first Kyrie and Christe. In its unremittent movement it sounds god-like; creative energy is unleashed, and has less need of the architectural props with which the first Kyrie and the Christe assert their confidence in the human instinct to control. That is why it's appropriate that Bach should return to an apparently archaic contrapuntal style. None the less, the piece is not in effect archaic, for its rhythmic drive and harmonic momentum generate a climax both in linear terms (through stretti) and in modulation. The fugue is thus a 'becoming', profoundly and ecstatically human; and in so being has fused the harmonic potency of the first Kyrie with the stepwise lyricism of the Christe. It is probably not fortuitous that the fugal subject begins with the B-A-C-H motive inverted; Bach writes his own signature into the apparently hieratic structure since, being the maker of the work, he is the people's representative as they call on God for succour. Without blasphemy, he draws an implicit analogy between Jesus as mediator between God and man and the artist who, in making the work, performs a godly act. After the invocation of Christ in the Christe, there's more hope that our plea to God will be answered; and this is manifest in the triumphant end of the second Kyrie. Bach concludes with another *tierce de Picardie*, a majestic F sharp major triad, which is, however, again succeeded by a false relation, balancing that between D and D sharp in the opening apostrophe, and that between D sharp and D natural in the transition from the first Kyrie to the Christe. This time the false relation is between the A sharp in the cadential triad that concludes the second Kyrie and the A naturals in the D major arpeggios that launch the Gloria on its resplendent course.

Though the dense texture of the second Kyrie is harmonically painful, the polyphony of the four voice parts, reinforced by orchestral doublings and additions, is in total effect richly, if equivocably, affirmative. Before examining it in detail, however, it will be helpful to consider the scheme of tonal relationships on which the mass—with psychological as well as musical consistency—is based. Not surprisingly, it is a circular scheme; even more significantly it may be diagrammatically represented, in the manner of a mandala, as a circle enclosing a cross. B minor and D major are tonal relatives, the complementary poles of suffering and joy which epitomize the human condition. Both may be intensified to their dominants, initiating a step towards the transcendence of the physical into the metaphysical. These relatives are a third apart; add the third below B and one completes a triad of G major, which is the subdominant of D and the submediant of B. This key of G major, usually signifying benediction in Bach's music, stands at the circle's centre. Its tonic complement, G minor, and its relative complement, E minor, complete the vertical line of the cross, bisecting the horizontal B minor-D major. E minor, the key of the Crucifixion, is G major's relative and B minor's subdominant, an anguish both lowered and deepened. G minor, the key of tragic consummation, is seldom approached in the work and is the home-key only of the penultimate movement, the Agnus Dei. (In a sense it's the last music we hear, since the final 'Dona nobis pacem' repeats the music of the earlier 'Gratias'.) Musically, psychologically and theologically the whole work gravitates *around* G major, the still centre which is the state of blessedness, and *towards* the tragic purgation of G minor. Of course the mass does not end there but in the world, or at least in the church where two or three or many thousands are gathered together. But in any event it ends not in B minor, but in a D major purged of merely mundane pomp and circumstance.

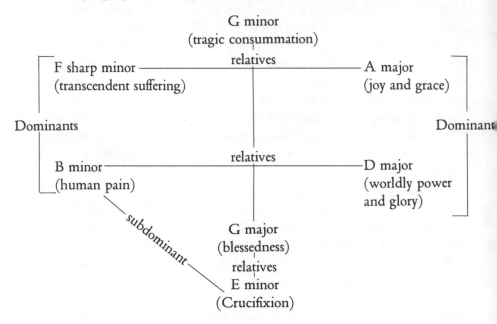

G minor
(tragic consummation)

F sharp minor ———————— relatives ———————— A major
(transcendent suffering)   (joy and grace)

Dominants   Dominant

B minor ———————— relatives ———————— D major
(human pain)   (worldly power
                                                      and glory)

subdominant

G major
(blessedness)
relatives
E minor
(Crucifixion)

It will be observed from the above that there are seven basic keys in this hierarchical scheme; and although all of them come within the normal tonal practice of the Baroque period, there's an appropriateness, which Bach undoubtedly relishes, in the fact that seven is the holy number of the Church, and that twice seven is fourteen, Bach's number in the figure alphabet. In any case, it seems to me that the total consistency with which Bach uses this key scheme — no less than the multiple cross-references of theme and motive which our analysis will reveal — makes nonsense of Smend's suggestion that Bach himself regarded the mass not as one work but as four; as we'll see, the strict repetition of the 'Gratias' music for the 'Dona nobis' is justified both doctrinally and in terms of musical structure. Perhaps Bach regarded either alternative as admissible. Kyrie, Christe, Kyrie; Gloria; Credo; and

Sanctus, Benedictus, Agnus Dei could be performed separately if occasion offered and, in Bach's own church, such occasions were the most he could hope for. This doesn't alter the fact that he conceived the work as an 'ideal' liturgy which should be performed in its entirety, thereby revealing the relation of the larger and smaller parts to the whole.

As a trinity Kyrie I (B minor), Christe (D major) and Kyrie II (F sharp minor) form the simplest kind of chiastic structure, rotating on the tones of a B minor triad. In the first movement of the Gloria, this is expanded to a blend of instrumental ritornelli and choral polyphony in three symmetrical stages, the outer two being in D and the inner one in A, so that the first section is a macrocosmic tonal extension of the Gloria motive—D–A–D—of the first bar. The Cross, in medieval iconography, was often represented as a Y-shaped tree of life, which it is, in addition to its being death-symbolic. So it is logical if paradoxical that, after the second Kyrie has fulfilled its humanistic purpose in revivifying an archaic style, the Gloria should open with a complementary reversal. Reputedly, the Gloria was a hymn sung by angels in excelsis on the night Christ was born. Bach sets it not to ecclesiastical counterpoint but as the most secularly resplendent round dance in Baroque music! There's a rhythmic parallel to this reversal. In the Middle Ages triple rhythm represented perfection, perhaps because of its Trinitarian implications, while the relatively infrequent duple rhythms were an imperfection. During the Renaissance, however, a duple, or quadruple, pulse gradually encroached, since it was basic to the development of harmony, which required the swinging pendulum of 'strong' and 'weak' beats on which dissonances could be prepared and resolved. The beat did not have accentual significance, being simply a tactus measuring time at about the normal speed of walking, or of the unagitated pulse. But it gave vertical sense to the flexibility of horizontal lines, whereby the music's equilibrium between the 'civic' and the 'divine' was effected. No longer was there a separate symbol for ternary rhythm, which was now indicated merely by appending a dot to the binary symbol; and the once divine Perfectio became associated with the all-too-human body. To a degree in church music, and almost invariably in secular polyphony, any textual reference to body movement prompts a switch from 'plain' or 'common' time to a triple pulse.

In the Baroque era, from the mid-seventeenth century to Bach's day, triple rhythms were preponderant in dance music itself, ousting, or at least holding their own with, the duple rhythms of the Renaissance. The paradox in Bach's Gloria lies in the fact that the heavenly dance in excelsis is in 3/8, whereas 'peace on earth' provokes a change to four-pulse common time. Though this is not exactly a return to medieval practice, ambiguity is its essence; for the worldly triple dance rises to ecstasy, while the interweaving polyphony of the common time section coheres into a march. That feet should tread the earth, even as the melodies soar to heaven, may be a paradox but is not a contradiction, given what we know, through his music, of Bach's mind.

St. John Chrysostom tells us that, in approaching the altar for divine communion, we should be 'ut leones ignem spirantes'. It would not be amiss to think of the orchestral prelude to the Gloria as lion-music analogous to, if much grander than, that in the middle section of the *consummatum est* aria of the *St. John Passion*. Arpeggiated and scale-flourishing violins are doubled by or alternate with flutes and oboes, while a panoply of three trumpets takes—to use an appropriate metaphor—the stage. D major was the heroic key of glory because it allowed, owing to the prevalence of open strings, for maximum resonance and brilliance on instruments of the violin family; and still more because it was the key of the natural trumpet, capable of considerable agility and of stratospheric heights. Military timpani, usually tuned to tonic and dominant, play with the trumpets, reinforcing body rhythm. None the less Bach's trumpets would seem to be well adapted to angelic music also, for their tone is jubilant yet pure, less brash or opulent than the modern valve trumpet, if more limited in number of notes. Certainly in the Gloria's opening paragraphs the trumpets reveal the divine exhilaration that Louis XIV's court composer Lully sought in his ceremonial overtures, the quick sections of which were habitually a round dance in 3/8. Louis called himself a 'roi soleil' because he played at being God. But Christ the Son was also a sun, associated with the birth of the new day and the seasonal processes of the year; and Bach's music, unlike Lully's, makes this divine-human equation manifest. The thematic material is built from D major trumpet arpeggios; the overall shape, however, rises up the diatonic scale from D to B, and then falls to E:

Ex. 115

So the arch shape of the two Kyries is repeated in rudimentarily diatonic form. Moreover the tune rocks through the interval of a fourth and then bounces up the scale to the major third. Though it would be fanciful to claim this as a permutation of the leaping fourth and scalewise third figure that appears in both the Kyries and the Christe, there's no doubt that we hear the theme *in relation* to that 'ecclesiastical cliché'; and that heard in that context the tune sounds open, untrammelled. The music glitters with arpeggios, parallel thirds and clattering scales; dissonances are minimal. Apart from a two-bar touch of E minor and half a bar's hint of G major, the D major tonality is unsullied during the twenty-four bars of the prelude.

The second Kyrie had been scored for four voices, rather than the five of the first Kyrie, probably because, in this ostensibly archaic style, Bach wished to give equal weight to each part. For the Gloria he returns to a five-part texture, the two soprano lines adding edge to the trumpets' resonance. The choral entries start with the trumpets in fugato; counterpoint is abandoned, however, after a two-bar canon between alto and tenor. All the voices chant 'Gloria in excelsis' in jubilant homophony, unambiguously in D major. A seven-bar ritornello, spicing the prancing arpeggios with parallel sixths, passes through B minor on the way to the dominant, in which key the two sopranos sing the original theme, also in two-bar canon, soon reinforced by the other voices. A motive of leaping fourth and descending scale is bandied in free fugato between the parts. Though it derives from the similar motive in the Kyries and Christe, its emotive effect is very different; having lost its lyricism it has become an animated dance, physically vivacious in the first soprano part, with its tipsily displaced accents. As the sharper dominant becomes established, the individual lines grow wilder in their ebullience: consider the bass's lurching sevenths, the alto's misplaced accents, the tenor's crazily angular approach to the cadence:

Ex. 116

The opening of the Gloria is a music of almost Handelian worldly glory; by this point, however, the sensual energy has become Bacchic, and the character of the music utterly Bachian. It's not surprising that a celebration of the wonders of creation should become itself a religious act. Vegetation myths survived in Christianity, and Catholicism, even in Bach's day, was not reluctant to acknowledge them. After another two-bar ritornello on the original theme, vocal fugato resumes with the fourth grandly stretched to a fifth. Modulation is still rudimentary; only a touch of B minor is necessary to carry us back from dominant to tonic, when the two soprano lines again sing the original version of the trumpet tune in canon. Excitement accumulates as the fourth motive blazes in parallel sixths. Sopranos leap through a sixth to the high B and explode in further displaced accents; we're reminded of those biblical goats and rams—symbols of virility as well as sacrificial victims—that cavort on the hills of Zion. The chattering semiquavers in the orchestra are unbroken during this D major peroration; the bass bounces through falling thirds and rising fourths.

At the cadence the time signature changes from 3/8 to ¢, and we move to the next clause of the text: 'Et in terra pax hominibus bonae voluntatis'. The texture changes from open arpeggios to stepwise moving quavers, the tonality flattens to the subdominant, and momentarily to the subdominant of the subdominant, before the transition to G major becomes a real modulation. The paradox lies in the fact that, while the flattening of tonality brings us down to earth after the D major splendour of the 'in excelsis', the word 'pax' promotes a religious-sounding polyphony, moving by step and aspiring slowly upwards. There is a secular precedent for such music since in Lullian opera the *scène de sommeil* was conventionally notated in common time, in stepwise moving quavers often in parallel thirds and usually phrased in pairs, as here. This is a natural musical symbol for sleep, which is in one obvious sense *pax*. But in Lullian opera the sleeping hero dreams; and his dream is often a vision wherein a god sets to rights the chaos created by blundering mortals, especially the hero himself. Bach's use of this convention in this context was probably not a conscious choice, but it is miraculously appropriate nonetheless, for here mankind as hero—or at least those men who are of 'good will'—looks upwards towards a vision, 'whence cometh my help'. Over a soft but sonorous pedal G, strings and then the upper voices doubled by flutes and oboes rise scalewise in parallel 6-3 chords, echoed by cellos and double basses and by the lower voices. Nor is it fortuitous that the paired quavers should recall the gentle semiquavers of the Christe; nor that the vocal ascent should create a modulation from G major to its relative E minor, the key of Crucifixion:

Ex. 117

For man's reaching up to God (which is beautifully conveyed even by the visual appearance of the music in score) is to be answered by God's descent to man, and his Crucifixion on our behalf. Again with allegorical appropriateness the ascending scales of the upper voices are, during the E minor episode, answered by inversion in bass and tenor. A 6–4 cadence in E minor induces repose in that the voices cease, and the orchestral basses settle on a long pedal. Above this, however, the upper strings, their quavers still slurred in pairs, drift upwards, their 6–3 chords clashing in hazy dissonance with the pedal notes. From the violins' high B scales descend in parallel tenths. At bar 120 a touch of B minor returns us to D major, initiating the Gloria's final evolution and resolution.

This is achieved, musically and theologically, through an interaction of man's prayer with God's death, beginning as an enormous fugue which stays in common time, but fuses the quaver scales of the 'Et in terra pax' prayer with the exuberant arpeggios and scales of the 'Gloria in excelsis'. This bears on the tempo of the 'prayer': its quavers must be more or less identical with the 3/8 quavers if the synthesis is to work. The theme starts from the *sommeil* quaver scales in G, cadences in D, and leaps into a trumpet-like arpeggio and a flurry of semiquaver scales, the figuration incorporating the familiar rising fourth and falling scale (Ex. 118).

The orchestral bass has an independent melodic part, mostly moving in level quavers; and the other strings and woodwind punctuate the polyphony with regular homophonic chords. These continue as the fugal entries of the long theme unfold: first in the alto (dominant), then tenor (subdominant), then

Ex. 118

bass (tonic), then second soprano (relative minor of the subdominant). The persistent chords in the orchestra give the music a march-like impetus, which metrically regularizes the polyphonic and rhythmic complexities; these are considerable, given the length of the theme and the variety of texture (and therefore mood) which the music encompasses. The semiquaver roulades grow wilder as the music again attains a purgatorial E minor, vacillating to A minor. In bars 134-40 savage cross-rhythms and suspensions, allied with lion-like arabesques in the bass, belie the word *pax*, or rather hint at its redemptive significance, since our peace can be attained only through Christ's pain. The complexity of the music reflects the complexity of reality: a super-human ecstasis in the winging roulades combines with human awareness of the world's glory in the bounding arpeggios. Even the human will seems, in the gradually strengthening march rhythm, to play its part in reaching divine afflatus. Furthermore, the overt return of the rising arpeggios in the orchestra leads to a modulation to the 'transcendent' pain of F sharp minor, and then to a sequence of dominant-tonic cadences falling sequentially from E to A to D to G. Thus the humanly ceremonial 'bowing' of the first Kyrie plays a part in this cosmic dance; the phrasing of the paired quavers is now with the beat instead of across it.

The rest of the fugue, fusing man's prayer with God's dance, indeed invokes St. John's *leones ignem spirantes*. Both the vocal and orchestral parts are now polyphonic, the quaver pulse unremittent. Rhythmic energy increases though the tonality moves flatwards through a cycle of fifths, from dominant to the subdominant of the subdominant. If this flattening roots us again to the earth, it also makes the assertion of the D major tonic the more imperious. In bar 139 the trumpets re-enter in long suspensions, then blaze the stepwise-aspiring prayer theme over a battery of kettledrums. Far from being a symbol of sleep, the prayer theme has become, if not a battle-cry, a song of triumph,

Ex. 119

unshakeable throughout the choral whirligigs. The word 'pax', isolated, separated by rests, becomes a yell of power; and the choir, doubled by trumpets, chants the prayer theme in ascending parallel thirds, answered by the basses in inversion. The thematic fulfilment releases an avalanche of semiquavers on the violins, which is controlled by the familiar touch of plagal subdominant in the approach to the final 6–4 cadence. Trumpets and drums, voices and violins are here not mere columns of air or vibrating gut or membrane, but a paean of created Nature, a hymn of the saints in glory (Ex. 119).

One cannot conceive of a 'Gloria in excelsis' more excellent or more glorious. Yet Bach, in setting the next clause of the text, achieves the inconceivable; and does so by a transition from a public to a private world. The relationship of the 'Laudamus te' to the 'Gloria in excelsis' thus parallels that between the first Kyrie and the Christe. The Gloria was a hymn of mankind and of created Nature; in the 'Laudamus' the individual spirit praises, blesses and adores God for his bounty, in that he sent his only begotten son to us *in human form*. The 'Laudamus te' is an operatic aria for soprano or treble, with a ritornello of dialogue between violin obbligato and string quartet. Yet it is remote from the rhetoric of opera, being an intimate song wherein the soul takes wing. The physical-metaphysical duality, which is also a unity, is manifest in the relation between voice and violin. The voice sings, in human aspiration; the violin, supremely capable of human expressivity, takes off into the heavens.

The key, A major, is the dominant of D, the key of Glory. Bach seldom — one might risk saying never — uses this key to express public majesty, but rather associates it with contemplative states, intimate or ecstatic or — as in this case — both. At first the continuo bass proceeds in level quavers, suggesting a quiet confidence comparable with that of the Christe. The solo violin begins with the familiar rising fourth and a decorated version of the scalewise descent, in the warm middle register. A balancing phrase introduces a lilting syncopation (echoed by the ritornello), and an upward modulation to the dominant. The violin floats down in demisemiquaver scales, but then rises to the heights, in a rhythm that creates an almost physical sensation of being airborne. The bass also rises up the scale through the sharp seventh; no dominant modulation has ever more radiantly embodied its upward movement! From the high E the solo line falls, flattening the seventh and landing not in the tonic, but in B minor. B is the dominant of the dominant, so although the tessitura has descended to the middle register, the upward feeling isn't entirely eradicated. Moreover the spiralling line cannot cadence into rest; B minor flows into D major, then back to the tonic A, with an exquisite lift

through an arpeggiated dominant seventh and dominant ninth. The violin —
regarded in the heroic age as the most humanly expressive of instruments —
lilts, its line almost breaking, in the intimacy of its tenderness. At the same time it
becomes a lark ascending, recalling the traditional image of birds as heavenly
messengers, and the equation between a bird (especially this heaven-seeking
one) and the liberated soul:

Ex. 120

Even now the return to the tonic is not effected. After a cadential trill a
diminished seventh of E minor is substituted for the expected tonic chord,
launching the violin-lark on his most extended demisemiquaver arabesques,
the line curvetting up and down as though winging just above the earth. The
ritornello instruments' interjected drooping sixths suggest that a fall is
imminent, and the lark does finally cadence on the A below middle C. Yet
although he's alighted, the lark cannot forget his heavenly aspirations. There's
a touch of dominant in the approach to the tonic cadence; and after it is
achieved, the violin line is lifted through an A major arpeggio, pointing its
upward resolution with the sharp seventh. After the E minor (Crucifixion
key) darkness, indeed because of it, the arpeggiated arabesque on the terminal
chord again promises flight.

When the voice enters the pattern of this human-celestial prelude is
imitated, but extended from twelve to eighteen unbroken bars. The voice's
version of the rising fourth theme is trill-garlanded, with semiquavers
caressingly tied across the beats, negating temporal pulse. An accompanying
figuration in the ritornello instruments consists of semiquavers slurred in pairs,
moving in parallel sixths or thirds: a musical image identical with the prayer
motive in the previous movement, and moving at about the same speed,
semiquaver equalling quaver. It's improbable that Bach was consciously

aware of this relationship; none the less it bears on the fact that we hear the 'Laudamus' as complementary, in terms of private experience, to the public statement of the previous movement. The slurred semiquavers sing in the continuo bass at the approach to the tonic cadence; the dominant modulation takes longer to establish than in the prelude, since it's in free canonic dialogue between voice and violin. The flighting of the 'lark' fuses with the slurred semiquavers, which the voice associates with adoration; the 6–3 oscillations over a pedal E are strikingly similar to those which initiate the previous movement's consummatory fugue:

Ex. 121

In bar 25 the violin-lark repeats his ascent to the heights, the soprano following in somewhat breathless syncopation. The mere human voice cannot attain to that cerulean region; but at least the cadence, which seems to be returning to the tonic, stays in the sharper dominant while the violin repeats the last four bars of its prelude at that higher pitch.

As the first statement of the aria ends in the dominant, not tonic, it isn't surprising that this aria da capo should share some of the characteristics of a sonata. The next sixteen bars might be called developmental in that they fragment the long theme, intensify its harmony, and modulate fairly frequently and widely. The first phrase bandies the rhythm of semiquaver and two demisemiquavers between voice and violin, modulating sequentially from E major to B and F sharp minor. The ritornello strings take up the slurred semiquavers of the 'pax' motive, often in 6–3 chords, and modulate sharpwards again to C sharp minor. A tritonal ascent in the voice part adds a note of anguish to the once serene line; but the cadence falls back to F sharp minor, A major's relative, and solo violin and strings repeat the syncopated ascent, mounting no higher, however, than the F sharp a seventh below the original E. Through further modulations to D major, B minor and back to F sharp minor, the voice's melismata grow longer, more asymmetrical, more tense in harmonic implication, until the voice is freed in a C sharp minor cadenza that obliterates temporal pulse:

Ex. 122

This cadenza carries us to a full close in the sharpness of C sharp minor.

The middle section of the aria centres around the 'suffering' keys of B, F sharp and C sharp minor, and breaks off at the sharpest point of pain, as though this were the most the human spirit may hope for, locked in its earthly coils. One might even say that, in the vocal cadenza, the arabesques are transformed from rising wings *into* coils, which they visually resemble in score. From these coils a da capo releases us, promising bliss *in potentia*. That this aria concerns human aspiration towards liberation from the flesh may help to explain why its da capo form should contain sonata-like development, though the threat of divisiveness within the psyche is not strong enough to call for a sonata-style recapitulation that heals breaches and reconciles opposites. The music simply stops at its maximum point of tonal adventure (C sharp minor); and voice and violin sing the aria, da capo, in sixteen bars that exactly balance the sixteen bars of the developmental middle section. Thematically, it's the same as the original prelude, only the hint of a dominant modulation is replaced by a fall to B minor and D major, which makes a *sub*dominant approach to the home tonic. The violin-lark's ascent to the heights, again haltingly echoed by the voice's breathless syncopation, thus occurs in A major; he wings up not merely to E, but to A *in alt*—a vertiginous height for the eighteenth century! The instrumental postlude repeats the last four bars of the prelude in the tonic key, but released into the higher octave. The solo violin doesn't, however, float through its arpeggiated lift on the final chord. For the time being, we're home, and earthed. In the next movement we give thanks again as members of a corporate society; but as individual spirits we won't forget that moment of transcendence, which envisages a state wherein time and being are no longer enchained.

Liturgically the 'Gratias agimus' begins the process of atonement, or 'at-one-ment', which Bach has prophetically encompassed in the 'Laudamus te'. That movement is a vision of bliss achieved within the individual psyche; the 'Gratias agimus' is a vision of mankind at one. A part of the Gloria and the whole of the Credo will be an aural enactment of this vision, of its fulfilment in history and myth; as we'll see, this is why the 'Gratias agimus' is musically identical with the 'Dona nobis pacem', the last music we hear in the mass. At this point Bach returns from A major, a key of grace, to D major, employed, however, in a manner very different from the Handelian pomp with which the Gloria had opened. He restricts himself to four parts (SATB), and uses the old-fashioned *alla breve* notation, as he had done in the second Kyrie. The theme consists of the simplest possible version of the rising and falling fourth motive, for in both directions the interval is filled in diatonically. The nobly swinging movement of minims is rock-steady, the fugal entries appearing in due order from the bass upwards. The movement is not a fugue in the eighteenth-century sense, with a defined theme that must be fully enunciated before the next entry. Bach rather offers us counterpoint in the sixteenth- and seventeenth-century manner, showing respect for the general principles, if not the specific laws, of species counterpoint. Yet the idiom is a high Baroque permutation of Renaissance ecclesiastical polyphony in that the metre is rigid and the counterpoint chained to the progression of diatonic harmony and tonality. The steady pulse and harmonic solidity are basic, though the imitative entries, moving by step, recurrently flow across the bar-lines. Curt Sachs has compared this spatial-temporal effect in high Baroque polyphony to the visual device whereby, in Baroque painting, the physical forms of nature frequently seem to be flying out of the frame. Nature's boundaries, in painting and music, are respected, yet at the same time denied. The comparison, and contrast, with the 'Laudamus te' is revealing. The upward flight of the 'Laudamus' was a personally expressive act, however freely the spirit sought for the voice and wings of a bird. The 'Gratias agimus' is not thus expressive. The pulse of the aspiring scales is regular, the imitative textures sonorously dissonant. The overlapping entries, with voices doubled by strings, oboes and bassoon, proceed inexorably 'out of the frame', as though the music were happening without our, or even Bach's, volition. The total effect is impersonal, or perhaps suprapersonal, even as compared with the gigantic fugue that concludes the Gloria, based on a similar stepwise rising theme.

We begin with four entries of the rising theme in stretto, at two beats' distance between the pairs of lower and upper voices, but with four beats' distance between the two pairs:

Ex. 123

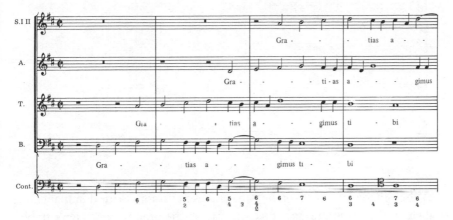

The entries, with their sense of inevitability, do not effect a modulation, though the passing dissonances are acute. The descending half of the theme generates a countersubject which quickens the crotchets to quavers. This doesn't impair the music's unity, since the countersubject is a free diminution and inversion of the original scale. The interlacing of subject and countersubject does, however, enhance the music's animation, and in an interesting way: for in bar 8 the sharp seventh leading notes clash with the C naturals of the quaver figuration, creating false relations analogous to those in sixteenth- and seventeenth-century polyphony. We've seen that the phenomenon of false relation sprang originally from tension between the medieval and Renaissance worlds. The medieval inheritance of modal monody came into conflict with the Renaissance desire for a humanly disposed harmonic order; collisions of flat and sharp third or seventh occurred fortuitously, but were later exploited with expressive intent, in association with painful or sometimes ecstatic experience. In this passage Bach's false relations, producing a near-simultaneous sounding of C sharp, C natural and B natural, have an expressive significance in relation to the Christian story yet are, in immediate context, a fortuitous coruscation that doesn't threaten the music's assurance. Dissonant pain is therapeutically absorbed in polyphony, the 'many voices' that create a corporate act of worship:

Ex. 124

Although the movement of the parts creates transitions to the dominant and relative, and to E minor and F sharp minor, the modulations aren't stable enough to function as new home tonics. The absolute regularity of rhythm and the inevitable recurrences of the theme, always in the same rising form and in the same temporal units, discount any suggestion of (eighteenth-century-style) sectional tonality; from bar 25 until the end the affirmation of the rising scale becomes irresistible. Trumpets, adding a fifth part to the ensemble, enter the canonic dialogue, thrusting upward to their high D. The more resolutely the entries follow one another in stretto, the greater is the harmonic tension which this affirmation can sustain. The double suspensions at bar 36 lead to definitive dominant cadences, and a kind of dominant enhancement persists throughout the final peroration, despite the fight between the upward-pressing sharp sevenths and the downward scales with seventh flattened. At the very end suspended sevenths and ninths give way to a 6-4 cadence, resplendent with trumpets and drums, hardly less glorious than that which concludes the 'In excelsis'. The liturgical manner of the 'Gratias' allows, however, for no trace of theatrical rhetoric; its impersonality serves as preparation for the fundamental drama of Incarnation, which is approached in the next sequence of movements.

The 'Domine Deus' and 'Qui tollis' are Annunciation music in that the one prophesies the 'Et in unum Dominum', the other the 'Et incarnatus', the keys (G major and B minor) being respectively the same. 'Domine Deus' is a turning point in the mass for both doctrinal and musical reasons: it's the first movement notated in G major, the key of benediction to which the mass gravitates. The words invoke God as Father and Son and prophesy, but do not finally enact, his descent into the human. The duet aria is scored for soprano and tenor voices, with flute obbligato and muted string trio ritornello, wherein the first violin sporadically functions in canon with the flute. This is the case in the opening vestigial canon, the wind instrument (through which blows the breath of life) representing the Father, and the humanly expressive violin the Son. That the violin's canonic entries are fragmentary may be Bach's way of indicating that incarnation is not yet complete. At first the canon is at the unison, the theme beginning with the habitual fourth, filled in scalewise and in descent, then moving in semiquavers through a rising third and falling fourth. The semiquavers are again slurred in pairs. The continuo bass, played pizzicato, is also thematic, beginning with a scalewise rise through a fourth in quavers, then falling a third, the bass notes interspersed with leaping sixths:

Ex. 125

The mood is gentle and equable, the pulse about that of the Christe. We don't hear the slurred semiquavers as sighs since they're concordantly on the beat; they rather suggest a smiling grace, especially when combined with the rising version of the fourth motive, and the delicately leaping sixths. This figure appears in imitation between violin and cello continuo, as the music modulates to the dominant.

The two-in-one canonic texture then dissipates. Quavers slurred in pairs take over from the semiquavers and turn into increasingly dissonant double appoggiaturas, which the flute lengthens from quavers to crotchets, yearningly resolving them upwards as the music returns to G major. Throughout this prelude the lilting semiquavers, whether slurred in pairs or in open arpeggio, remain unbroken, and the cello's pizzicato bass tiptoes with cat-like delicacy. The serenity is not quite absolute, however, since the intrusion of the appoggiaturas — especially the last one in the prelude, when the sharp seventh resolves upwards against the descending flat seventh in the bass — has humanized the impersonal music. Later it becomes evident that this darkening is a faint prophecy of the pain inherent in God's mortal incarnation.

The prelude covers sixteen level bars. The voices enter in canon at the fifth, the tenor personifying God the Father ('Domine Deus, rex coelestis'), the soprano personifying the Son ('Domine fili unigenite'). Their theme begins with the descent by step through a fourth, in quavers, while the continuo repeats its original motive, which starts with the scale inverted. In the second bar Father and Son abandon their brief canon to entwine in parallel sixths, then tenths; the instrumental canon, however, resumes. As the voices move together in a syncopated rhythm recalling the 'Laudamus te', the music modulates flatwards to the subdominant, then cadences in the tonic. A ritornello passage repeats the phrase with the crotchet appoggiaturas, now in the tonic, and the vocal canon resumes with soprano and tenor parts inverted. Otherwise the repetition is literal. Having modulated to the dominant the vocal canon sings at the octave; back in the tonic it's still at the octave but with the entries in reverse order. There's a touch of subdominant at the syncopated passage and a lovely chain of decorated suspensions at the return to the tonic. Father and Son 'weave the garlands of repose', in Marvell's phrase, until on the words 'altissime' and 'omnipotens' they fall in parallel thirds, not in lament, but in content. In the next bar, however, canon at the octave and at the unison injects an unexpected tension: the suspended minor second in the unisonal entry prompts diminished seventh formations and triple appog-giaturas which cadence in G minor, the mass's first reference to this key, which is to be so crucial, if rare, in the tonal scheme (see chart on p. 178). Its emotional effect is here disproportionate to its fleetingness. When G major returns the shape of the vocal canon at the octave is slightly changed so that it combines the scalewise descent with the tender appoggiatura. The tenor has an octave leap and turn on the words 'Rex coelestis', before the caressing syncopations return with the voices in parallel tenths. As postlude, the unisonal canon between flute and violin is repeated without the dominant modulation, so the triple appoggiaturas occur a fifth lower. The final cadence is prefaced by a momentary subdominant.

While this duet looks superficially like the first section of an aria da capo, it does not behave as such. Apart from the decisive modulation to the dominant in the prelude, it displays comparatively little tonal movement or 'architectural' order. Though it is not mainly structured by its counterpoint, as was the previous chorus, its form is a compromise between traditional ecclesiastical polyphony and contemporary Baroque dance. The gentle motor rhythm (to which the unusual pizzicato bass contributes) is unruffled, seemingly eternal—godlike if we remember that a motor is not necessarily a machine, but something that imparts motion and therefore life. Owing to the recurrent returns to the tonic and to incipiently canonic organization, the duet lacks the sense of progression typical of the 'Laudamus te'. This is to the point, for whereas the 'Laudamus' concerns an individual spirit's aspiration towards godhead, the duet—like the previous chorus—is a doctrinal statement. None the less, since the doctrine is that of Incarnation, the music reveals those tentative intimations of the Word made flesh; and in what looks as though it's going to be the aria's middle section, the hints become more than tentative. The key changes to E minor, anticipating the Crucifixion. The voices move more urgently in syncopated parallel thirds; the flute makes no reference to canonic falling fourths but traces chains of slurred semiquavers which, in duet with the voice, emulate faint sighs. The bass, having stood still for a bar at the crucial modulation to E minor, moves more energetically, modulating to A minor, through which the tenor droops in a diminished seventh, his line angular, almost distraught. A four-bar ritornello repeats the passage with crotchet appoggiaturas both rising and falling. This returns to A and E minor when the voices enter in syncopated, panting parallel thirds, with an agitation of mordents and trills. The music now has a passionate involvement it hadn't previously touched on, or needed, in the 'doctrinal' first section; and the passion increases with a sharpwards modulation to B minor. The bass leaps urgently as the slurred semiquavers thrust upwards. The voices' cadence on the octave clashes with the major seventh of the appoggiatura; the ritornello parts abandon their flowing line for punctuating quaver chords, separated by rests. The voices' final canonic entry, at only one beat's distance, has become an arpeggiated cry, falling through a B minor triad, then through a phrase wrenched over a minor ninth (Ex. 126).

Such passion is prophetic of the Passion, and defeats doctrinal expectation. For this middle section proves to be no middle, since there is no da capo! Instead, the falling triad of the last canonic entry, breaking the bar-line, becomes the impetus to the next movement, the 'Qui tollis'. This is a kind of music we've not previously encountered in the mass. Far from being doctrinal, it is dramatic, even operatic. Christian faith cannot make do with doctrine alone: the Word must become flesh.

Ex. 126

The text of the 'Qui tollis' tells us that God manifest in Christ bore the sins of the world, and so had pity on us miserable offenders. The music that Bach creates for these words at once enacts our sorrow and our plea, and gives intimation of Christ's suffering on the Cross. The texture is that of fugato, though the movement is not a fugue. The distinction matters, because in a fugue proper—especially in an archaic ricercar-type fugue such as Bach writes for the second Kyrie and the 'Gratias agimus'—contrapuntal order is paramount, a linear many-in-oneness with which tonality merely accords: whereas in this fugato the evolution of harmony and tonality conditions the counterpoint. Humanly orientated, the music makes suffering incarnate. This is evident in the theme itself, which derives directly from the soprano's cry, at the end of the previous movement, on the words 'Agnus Dei'. A B minor triad descends, low in the alto's register, from the weak third beat to the first; reiterates the low tonic three times; stretches in pain through the minor sixth, which is tied across the bar; droops under its own weight to the sharpened D—through a diminished fourth. Falling minor triads have, throughout European music, traditionally been associated with death and dissolution ('ashes to ashes, dust to dust'), possibly because their lower partials root us darkly to the earth; they're obsessive in the late music of Brahms, but have a similar significance in so very different a composer as Stravinsky (consider the opening of *Oedipus Rex*). In this passage from Bach's mass the falling triads sound as though they want to let go, to sink to rest ('Why hast thou forsaken me?'). But the leap through the minor sixth screws up energy in a manner distinct from the tensionless lilt of the sixths in the bass of the 'Domine Deus'; and although the phrase declines again it doesn't relax, since the fourth it falls through is chromaticized:

Ex. 127

Moreover the effect of the single theme cannot be separated from its relationship to the other entries, each of which increases the tension. The tenor's entry in the second bar acutely clashes, as it rises through the sixth to C natural, with the violins' sustained B, and in the next bar creates a dominant minor ninth with the bass's B and the alto's D sharp. Unrest is manifest too in the fact that the first four bars modulate twice, to subdominant and dominant, while duality is emphasized when the words 'miserere nobis' are set, first to a modified version of the original theme, then to a countermotive. The 'Qui tollis peccata mundi' phrase falls, painfully to rise; the 'miserere nobis' phrase simply descends, once more through a fourth, sometimes perfect, more often tensely diminished. The drooping quavers of the 'miserere' are phrased in pairs, and are usually dissonant appoggiaturas: the tears that were implicit in the slurred semiquavers of the 'Domine Deus' have become explicit.

The counterpoint here and throughout the movement is dramatic rather than organizational. The entry of each voice sounds personalized: 'many voices' join in lamentation but, given the renewed harmonic impact, each voice is an individual creature. Balancing this is the effect of the orchestral parts, which sway like a pendulum in the 3/4 time, with a figuration of rocking quavers (often through minor thirds) in middle register. The regular pulse and rocking figuration go on, like the turning earth or a softly beating heart, while it's the increasingly lacerating entries of the counterpoint that threaten disruption. This becomes the more pointed when, in the seventh bar, two obbligato flutes appear, twining in alternation through level semiquavers. Their relationship — poised above the dark string sonority and the low tessitura of the voices — to the winging flute of the 'Domine Deus' is unmistakable. In so far as the 'Qui tollis' is prophetic of Incarnation and Crucifixion, it may not be fanciful to hear this composite flute melody as the holy dove, hovering over the slain God. Certainly the flutes' continuous stepwise movement contrasts with the choir's passion-broken utterances, though later the flutes are affected by the pain the voices create.

Thus at bar 16 the flutes are momentarily stilled by the harmonic shudder generated by the weird modulation from F sharp minor to C major, which proves to be an operatically Neapolitan approach to B minor:

Ex. 128

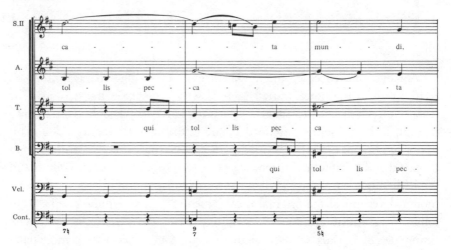

The shock affects the voices themselves: the bass falls through a diminished instead of minor third, yearns up through a diminished seventh instead of sixth; the 'miserere' phrase strains through a tritone; the alto and tenor clash painfully on a major seventh. When the flutes flow again, their semiquavers are gradually changed into tears, as though the Holy Ghost is not Itself responsive to human suffering. For the rest of the movement the flutes alternate between weeping (their semiquavers phrased in twos) and benediction (their semiquavers phrased in fours). This ambiguity becomes the more poignant when, at bar 30, the music centres on the 'transcendent' key of F sharp minor. Neapolitan touches of G major within the F sharp minor tonality are here almost physical, felt in the solar plexus; and they affect the vocal entries too — consider the diminished third in the soprano:

Ex. 129

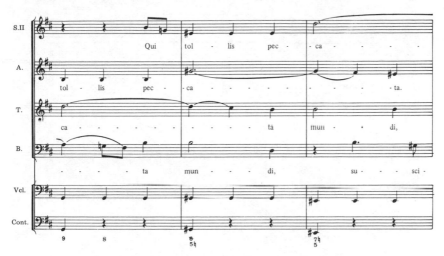

Yet the effect of the intensified harmony and sharpened tonality is far from negative; on the contrary greater momentum is induced in the lines, so that the vocal phrases swell instead of drooping. The burgeoning enacts the words 'suscipe deprecationem', energy being prompted by the fact that the 'suscipe' phrase begins with a stress on the second beat, in sarabande style. Though the lines are still riddled with angular sixths and diminished sevenths, they now flow and grow, carrying us, through the soprano's succession of unbroken quavers, to the further sharpness of C sharp minor, dominant of the dominant. In the orchestra, dissonance is still rife; the flute obbligato, however, expands lyrically, so that the tears may also be heard as fluttering wings.

The cadence in C sharp minor at bars 41–42 is the movement's climax; and it's significant that the piece has a climax, as the two previous movements had not. The remaining nine bars descend to F sharp minor, with stabbing dissonances between the obbligato parts and the string harmony; with abysmal descents in the bass through a tritone and a major seventh; and with a whole bar of Neapolitan G major as approach to the F sharp minor cadence. The almost visceral perturbation of this harmony is counteracted by the fact that the flutes' semiquavers are, for the first and only time, an arpeggiated rise:

Ex. 130

From the depths we are lifted up, despite the soprano's and alto's tritonal declensions, on to a dominant minor ninth. After the noble broadening of a hemiola rhythm, the final triad becomes major, a *tierce de Picardie*. Thus this movement, though ostensibly a lament, ends not merely in the dominant, a fifth higher than the key it started in, but also in the dominant major. Bach's prophetic vision — though we cannot fully understand this until we reach the 'Incarnatus' and 'Crucifixus' of the Credo — is wonderfully timed and placed. The 'Qui tollis' is the mass's climax up to this point, realizing, in the here-and-now of experience, through operatically dramatic techniques, what had been epically envisaged in the first Kyrie (also in B minor). For the first time it returns to the immediacy of the work's opening apostrophe. Then, we lifted our hands 'unto the hills'; now, we bow our heads and suffer with Christ, growing through (harmonic) anguish to (melodic) life.

But it is not yet the time of fulfilment; and Bach follows this moment of crisis with two rather curious movements that deliberately lower the emotional temperature. The text of the 'Qui tollis' has paid homage to Christ because he 'taketh away the sins of the world', the best reason we mortals can have for gratitude. The liturgical words then proceed to tell us that 'he sitteth at the right hand of God', and that 'he alone is the highest'. So if the 'Qui tollis' concerns Christ's coming to terms with our mortality, the next two arias are about his relationship to the Godhead. Inevitably, they remove Him from us, presenting Him impersonally, as contrasted with the immediacy of the 'Qui tollis'. Yet at the same time they relate His heavenly to man's mundane glory: both pieces are stylized arias da capo such as were sung to worldly lords and masters in heroic opera. The kingly aspects of Christ, once he's descended to earth, betray affinities with those of the absolute monarch who played at being God in the heyday of the heroic age. Theoretically and ideally there may be a serious point in this since a king is God's representative; but there's also a suggestion—especially in the second aria—that Bach is retrospectively debunking moribund gods before the reality of Christ can be revealed. This does not mean that he was being consciously ironic. As far as we know Bach was politically indifferent, though he occasionally indulged in petty sycophancy when necessity prompted it. In the last resort he honoured only his muse and his heavenly master.

The formality of the 'Qui sedes' seems, as so often in Bach, to be triggered by the words' physical, visual image, that of Christ 'sitting', enthroned, at the right hand of God. Surprisingly, the key is B minor, not the royal D major. This may suggest that Christ, even in heaven, still bears the weight of our sin, a view supported by the fact that the obbligato part is for oboe d'amore, an instrument of love, as its name indicates, yet also of melancholic timbre. The expressivity of the oboe d'amore is not to be confused with that of the modern oboe. Though a third lower in pitch, and thus mellower, it is also tenderer, less pentrative in timbre. There's a quality about it that one might call pristine (Richard Strauss, having heard the instrument in a revival of the *Matthew Passion*, used it to personify the dreaming child in his *Sinfonia domestica*). Love-oboes, like love-viols, are as much spiritual as sensual. Another paradox is that the 'Qui tollis', begun in B minor, had ended in its dominant, with the major F sharp triad of the *tierce de Picardie*. This chord followed by the B minor of the 'Qui sedes' is translated back into a dominant, so that Christ in heaven, as compared with Christ incarnate in the flesh, is a deflation—lower in the cycle of fifths. The Jungian notion of God's need to become man may be relevant here. In any case the prelude to the aria is grave, chaste, ceremonial, at first made up of short phrases on the oboe, answered by 'bowing' motives in a string quartet ritornello. The oboe's melody begins with a chromatic wriggle and descends a fourth, answering this with a diatonic wriggle and descent through a fifth. Rising through a dominant seventh, it flows syncopatedly down the scale to cadence in the relative major:

Ex. 131

The theme has an affinity with the 'wedge' shape of the first Kyrie, though the 'Qui sedes', being formally disposed in short clauses, has none of the Kyrie's interior energy. The answering period begins with a touch of the relative's dominant, but stays in D as the first clause's falling intervals are balanced by rising sixths. This gives a lift to the tune; promotes a momentary modulation to E minor; and flows into continuous semiquaver figuration, alternating scales with thirds. The final clause combines the initial wriggle and falling intervals with the unbroken semiquavers. But the 'bowing' motives return in the strings, preserving the cool, formal lyricism. It's as though the aria offers an idealization of the Man-God phenomenon, telling us that God's salvation, presaged in the 'Qui tollis', is 'not of this world', whatever a Louis XIV may have thought or hoped. This must also be why the aria's loveliness sounds, in its remoteness, sad.

The voice is an alto; and this is one of the occasions on which a boy's voice is more appropriate than a woman's. He begins with the phrase the oboe had sung in the prelude, and the oboe echoes him. After the modulation to the relative, however, there's a further modulation flatwards to G major, then to E minor, and so back to the B minor tonic. The first vocal episode ends with the rising sixth motive, which closes into a fifth and cadences in the dominant. The oboe repeats the prelude in F sharp minor and A major, telescoping the material to reduce it from eighteen to twelve bars. So far the oboe has had more say than the voice, and one of the oddities of the aria is that the voice never becomes fully articulate. At bar 43 there's a thirteen-bar section beginning in the dominant and moving by way of A major to D major. After an octave leap the alto gets locked in roulades based on the original wriggle and falling interval; but after an appoggiatura-weighted cadence, starts off again with the original theme. It looks as though the voice, declaiming the words 'miserere nobis', will at last come into its own, since in four bars it modulates from D major to E minor to B minor, with appoggiaturas tied across the beats and upward-aspiring sixths and octaves. Yet if this threatens to be an emotionally involved middle section, it peters out in an adagio cadenza. An almost decorative impersonality is reasserted at *tempo primo*, and although there's a slight heat in the diminished fourth on the word 'miserere', it's not sufficient to counteract our sense that the kingly Christ, sitting as if sculptured at God's right hand, cannot hear our plea very clearly. The contrast with the emotive commitment of the 'Qui tollis' is striking. It may be that Bach is intuitively redressing the balance, reminding us that God works in a mysterious way and we shouldn't presume on acquaintance with him.

The companion aria, 'Quoniam tu solus sanctus', makes the same point, more boldly. It is in regal D major, scored for a noble bass soloist with obbligato on corno da caccia and two bassoons. The corno da caccia was by provenance feudal and kingly and Bach clearly thought, with Mattheson, that bassoons were stately instruments. In modern performance, however, the aria is usually a thorn in the flesh, for the bassoons, in dialogue with the bass voice, sound gruff rather than grand, while the horn solo is nervous and precarious, if not on the verge of risibility. Terry thought that Bach's corno da caccia was a large, coiled modification of the old *Jagdhorn* of Praetorius's time, braver in tone than the customary *Waldhorn*. Though the part Bach writes for it may have been less hair-raisingly difficult on the original than on a modern instrument, one suspects there must always have been, in performances of this part, a disparity between the ideal and the real. This may be in part what the aria is about, which is not to endorse any naively political view that Bach wanted the obbligato to sound nasty to indicate his disapproval of a feudal aristocracy! The latent irony is rather between man's royal pretensions to divinity and his inevitable human frailty; and we cannot evade this serious, even solemn, irony since it is inherent in the sounds themselves. Though the words are about 'Deus *altissimus*', up in the heavens, what we hear is low, even grumpy. Moreover it may not be too fanciful, in view of the fact that Bach nowhere else employs two bassoons as duettists, to relate these two 'woods' or fagotti to the two trees—that of life, and that of knowledge of good and evil. In this case the celebration of God's separateness is also a celebration of man's fall.

The horn's preludial theme is grand, with an expansive octave leap and cadential trill; in the balancing clause the octave is contracted to a seventh. The nobility of the theme is, however, tempered by the chugging stepwise movement and repeated notes of the bassoons, and by the arduous character of the figuration when the horn moves into semiquavers:

Ex. 132

The twelve-bar theme stays in the tonic except for flickers of dominant and subdominant at the moment when the theme brings in the familiar rising fourth and falling scale. The bass voice doesn't open with the octave leap but substitutes a godly fifth, moving up to the sixth, then down a seventh; again there's a cadential trill. In dialogue the voice tends to answer the horn's octaves with arpeggiated sevenths, as though he cannot quite make what Milton called the 'perfet diapason'. The voice does better than the horn, however, with the semiquaver figuration; and the spacious thirty-two bar paragraph is on the whole positive in effect, the dominant modulation being reinforced by 'dominant enhancement'.

At bar 53 an ornamented version of the original motive leads to an extensive middle section. At the mention of Jesus' name, the vocal line, moving through E minor, is fragmented and harmonically more anguished, with diminished sevenths—as though the invoking of the living Christ has awakened memories of the reality of Incarnation, evident in the 'Qui tollis'. The wider tessitura of the voice strengthens this sense of involvement, though only momentarily; for after a modulation to B minor there is another ritornello, wherein the obbligato's repeated note figure grows ever more naggingly obtrusive:

Ex. 133

Assertive, wilful, in a sense heroic, it carries a distinct whiff of the Old Testament God of Wrath; one encounters similar figures, in Hebraic contexts, in the oratorios of Handel. The bass tries to get the better of it by starting again with the ornamented phrase he sang at bar 53, a tone higher, but in B minor instead of A major. Again the reference to Jesus' name prompts him to widely flung melismata and richer harmonies, in F sharp minor; again the obbligato's reiterations are insistent, but positively so since they lead into a da capo which is strict except that the voice's roulades on the word 'Dominus' are extended, driven by those repeated quavers. The postlude is also strict; the hieratic nature of this 'Deus solus' allows minimal opportunity for growth and change. Indeed the entire da capo is in D major, except for the fleeting tinges of dominant and subdominant already referred to. The total effect is slightly monstrous — especially when the horn cracks, as it usually does. The God of Power seems larger than life and too big for his boots, as did the absolute monarchs who tried to emulate him in mundane terms. Yet psychologically and theologically the aria makes a point: the Old Testament God has to be contained within the New Testament if the latter is to be valid. Power, no less than compassion, is an attribute of divinity, the more so when that power cannot of its nature be humanly comprehensible. The implications of this are revealed in the immense chorus that concludes the Gloria. Significantly, the royal aria leads into this chorus without a break, for the chorus is an epic, public statement of what the aria has said, with inevitable inadequacy, in idealized and abstract terms.

The 'Cum sancto Spiritu' bursts upon us, still in the aria's triple metre though speeded up, and with the aria's pompously nagging repeated notes now hammering away ebulliently in the strings. Man as monarch, playing God, may look and sound a fool; mankind, exulting in strength, awes and even terrifies. What in the aria had seemed stilted—on stilts, too tall to be true—now releases a torrent of energy. The vocal themes enter pell-mell, with at first no attempt at fugal organization. They're all openly arpeggiated, bouncing through fifth, sixth and octave. Three trumpets answer the arpeggiated phrases; two pairs of oboe and flute plus bassoon inject scales into the strings' arpeggios and hammerings:

Ex. 134

In the fifth bar the voices' arpeggios coalesce in a sustained tonic triad, only the bass continuing to prance in quaver arpeggios. Trumpets blast the repeated quavers in militant modulations to the dominant and the dominant of the dominant; beneath the chorus's sustained triads the instrumental bass cavorts wildly. The lilting figure in parallel sixths or thirds, previously heard in the 'Laudamus te' and 'Domine Deus', adds to the joyousness, both vocally and instrumentally; in diminution on flutes and oboes it becomes skittish, a gambolling of those rams and goats on the scriptural mountains. The chorus reasserts its sustained triads, first trumpet arpeggiates to the scalp-prickling top of its register, woodwind twiddle in parallel thirds, strings cascade in semiquaver arpeggios and the bass pounds the repeated quavers in descending chromatics. The excitation is fearful, like the wrath of God. Passing modulations from A to D to E minor don't disturb the dominant affirmation, which climaxes as a stratospheric trumpet chuckles in the diminished rhythm previously heard on the woodwind:

Ex. 135

At this point there's a respite, the tutti giving way to an extended choral fugato accompanied only by continuo. The vocal theme — proceeding from tenor to alto to soprano 1 and 2 to bass — translates the free arpeggios into the familiar rocking fourth or fifth (A D A), spilling into vast semiquaver roulades. Modulation flatwards from dominant to tonic to subdominant is balanced by a transition to the relative minor and an instrumental ritornello. The woodwinds' syncopated parallel thirds seem intoxicated by the yea-saying amens. Rapid tonal movement on the sharp side of the tonic leads to a dionysiac dismemberment of the theme, fragmented fourths and fifths being rapped out within the swirl of semiquavers. Even when the tonic is re-established in bars 97–100, the sweep of the paragraph evades any sense of resolution. Amens shoot up through a fourth, pounce down an octave. The last statement of the sustained choric triads changes consonance to a diminished seventh; the hammered quavers again descend in the bass, the strings cascade and the woodwind twiddle even more corybantically. In the final peroration the first sopranos sound crazed by their semiquaver arabesques, doubled by trumpets; the second sopranos leap through a fourth on to the accented second beat; the bass pounds up the scale sequentially, through a fourth. In the approach to the cadence the pounce on to the second beat is stressed by the trumpets' tipsy triplets.

There's an element of danger in this music's power and glory, which makes it very different from Handel's Augustan assurance. Early Christianity had absorbed into its mythology pagan fertility rites: the creation of the world in six directions and three dimensions became the primordial crucifixion of the Logos (Rev. 13:8), and creation itself is a sacrificial act in that it is God's assumption of finite limitations whereby the one is dismembered (like Orpheus⁄Dionysos) into the many. The sun was regarded as the *typus Christi*, and Christ's birth was a *natalis invicti solis*. Moreover, the Christian year was integrated with the sun's cycle. According to tradition Christ the Son⁄Sun was born at midnight, at the winter solstice, when the sun, at its lowest meridian, is about to begin its upward journey. Pagan spring, summer, autumn and winter festivals become Christian Advent, Christmas, Epi⁄phany, Lent, Passiontide, Easter and Pentecost. Easter parallels the vernal equinox. Forty days later the Church celebrates the ascent of Christ into heaven; at Pentecost it celebrates the descent of the fire of the Holy Spirit. Since the Church, from time immemorial, incorporated so many of the seasonal processes of the year into its calendar, it's not surprising that Bach's superabundant creativity should make of the corporeal affirmation of these amens an ecstasis not dissimilar to the orgies of so⁄called primitive peoples, or of the Eleusinian mysteries. Intuitively, his fecundity recalls memories the Church had suppressed or forgotten. Midsummer Day significantly dropped out of the Christian calendar, but is surely vibrant in the closing pages of the 'Cum sancto Spiritu'. Bach sometimes seems superhuman simply because his humanity is total. He evades nothing. Spiritual heights and sensual depths — the nouns and adjectives may be reversible — prove to be complementary sides of an ever⁄new⁄minted coin. In this Bach, although buttressed by his faith, is closer to Beethoven than one might imagine.

There's something here of Blake's energy that is unknown and unknowable; or in biblical terms of the wrath of God that is to find much wilder manifestation in the Gloria of Beethoven's *Missa Solemnis*. Bach's energy, being allied to his faith, is more positively directed than Beethoven's; and even this 'Cum sancto' has traditional roots in that its large⁄scale structure mingles contrapuntal organization with (concerto⁄grosso⁄style) dispositions of material centred on the tonic, dominant, relative and dominant of the relative. None the less there is no movement in Bach that *sounds* less sectional, that so sweeps on in (nearly if not quite) unbridled force. It's an apotheosis of the dance if ever there was one; and this despite the fact that Protestantism, far more oppressively than Catholicism, had banished dance from worship in accord with its denial of the flesh. Bach, as a man who sired many children, must have had some misgivings about that; certainly his music, whatever dogma he intellectually subscribed to, reinstates dance as 'a play of Powers made visible' (Langer). With their exuberant bodies, men dancing bridge the chasm between this world and the world of chthonic forces; they dance not merely with one another but, in Curt Sachs's phrase, 'with the world, with music, with light and rain and earth'. In this sense sensual dance is a sacral act, and Bach's blood, nerves and sinews were wiser than his Church. In this chorus he responds to an older rhythm which St. Bernard referred to when he wrote:

> Jesus the dancers' master is,
> A great skill at the dance is his,
> He turns to the right, he turns to the left,
> All must follow his teaching deft.

Here, as in Bach's 'Cum sancto Spiritu', Jesus is also Orpheus-Dionysos. Even in Christian Europe one means of approaching God was admitted to be the negation of intellect; as Ficino put it in his commentary on Plotinus's *Enneads*:

> the spirit of the god Dionysos was believed by the ancient theologians and platonists to be the ecstasy and abandon of disencumbered minds, when partly by innate love, partly at the instigation of the god, they transgress the natural limits of intelligence and are miraculously transformed into the beloved god himself: where, inebriated by a certain new draught of nectar and by an immeasurable joy, they rage, as it were, in a bacchic frenzy [*ubi novo quodam nectaris haustu, et inexistimabili gaudio velut ebrie, ut ita dixerim, debacchantur*]. In the drunkenness of this Dionysiac wine our Dionysos expresses his exultation . . . To imitate his quasi-Orphic manner of speech [*quasi Orphicum dicendi characterem*] we too require the divine fury. And by the same prayer let us implore the Trinity that the light which God infused into Dionysos, in answer to his pious wish that he might penetrate the mysteries of the prophets and apostles, that the same may also be infused into us, who make a similar supplication.

So an appeal for Bacchic abandonment turns into a prayer to the Trinity ('*eadem prorsus oratione trinitas obsecranda*'), and leaves us in no doubt that in order adequately to perform the 'Cum sancto', and the many comparable passages in Bach, we must learn to swing no less than do, in our own day and world, black and brown North and South Americans as they worship God in the corybantic revel of gospel song and dance. It's worth noting that Gesner, rector of St. Thomas's School and sometime critic of Bach's management of his academic duties there, remarked of Bach's direction of a rehearsal that '*the rhythm takes possession of all his limbs*. I believe that my friend Bach must have many men like Orpheus within him!' There's a whiff, one suspects of disapproval in this comment; and it's fortunate that the rector never heard the 'Cum sancto', which might well have finished him off. Yet, as we've seen, Bach's sensual ebullience was not a Christian. Altar dances of celebrants were encouraged in the second century by Justin Martyr, in the third by Clement of Alexandria, and in the fourth by Eusebius of Caesaria. Whether they attained the orgiastic fervour implicit in Ficino's adaptation of Plotinus and no less in Bach's 'Cum sancto' we shall never know since protesting voices, which later became Protestant, were soon raised against dancing within the sacred precincts. Today, dance is legally ordained by the Roman Church only in the altar rites of angelic little boys who, in Seville, enact the Easter Resurrection. None the less orgy returns to the American Church, and hence to ours, by the black back door; 'with dances and hymns in the city and in the country' we now 'give honour to God' in gyrating to jazz and rock, and Jesus Christ is himself a Superstar. The Church receives back what it had foolhardily surrendered; though for those who have ears to hear and limbs to cavort Bach's Gloria is a present excitation far more powerful than anything our jaded world can offer.

That the 'Cum sancto Spiritu' outdoes in sheer stimulation anything we've so far heard in the mass justifies its position as halfway house. Looking back, we see that the first part—Kyrie, Christe, Kyrie—is an immense ternary structure wherein two fugues enclose an aria. Kyrie I is a fugue with architectural elements derived from concerto grosso; the Christe, being a duet, is an aria which is also contrapuntal; Kyrie II is purely and archaistically fugal, yet at the same time more dramatically intense than the first Kyrie. The keys of the three movements are B minor, D major and F sharp minor: key-notes which form a B minor triad. The Gloria consists of eight movements, half of which are choruses, half arias. The first chorus in D major deals paradoxically but grandly with the relationship between earth and heaven. The first aria ('Laudamus te') is an intimate communion between the soul and Christ, in the dominant A major, which leads to a D major chorus of gratitude, in old-style *alla breve* notation. The next aria, in G major, the subdominant, is a duet concerned with God as Father and Son, and therefore potentially with the Incarnation, which is prophetically envisaged in the 'Qui tollis', a dramatically human chorus centred again on B minor, but ending in the dominant major. Two formal arias, one in B minor, the other in D major, redress the balance, invoking Christ in relationship to the Godhead rather than to humanity. But formality releases inhibition, and the final 'Amen' chorus, gloriously in D major like the first chorus, is a paean of creation that seems almost pre-Christian, if not overtly pagan, in its abandon. This may be an accurate statement, since the purgatorially Christian elements in the story are, in the Gloria, 'annunciated' but not fulfilled. The tale is told and the Passion suffered during the next part, the Credo, which repeats, but this time completes, the Gloria's symmetrical pattern.

The Credo is an affirmation of faith which, as well as stating what the Church believes, tells us why, and so recounts the story. It begins, however, with doctrine: 'I believe in One God'; and Bach treats it with appropriate austerity, notating in old-fashioned *alla breve* style, in five parts, for most of the time with continuo only. He uses as a fugal theme the original plainsong melody, which is effectively related to the thematic germs that pervade the mass—it begins with falling minor third followed by a stepwise undulation. He presents the theme in long notes, as in a traditional cantus firmus motet; the music is even ambiguously modal, in mixolydian A major with two instead of three sharps in the key signature, so that the seventh is habitually flattened. In the more decorated extensions of the theme sharp sevenths sometimes appear, clashing in false relation; the mixolydian flavour of the final plagal cadence is, however, unambiguous. The scholasticism of the fugue is theological as well as musical. Since in the figure alphabet CREDO equals 43, Bach makes forty-three entries of the plainsong melody, which represents God's law. That Bach, in his harmonic-polyphonic texture, imposes a rigid metre on the plainsong makes the law seem—as perhaps it is—irrefrangible; and although the harmony's suspended seconds and sevenths are often sharply dissonant, these clashes are not expressive but rather inexorable occurences within the unfolding counterpoint. Complexity is increased when two violin parts, also thematic, are added above the voices. Inevitability is stressed by the unbroken surge of the continuo bass, which moves up and down the scale in immense waves, sometimes with sharp sevenths in the ascent, flat sevenths descending. The continuous bass has something of the effect of a passacaglia, though it is not an ostinato. In the combination of strict counterpoint with the passacaglia-like bass there's a profoundly Bachian reconciliation of opposites; the inevitability of God's law, the energy of the human will, and a 'natural' creativity that we can imagine to be independent of either, seem wonderfully to co-exist.

Since this is a deliberately old-fashioned piece there is little modulation, apart from incidental dubieties caused by the ambiguous sevenths. None the less the 'doctrinal' movement is not without dramatic event. The appearance of stretto within the imitations gives energy to the theme's (non-plainsong) tail; bass, tenor and alto drive across the bar lines, leaping through sixths and octaves, and this stimulates real modulations to the dominant and to what would be the relative (F sharp minor) if the main key were simply A major instead of A mixolydian. Thus the counterpoint creates a climax; stretti run disciplined riot (another paradox) when the tonic is re-established and the plainsong theme rings augmented in the bass, answered by second sopranos and altos in parallel sixths at a beat's distance from the first sopranos, who are at another beat's distance from the tenors:

Ex. 136

There's a tentative modulation to the minor of the subdominant — that 'crucial' E minor — as the violins grow rhythmically more alert and harmonically more dissonant. They toughen the final 6–4 progression with appoggiaturas on sharp seventh and flat sixth.

Despite its culmulative animation this cantus firmus opening to the Credo sounds, after the orgiastic conclusion to the Gloria, like a call to order; and it is so in that Bach maintains a close hold on his numerology. There are 45 bars in the cantus firmus passage, 84 in the succeeding 'Patrem omnipotentem'. 45 plus 84 make 129, which is three times 43, the number symbolizing Credo, thereby conforming to the threefold repetition liturgically prescribed. Moreover, 84 is seven times twelve: the holy number of the Church multiplying the number of apostles (Bach scribbled 84 in his score, presumably to check up on his arithmetic). None the less submission to God's law is not inhibitory, if voluntarily assented to; and the text's reference to the Father Omnipotent prompts the music to a glory perhaps even more positive, because simpler, than that of the Gloria itself. Though the key signature of two sharps is maintained, the beginning is in unambiguously diatonic A major. The texture is homophonic; the melody has sturdy repeated notes and bounding arpeggios, the vocal bass being especially agile. At first the basses carry the text, while the other voices raise three shouts of 'Credo in unum Deum' in doubly Trinitarian symbolism, for the number of voices uttering these affirmations decreases from three to two to one. Meanwhile there is a dialogue of oboes and violins in split crotchet arpeggios and the continuo bass drives through quaver scales, frequently rising through the habitual fourth. Trumpets, and eventually drums, enter thematically when the words describe the Father Omnipotent as maker of heaven and earth. D major is again the home key (which may explain why Bach didn't add the extra sharp at the A major opening of the 'Patrem'). The word *invisibilium* suggests a passing modulation to the numinous G major and a transitory survival of false relation:

Ex. 137

In the final pages, however, resplendently scored for a trinity of trumpets, two violins and viola, two oboes and continuo bass with four-part chorus, dominant assertiveness carries the day. Upward shooting fourths climb in stretto. During the final peroration, back in D major, the rising scale motive, pushing up a fourth through the sharp leading note, sweeps all before it. Harmonic consummation brings divine law back to earth; one can hardly say *down* to earth when the melodic movement is unremittently upwards. This leads inevitably into the sequence of the next three movements, which are the mass's heart, enacting what was annunciated in the Gloria's 'Domine Deus' and 'Qui tollis'.

Ex. 138

Like the 'Domine Deus', the 'Et in unum Dominum' is a duet aria that, beginning as doctrine, renders doctrine incarnate. The key is again G major, the lower mediant to B minor and the subdominant to D; these three pivotal keys of the mass form a G major triad, complementary to the B minor triad formed by the key-notes of the two Kyries and Christe. As in the 'Domine Deus', the movement is again in level quavers, at about the speed of an unagitated pulse. The scoring is for a pair of oboi d'amore and a pair of violins, in free canon, with an independent bass line in dialogue with the violas. The canon begins in unison at one beat's distance, symbolizing the mystic union of Father and Son. Appropriately enough the Father is given greater weight than the Son, the first entry being scored for the two oboes doubled by first violin, the second entry for second violin only. None the less the theme—which begins with an undulation and then climbs through a fourth—is so subtly and intimately entwined with itself that the ear can hardly separate the voices. The parts become more clearly defined when, having modulated to the dominant, the canon is at the octave; the texture of level quavers and flowing semiquavers is limpid. The vocal entries — for soprano and alto, which are better matched if male rather than female — also begin in canon at the unison moving, after the scale has ascended its fourth, to canon at the fourth (Ex. 138).

The instrumental canons continue independently, now equally weighted: first oboe is doubled by the first violin, the second oboe by the second violin. This time the modulation to the dominant leads on to its relative, B minor, and that to its subdominant E minor, which is of course also the relative of the original G major. During the E minor episode the vocal canon is at the third, producing semitonic dissonances in suspension:

Ex. 139

This emotional colouring — a tender pain that is also a caress — may be prompted by the mention of Jesus' name.

The first section of the duet ends with a full close in the dominant, in which key there's a six-bar ritornello again in canon at the unison. When the voices return, also in unisonal canon, they acquire deepened energy since their phrases, trill- and turn-garlanded, expand across the bars as the music modulates to B minor. Intermittently the two violins interject the ardent syncopated motive in parallel thirds or sixths, familiar from the 'Cum sancto'. This grows gradually more obtrusive after the next canonic entry, when the theme is modified so that it begins with a falling minor third. Patterns of rising fourth and falling scale are dovetailed into the texture; there's a definitive modulation from B minor to the Crucifixion key of E minor at the words 'Deum verum de Deo vero'. Here the voices are in parallel sixths in the syncopated rhythm, while violins and cello prophesy God's descent to earth by falling through arpeggiated dominant sevenths:

Ex. 140

Back in the tonic major, we seem to be embarking on a da capo, but the instruments' unisonal canon turns into a vocal canon at the fifth which emphasizes the words 'qui propter nos homines' by repeated notes and the interval of a falling fourth. Both voices and instruments enact the divine descent in canonic falling scales, now stretched beyond the fourth to cover a major ninth. The motive of rising and falling fourths is, however, reaffirmed with an unexpected turn from the tonic to its minor:

Ex. 141

This is only the second appearance of G minor in the mass; and it's the point on which the whole structure pivots, since it immediately precedes the Incarnation, Crucifixion and Resurrection, and annunciates the ultimate transcendence which is to come in the Agnus Dei, the only complete movement notated in G minor. For the first time in the aria the level quaver movement is disturbed. The minor modulation is deepened by subdominant enhancement to C minor, with an emotive Neapolitan cadence to lead back to the tonic. The heavenly descent on the instruments now passes through dominant sevenths of G minor; after the cello has fallen through thirds from A to B flat, while the canonic voices have risen through the thirds of a dominant seventh, tension is released by way of a still more emotive German sixth. So, far from being a restatement of an absolute, this presumptive de capo has proved to be a development, an event at once cosmic and human. A four-bar instrumental postlude takes us back to the level movements of quavers and semiquavers in G major, though not to the original canonic theme. The main motive is now a scale that descends—echoing the 'de coelis' phrase—through a fourth and rises a third, with chromatic sharpening. Even if this is not an intentional prefiguring of the Resurrection, the musical imagery is remarkably apt.

In this crucially central duet there's a mingling of pictorial symbolism (the descent of Christ the Dove) with mathematical symbolism (canons two in one, doctrinally significant grouping of entries etc.), and with an allegorical deployment of tonality (the modulation to G minor). These devices universalize the experience that has passed through Bach's imagination; and in so doing function, as Arnold Schmitz has demonstrated, in a manner that resembles the techniques of rhetoric. Bach imbibed rhetoric as part of his normal education. He was a personal friend of Magister Birnbaum, who taught the subject at Leipzig University; and Birnbaum tells us that Bach 'so perfectly understood the resemblance which the performance of a musical composition has in common with the rhetorical art that he was listened to with the utmost satisfaction when he discoursed of the similarity and agreement between them; but we also wonder at the skilful use he made of them in his works'. The manuals of rhetoric, medieval in origin but periodically revised and updated, had as their aim: 'docere, delectare et movere'; Bach's music, like rhetoric, teaches, delights and moves by objectifying the complexities of mind and senses by means of the symbol. To a degree, of course, all art does this; what makes Bach's art rhetorical in the technical sense is its high measure of conscious stylization. As early as 1593 Peacham, in his *Garden of Eloquence*, had compared the rhetorical device of symploce to 'Musicall Repetition'; Bacon, in *The Advancement of Learning*, remarks: 'Is not the trope of music, to avoid or slide from the close or cadence, common with the trope of rhetoric, of deceiving expectation?' When seventeenth-century treatises drew elaborate analogies between the figures of rhetoric and specific melodic and harmonic conventions in music the point was to codify the techniques, and implicitly the meanings, of an art that is of its nature intellectually elusive. This accords with one aspect of the Baroque approach, but it would be misleading to circumscribe Bach too rigidly with contemporary practice. Though his mind functioned spontaneously in analogical terms, we don't need to interpret his symbols as rhetorical devices of persuasion; we merely need to respond to them. At the end of this duet the explicit symbol of the divine descent cannot be experienced simply as a musical analogue, but only in relation to the musical events as a whole, including the surprising yet inevitable modulation. In Bach even symbolical minutiae tend to have musical significance also. In this place we cannot always aurally follow the canonic precedence of the Father over the Son, but we can hear the differently tongued and bowed phrasing of the oboes and violins (staccato on woodwind, pair-slurred on strings). The simultaneous unity and duality of the Godhead is thus an aurally apprehensible fact; and the music is the livelier for it.

In the original version of the Credo Bach included the words 'Et incarnatus' within the 'Et in unum Dominum' duet. Later he revamped the words 'Qui propter . . . nostram salutem descendit de coelis' to fit the last section of the aria, and turned the 'Incarnatus' into a separate movement, taking care that it covered forty-nine (seven times seven) holy bars. The modification slightly upsets the chiastic symmetry of the whole Credo, but compensatorily establishes a link between the Gloria's 'Qui tollis' and the Credo's 'Et incarnatus'. Again, the Credo fulfils what the Gloria annunciates; and the experiential sense this makes must have been more important to Bach than mathematical exactitude. The 'Et incarnatus' resembles the 'Qui tollis' in several ways. It too is in B minor and in triple time; it has a bass pulsing in crotchets, with obbligato strings in quavers. The choral parts are again in fugato, though the movement is not a fugue; and again the theme is based on those falling minor triads that are a musical symbol of death, which in this case is also a birth. The Word dies into the Flesh that the Flesh may become Word: an aural event which occurs during the sequence of the 'Et incarnatus' and the 'Crucifixus'.

For eight bars the continuo thuds darkly on a dominant pedal; violins weep in unison, one detached quaver being followed by two pairs that form upward appoggiaturas. The vocal entries steal in, building tension from arpeggios falling through an octave, seventh, diminished seventh and diminished octave. A German sixth effects a modulation to the 'enhanced' pain of F sharp minor:

Ex. 142

A cadential minor ninth, felt almost physically in the bowels, recalls the similar cadence in the 'Qui tollis'; and an F sharp minor pedal introduces a repeat of the ritornello in the dominant. When the bass moves again, however, it promotes passing notes, suspensions and modulations that enact the laceration of human birth 'ex Maria virgine'. The rich harmony and texture of the five interlocking parts makes manifest God's need of man (or rather woman) for his fulfilment; the pain is released as the phrases stabilize, after a transitory modulation to E minor, in a hemiola cadence back to the tonic. The violins weep as at first over the pulsing tonic pedal; but when the chorus sings 'homo factus est' their phrases for the first time rise instead of fall. The bass mounts through a third to the fourth, sopranos expand in an upward E minor arpeggio, and the obbligato's weeping is no longer unisonal but in three-part canon between first violin, second violin and cello:

Ex. 143

The equilibrium between negative and positive forces is, in these concluding bars, wonderfully subtle. The bass throbs in 'heaviness of soul' until it finds release in emulating the violins' weeping which is never whimpering; the voices' fugato faints into those broken thirds and astonished semitones; yet from dissolution flowers the radiance of a *tierce de Picardie*. The passage enacts awestruck wonder: 'But the Lord is in his holy temple: let all the earth keep silence before him' (Hab. 2:20). Paradoxically, that B major triad proves to be no final resolution, but rather initiates the mass's central crisis and crux: for though it seems to have absolved pain in silence, it turns into a dominant of E minor, and so leads to the 'Crucifixus' itself.

This is also incarnate in a fugato chorus, in four vocal parts since Bach omits the first sopranos, whose tone is presumably more brilliant than the seconds. There are obbligato parts for two flutes, two violins, viola, with continuo. The metre, being notated as 3/2, is slightly more urgent than the 3/4 of the 'Incarnatus'; but the music's drooping quality is more oppressive since both the bass and the vocal lines are chromaticized. Appropriately enough, this is the most chromatically passionate music in the mass; at the same time any disintegrative tendency is resisted because the piece is a passacaglia, built over an ostinato that has illustrious parallels in music history. As a ground bass it appears in the lament of Purcell's Dido; in Mélisande's death scene in Debussy's opera; in the 'Thebes is dying' chorus from Stravinsky's *Oedipus Rex*. The figure pervades Gesualdo's *Moro lasso*, Purcell's funeral lament for Queen Mary, Elgar's threnody on Gerontius's death. The universality of the motive, not necessarily in a Christian context, is significant; and Bach's version is the most sublime, and the most heart-rending, of all. He gives it specifically Christian implications, since he repeats the ostinato thirteen times, a number which traditionally stood for Christ and the twelve apostles. More fundamental, however, is the fact that thirteen is a number at once unlucky and lucky, for God's fall into flesh, like Adam's fall into sin, is a *felix culpa*.

During the preludial statement of the four-bar bass, flutes and strings 'break' triads between them, and continue their pattern after the voices have entered. The triads mostly descend; and the rests in all the parts are catches in the breath, between sighs. The vocal entries also descend from highest to lowest; their theme is not so much a melody as an harmonic event—a semitonic drooping, usually on a dissonant appoggiatura. The substance of the vocal music, as well as of the instrumental parts, is thus physiologically a sigh; yet at the same time the sigh becomes liberation, since the chromaticism, in dissolving tonality, opens harmonic horizons. The fall from the flat sixth to the fifth is answered in the alto by a descent from the phrygian F natural to the tonic; and the F natural coincides with the C sharp (enharmonically identical with D flat) in the continuo's ostinato. This is the first of a series of enharmonic mysteries that transform pain into peace. At the ostinato's fourth repetition the theme appears in inverted permutation, moving up through an augmented second and the leading note to E, the highest note the sopranos attain. On 'etiam pro nobis' the entries fall in a gentle cross-rhythm, with chromatic alteration. Often the overlapping entries create piercing dissonances of a suspended minor second or major seventh. The harmonies are at once humanly emotive and divinely magical — for instance the D seventh chord in bar 13:

Ex. 144

In the next bar there's an emotional German sixth; and these altered harmonies mean that the expected cadences do not resolve, so the paragraphs grow larger and longer: harmonic disturbance itself generates lyrical expansion. 'Technique' and 'experience' are one. The 'flesh' of harmonic stress becomes a birth of lyrical song, which is the Word; thus the music acts out a miracle. Climax comes when the sopranos lift through a fourth to another high E, to be released with an octave descent on the world 'sepultus'. The descent is appropriate enough; the sense of release is a holy paradox.

Up to this point Bach has adapted this passacaglia from the lamentation chorus in his early cantata *Weinen, Klagen*, which was originally in F minor.

The final section, however, is newly composed; and makes the miracle manifest. The 'Crucifixus' motive is now syncopated on the second beat, in sarabande rhythm; and the sixth degree of the scale resolves on to the fifth, not by a semitonic descent, but by way of a diminished third—precisely the interval that had played so significant a part in the intensity of the two Kyrie themes. In effect the C natural and A sharp are double appoggiaturas, up and down, to B. The strange harmonic progressions that result from this—they sound like a B flat first inversion, a dominant seventh of G flat, a 7—5 chord over the dominant B and a dominant minor ninth over the tonic—make the lines flow in contours that increasingly embrace the fourths, stepwise and intervallic, that pervade the entire mass. In context it is the most lyrically fulfilled music we've ever heard; we lift up our hearts in song:

Ex. 145

And although, as Christ is buried, the vocal parts droop to their lower register, decline is again consummation. At last the bass moves into unison with the continuo's chromatics, and by way of a German sixth (soprano drooping down through E flat, bass pressing up through C sharp) the last two bars transport us from the passacaglia's E minor, and its chromatic instability, to the bliss of G major, its relative:

Ex. 146

As transubstantiation occurs, the pulse stills, the breath is stopped. There is no more remarkable example of the physiological and psychological impact of tonality, whether we consider it in relation to this magical moment or in the context of the mass as a whole. During the final five modulatory bars the pendulum of flutes—which were traditionally instruments of mourning—ceases, leaving the voices supported only by the continuo. Yet in the tomb-womb of this enveloping darkness, G major becomes haven and heaven. Christ's Easter and the Persephone myth meet; the new birth germinates in the gloom of the cave. We'll have occasion to explore this theme more deeply when discussing, in *Beethoven and the Voice of God*, Beethoven's less explicitly doctrinal, more inwardly psychological, response to Christian communion.

The Cross is a *speculum aeterni Patris*, not merely of the Father, but of holiness itself. The story of Christ's life, death and resurrection resolves the human problem adumbrated in the Book of Job—that of the guiltless suffering of the righteous. The rational and irrational, the revealed and the unrevealed, exalted love and fearful wrath, intimate communion and total otherness, are here as one. For Luther himself God was '*absconditus et incomprehensilibus*' yet not, since Christ's death, '*ignotus*'. This is why, against apparent odds, 'Christians are a blissful people who can rejoice at heart and sing praises, stamp and dance and leap for joy'. In Luther's homely metaphor, faith makes man one cake with God, holding him '*sicut anulus gemmam*'. The continuity of Bach's textures, the consistency of his figurations, are musical synonyms for this *adhaesio Dei*; faith proves stronger than the awareness of

God's otherness. In this Bach's and Beethoven's responses to the *mysterium tremendum* are opposite, if complementary. For Beethoven the consequences of the Resurrection are manifest only in a *testimonium spiritus sancti internum*; any consequences for the world at large must be partial and incomplete, as the inconclusive end of the *Missa Solemnis* demonstrates. For Bach, on the other hand, the consequences of the Resurrection may be immediately apprehensible in the life of the body politic. Thus, after the suspiration and cessation of the 'Crucifixus' in that wondrous G major, the return to D major is a positive animation, and at the same time a return to normality. The dying⁄into⁄life of the 'Crucifixus' releases our human rejoicing on the seasonally renewed earth. The 'Et resurrexit' has close affinities with the orgiastic chorus that concludes the Gloria, just as the previous three sections of the mass had been prefigured in the Gloria's Annunciation. The elements of fright and fear in the Gloria chorus have, however, mostly been dissipated, for Christ⁄Osiris has freed us.

The five⁄part choral entry is off the beat and homophonic. In the top voice the familiar rising fourth is now jubilantly succeeded by a rising, not falling, third, and by a triplet turn, to end with a fourth in descent; the bass bounds in octaves. After a brief trumpet⁄and⁄drum⁄resounding ritornello, the chorus extends its rising fourth theme in fugato, surging into immense roulades of semiquavers, which soon undulate in waves of 6–3 chords. Meanwhile the quaver 'hammering' typical of the 'Cum sancto' chorus affirms itself on strings:

Ex. 147

In this context the assertiveness is not minatory, but as life-giving and irresistible as a mighty river. This remains true through modulations from the dominant to F sharp and B minor, since the increased tonal tension is offset by a blaze of flutes and trumpets in parallel-third triplets, and by long semiquaver undulations that amount to written-out trills. When the hammering motive thumps in the bass, the vocal bass compensates with a bubbling agility. After a full close in the dominant, the original ritornello is repeated in that key, but more quietly scored, modulating to B minor. The basses alone sing the 'Et iterum venturus' phrase, in a style more rhythmically involved and harmonically distraught, moving through F sharp minor. This has the effect of a brief middle section; a da capo of the original D major chorus starts abruptly, without any transitional modulation. All the elements of the first section recur, more briefly but more exuberantly. Triplets and written out trills sizzle; hammering quavers move chromatically up the bass, whereas in the Gloria chorus they move down.

The public rejoicing of the 'Et resurrexit' is followed by an aria concerned with the joy of the individual soul, just as the jubilation of the first Gloria chorus had been answered by the intimacy of the aria 'Laudamus te'. Moreover, the key of the 'Et in spiritum sanctum' is the same as that of the 'Laudamus' — A major, the key of grace, which is dominant to D major's pomp. This time, however, the voice is bass, not soprano, and the obbligato instruments are two oboi d'amore, not a violin. The interlaced oboes may symbolize harmony between the Catholic and Protestant churches; certainly the music is tenderly if undemonstratively loving, in a pastoral 6/8 such as Bach often uses for his Christmas music: if the 'Et resurrexit' depicts a world reborn, the aria is perhaps a birth in the individual spirit. The theme is a simple version of the pervasive rising fourth, followed by another fourth in gentle descent. The pulse is level throughout, and movement at first is mainly by step. The obbligato lines stretch through occasional sixths and sevenths as they move to the dominant, but the gestures suggest an angelic wafting rather than physical pain. Melodies like this—especially in A major which, with its three sharps is a Trinitarian key complementary to E flat major's holy peace— are often associated by Bach with the flight of angels. If this aria hasn't the ecstasy of the 'Laudamus te', the reason is that it doesn't need it; it's beyond yearning, for the spirit is whole, and home. This may also explain why it's a formal da capo aria that, unlike the two duet arias, ends where it began.

When the voice enters it too flows equably, the oboes twining around it in chains of suspensions; cadential bowings suggest a spiritual *cortesia*. The first section ends with a ritornello in the dominant, the oboes chiming in parallel sixths. The middle section, beginning in B minor and moving to F sharp minor, is slightly less serene, for the vocal range is wider and the stepwise movement is more disturbed by arpeggio formations, including diminished sevenths. Yet this retrospective emotion makes the radiance of the da capo the more moving, especially since it's exquisitely modified by written-out ornamentation. The voice and oboes weave garlands of peace to symbolize the unity of the Church. A delicate touch of B minor evades the first section's dominant modulations, while the voice's cadenza plangently incorporates the diminished seventh of the 'middle':

Ex. 148

In the final ritornello the oboes' parallel thirds bring balm.

The Credo concludes with a large-scale chorus which, like its first chorus, begins with doctrine and ends with drama incarnate. The 'Confiteor' reasserts the law in an *alla breve* fugue over a regularly marching, though not ostinato, bass. A plainsong cantus firmus is introduced later, as a rock to cling to as we confess our sins and hope for a life to come. As compared with the first equivocally modal cantus firmus chorus, this is from the start more clearly tonal; it is in F sharp minor. The entries proceed in symmetrical stretto from top to bottom. The theme, undulating through a second and cadencing on a high suspension, is traditionally ecclesiastical, and the answers are tonal, not real, changing the semitone to a minor third. Despite the rigidity imposed by the metre and the severity of the counterpoint, the texture is ripe with double and triple suspensions; and after a half-close on the dominant, approached by a German sixth, the theme is modified to repeated notes falling a fifth and lifting a fourth, while the bass rises in chromatic heat, agitated more by the heinousness of our sins than by the hope of their remission:

Ex. 149

Rapid modulation—through B minor, C sharp minor, D major and E minor—perhaps suggests that our sinfulness threatens to undermine the law. This certainly seems to be happening when a rising chromatic bass settles on a C sharp pedal, over which interweaving polyphonies, praying 'in remissionem peccatorum', create painful triple suspensions and sobbing augmented fifths:

Ex. 150

Compensatorily, the plainsong cantus firmus, 'Confiteor unum baptisma', enters in canon between bass, alto and later tenor, forestalling chaos. This time, however, Bach's and our personal apprehension proves more powerful than doctrine; frightened dismay at our sin creates an extraordinary deliquescence in chromatic sequences, crumbling from B minor to A to D to G to E minor in the space of four bars. The counterpoint evaporates; a harmonic and tonal drama is enacted in a passage marked *adagio* wherein, over a throbbing bass recalling that of the 'Crucifixus', the music modulates weirdly through D and G minor:

Ex. 151

Bach then strays to the remoteness of B flat minor and so, over a falling chromatic bass, to an oscillation between D and A minor. The words say that we *hope* for the resurrection of the dead, but all the vocal parts are in declension, the bass plummeting from its high D to low G sharp in the space of one bar.

Very slowly, on the word 'expecto', the voices rise through a third, with a mysterious enharmonic change from C natural to B sharp, leaving us lost in time and space. The ambiguity of this aspiration is emphasized by the excruciating suspended minor second between first and second sopranos, and by the fact that the bass line continues to fall. Except for the end of the 'Crucifixus', this is the most wondrous moment in the mass; and it reveals why Bach is the greatest of religious composers. He lived in an age of faith and composed for God's glory; yet faced (in the text) with the prospect of a 'world to come' and of judgement on the quick and the dead, he betrays this tremor of fear and dubiety, which dams the forward movement, slows the pulse, disintegrates harmony and tonality, resolves —if resolve it does —only on that

German-sixth-approached dominant triad. Bach the Christian is here, within the liturgy of the Catholic Mass, a Protestant humanist, even a post-Faustian man aligned with Beethoven who, in composing religious music, explores the conflicts of sonata within the 'closed' structures of the Baroque. We remember that Bruckner, probably the greatest religious composer since Bach and Beethoven, to whom he owed much, was a man of faith living in a moribund Catholic feudalism; he expressed his belief not only through liturgical settings but also through the dualistic medium of symphonies which are, after all, sonatas, however sublimely they may also be construed as symphonic hymns. Basically, Bach's mass preserves archaic contrapuntal forms and the monistic architecture of the Baroque. This strange passage, however, is a dramatic event in time, in much the same sense as is the climax of a sonata development; certainly it would be at home in a Beethoven mass. Bach's faith, it would seem, is vividly real to us precisely because it admits to the possibility of doubt.

And in this immediate context, doubt remains unanswered. The dominant triad leads abruptly to D major; human anxiety and terror are swept aside, but not by a transcendental revelation such as we experienced in the 'Incarnatus' and 'Crucifixus'. For the power and the glory return in an astonishingly physical image. The dead leap from their graves in sprightly, almost frisky arpeggios: one can almost hear, in the edgy interplay of trumpets, flutes, oboes and strings, the rending of shrouds and the clatter of discarded coffins. The introversion of the previous section is replaced by an extraversion as naive as that depicted in the resurrection paintings of Stanley Spencer, or of the medieval painters who were his model. All movement is upwards, the harmony is consistently tonic and dominant. The resonant homophony is succeeded by fugato — by the simplest possible stretto on that root interval of rising fourth:

Ex. 152

Repeated note figures — perhaps reforged from the repeated notes in the second section of the 'Confiteor' fugue — add determination; yet the rudimentary homophony, the simple dominant assertiveness, would seem to express the will to believe, rather than a mystical act of faith. Bach had encompassed *that* in his musical enactment of Christ's incarnation, death and rebirth. What he's now concerned with is the public consequences of that event, 'throughout all generations'. The amens thrust scalewise up their fourths, through the sharp leading note, in potent minims and in quaver figuration. The sopranos' high As are a triumph — gratefully experienced in terms of the earth on which we dancingly tread. Having had our moment of transcendence we can return to the world, publicly to confess our guilt and to avow our belief restored.

The 'chiastic' structure of the Credo may be expressed diagrammatically:

Credo in unum Deum	plainsong cantus firmus	mixolydian A
Patrem omnipotentem	dance-rhythm fugato	D major
Et in unum Dom- inum	duet aria	G major
Et incarnatus	choral fugato	B minor
Crucifixus	choral passacaglia	E minor
Et resurrexit	dance-rhythm fugato	D major
Et in spiritum sanctum	aria	A major
Confiteor unum bap- tisma	plainsong cantus firmus	F sharp minor
(Et expecto)	dance-rhythm fugato	D major

The telling of the tale is thus enclosed within two arias, which are in turn enclosed within the law and its public manifestation. Inside the psyche, we have enacted the story: what remains is ritual communion itself, which takes place during the mass's fourth and last part, the Sanctus, Benedictus and Agnus Dei. The Sanctus is Bach's ultimate fusion of earth and heaven. It exploits the panoply of heroic power, being majestically scored for three trumpets, three oboes, strings, drums and six-part chorus; yet its sublimity is distinct from the mundane glory of the Credo's conclusion. Doctrinal elements are present in the division of the band into trinities of trumpets, oboes and strings; while the six-part chorus also divides into two threes (soprano 1, soprano 2 and alto 1; alto 2, tenor and bass). The six-part scoring was probably suggested by the six-fold wings of the seraphim in Isaiah, and by the vision of St. John Chrysostom:

Thou art surrounded by thousands of Archangels and ten thousands of
Angels, by the Cherubim and Seraphim that are six-winged, full of eyes,
and soar aloft on their wings, singing, crying, shouting, and saying
Agios! agios! agios! Kyrie Sabaoth
Holy, Holy, Holy, Lord God of Hosts!
Heaven and Earth are full of Thy Glory!
Hosanna in the Highest!

God 'maketh his angels spirits, and his ministers a flame of fire'. So Bach's
trumpets blaze like the suns that form the angels' haloes; and though
movement is regular, and physical, it doesn't have the driven volition of the
Credo's end, but rather swings of its own momentum, like a gigantic censer
wafted by God Himself over his cosmos:

Ex. 153

The three upper voices sway up and down through a third, in triplets, usually in parallel 6–3 chords: the Trinitarian symbolism is inescapable, even in detail. Alto 2 and tenor swing up through a third; the bass falls on the beat through a noble octave. Milton's 'perfet diapason' and Bach's symbol for the perfection of God. In its second clause the bass grandly falls scalewise through a fourth, as though by its own weight. Having reiterated a dominant triad three times (of course), it climbs back through a fourth from A to D. The planetary movement of the upper voices is maintained until they stretch their falling third to the seminal fourth, counterpoising the octaves in the bass. Despite the dominant enhancement, this immense paragraph has been rooted in D major. At bar 17 the bass's swinging octaves are partially chromaticized, occasioning momentary modulations to B minor, G major and E minor. The bass octaves stab in brazen dissonance with the upper voices' sustained triads. The effect is of Byzantine splendour, even terror, for this music evokes God's *majestas*, not a personified Christ. At bar 30 canonic entries, descending through triplet-garlanded fourths, peal like giant bells. But the bass's octaves swing unremittent, in vast arches, until the vision ends with a real modulation to F sharp minor, the upper mediant, and dominant of the relative. The bass line rolls and reverberates in triplet arabesques, covering a wide range and cadencing with a plunge through a diminished seventh.

There is a residue of arcane number symbolism in the Sanctus's obsession with sixes or with pairs of trinities. Traditionally, three is the number of creation, which finds an (in the strict sense) vulgar manifestation in the 'ready, steady, go' of our childhood games. To be 'ready' is the idea in the mind of God; to be 'steady' is to form life in substance; to 'go' is to send forth the manifestations of life in time and space. The Jewish Book of Zohar tells us that 'three emanates from one; one is in three; one is in the midst of two, which draw their sustenance therefrom'. The same notion is more poetically expressed in the *Anthroposophia theomagica* of the English seventeenth-century mystic Thomas Vaughan, who was one of the formative influences on Blake:

God the Father is the Metaphysicall, Supercelestiall Sun, the Second Person is the Light, the third is Fiery Love, or a Divine Heate proceeding from both. Now without the presence of this Heate there is no reception of the Light, and in consequence no influx from the Father of Light. For this Love is the medium which unites the Lover to that which is beloved, and probably it is the Chief Daimon which doth unite the Rulers of Spirits. I could speak much more of the offices of this Loving Spirit, but these are grand Mysteries of God and Nature, and require not our discourse so much as our reverence.

I've used the metaphor of blazing in reference to Bach's Sanctus; what it blazes with is surely this 'Divine Heate' and 'Fiery Love' which create concord. The six parts, divided into two threes, remind us that according to alchemical theory the symbol of the soul is a double triangle wherein matter is prepared as a trinity and the spirit, already a trinity, absorbs it. For the Pythagoreans too the soul was a double triangle in which spirit and matter are blended; and the number six represented harmony, the perfection of parts, peace, health and truth—and by analogy marriage.

An obsession with trinities, being rooted in the psychology of number, not surprisingly predates Christianity by centuries. Pagan manifestations include the three Fates and three Graces, triple-headed Cerberus and Hecate, the three sons of Osiris, the tripod of Apollo, the three goddesses in the Judgement of Paris. Making the transition from the pagan to the Christian world Ficino remarks that

> the Trinity was regarded by the Pythagorean philosophers as the measure of all things; the reason being, I surmise, that God governs things by threes, and also the things themselves are determined by threes. Hence the saying of Virgil's: *numero deus impare gaudet*. For the supreme maker first creates single things, then seizes them, and thirdly perfects them [*primo singula creat, secundo rapit, tertio perficit*]. And thus the single things also flow first from the perennial fountains as they are born, then they flow back to it and seek to revert to their origin, and finally they are perfected after they have returned to their beginning. This was divined by Orpheus when he called Jupiter the beginning, middle and end of the universe: the beginning because he creates, the middle because he draws his creatures back to himself, the end because he perfects them as he returns.

Interestingly enough Garfurius's famous pictorial representation of the Music of the Spheres, published in his *Practica musicae* of 1496, groups the musical modes in threes (associated with the three times three muses) around a triple-headed serpent who represents devouring time; the whole cosmos swings in a triadic dance, supposed to have been set in motion by Apollo himself in his battle against the Python.

Certainly devouring time, though seemingly defeated as the cosmic dance of Bach's Sanctus swings in the heavens without apparent human volition, is not finally conquered, for the chorus is a man-made artefact which must be subject to mortality. It ends, indeed, with a critical modulation to F sharp minor; and after a full close in the new key the tempo suddenly switches, for the 'Pleni sunt coeli', to a brisk 3/8. Now despite the Trinitarian symbolism in the Sanctus's disposition of parts and threefold repetitions, its temporal dimension is an inexorable quadruple pulse, which is understandable if we recall what we said, *à propos* of the Gloria, about physical and metaphysical analogies in the metres of post-Renaissance music (see pp. 176–7). For the Pythagoreans, four, the tetrad, was the greatest miracle, the 'Son of Maia', a result of the interaction of life and substance. The concept of the squared circle is analogous: a process which is enacted in the Sanctus's synthesis of three and four. In medieval alchemy, four was the number of the cosmic Christ, impaled on a cross or tree on which he defines the figure '4' with his head, outstretched arms and nailed feet. His Name is inscribed on the Cross in four letters; four guards dice for his garments, three women at the foot of the Cross complete a quaternity with Christ on it; there are four Gospels; twelve disciples form a trinity of quaternities. Though we don't think of such matters as we listen to the Sanctus, we're affected, even perturbed, by the abrupt shift from that awesomely swinging four pulse to the jolly 3/8 of the 'Pleni'. This metre, we've noted, was that of the fast round dance in fugato that formed the second part of the heroic French overture. In this case, the music cannot even be designated as heroic. Far from being cosmic, it's merrily mundane; and is in fact borrowed from a secular cantata composed to praise a worldly Lord. In the Sanctus Bach uses the materials of earthly pomp to create a divine celebration. That music takes place in a baroquely heroic heaven, if ever any music did or could. In the 'Pleni' we're back in the world, perhaps in our literally palatial church, rejoicing at God's bounty in our own terms. Of course the tonality switches back from F sharp minor to D major; and of course the fugato theme is arpeggiated, spreading into brilliant roulades. Its characteristic interval, however, is the rising major sixth, even gayer than the habitual fourths and fifths:

Ex. 154

though the cadence is dignified by the broadening of a hemiola. After three normal entries, the second soprano and first alto enter in parallel thirds, which tenor and bass answer in parallel tenths, reaching the high A. Decorated fugato restores the basic motive of rising fourth and falling third, with only an occasional dissonant suspension, and no modulation beyond conventional turns to dominant, relative and subdominant. The subdominant modulation produces a brief resurgence of the parallel 6–3 chords of the Sanctus. Though exciting, it hasn't the Sanctus's grandeur, which is more than we on earth can aspire to. The bass has rising chromatics to animate the final peroration, which leads into the 'Osanna', also derived from a secular cantata.

It is the same kind of music, too, except that it's more magnificent still in being scored for double chorus in eight parts, and in adding flutes to the trumpets, oboes and strings. The metre is still 3/8, and the theme begins with the most rudimentary version of the arpeggio, all the voices yelling in octave unisons as they leap through a fifth, then fourth, then down the fourth again. It's as though the traditional synonym for God (which the fifth is) has received a mundane apotheosis. One chorus or the other intermittently returns to this fundament, but the total effect is of worldly excitation. The notion of the 'double' choir itself emphasises duality, which is our mortal lot: and although this duality is grandly disciplined, architectural order gives way to the hurly-burly of life-as-it-is. None of the 'glory' movements modulates so frequently, between D, E minor, B minor, F sharp minor and the dominant, often in two-bar sequences. The effect—given the continuity of figuration, the divisive antiphony and rapid roulades—is of milling crowds, of the 'hosannaing' of multitudes as Jesus makes his last entry into Jerusalem. So, though the final ritornello, reasserting D major and the basic fourth-fifth motive, is again formal, there's a whiff of danger in the long trumpet trills. It's only this awareness of the unknowable, even in the miry midst of our lives, that has made the *mysterium sacrum* of the mass's heart possible.

This being so, it's interesting that the setting of the Benedictus should not be in G major, the key of blessedness, but in B minor, the dark key of suffering; and that the Agnus Dei, the ultimate sacred moment of the ceremony, should be in G minor, not major. Both arias are among the supreme tragic statements of European music, in which all passion is spent because it has all been lived through. The Benedictus is for tenor solo (the only time in the mass), with an obbligato part which (for the only time in the mass) is unspecified by Bach. It's often played on violin and the simultaneously human and angelic character of the line, floating across the strings, is beautifully suited to that instrument. It looks more like violin than like flute music; on the other hand, the compass nowhere exceeds the flute's range and since Bach seldom, if ever, wrote for solo violin without exploiting the potential of its G string, a flute may well be here the better choice. A further point in the flute's favour is that Bach specifies violins as the obbligato instrument of the Agnus Dei. A contrast of timbre between the two arias seems desirable, and deepens the Agnus Dei's poignancy.

The use of flute for the prelude to the Benedictus conditions our response to it. It is one of Bach's 'flight' arias: a solo line takes off from a slow, level bass, wings upwards through broken arpeggios, descends through a sixth, flows into liquid triplets. The beat is latent; the melody would be airborne, like that of the 'Laudamus te'. The white tone of the flute stresses its role as angelic messenger; the bird lifts and hovers, breaking the time barrier, as though enacting the flight of the soul 'who cometh' in the name of the Lord. There's contrast between the convoluting triplets, and then demisemiquavers, through which the line wings in an immense spiral, and the arpeggiated descents, which usually involve dissonance. In the cadence the broken sixths and upwards appoggiaturas create a tender pain:

Ex. 155

A similar equivocation is found in the tenor's line, which is in dialogue with the flute. The two lines, interlaced, create a continuous soaring; at the same time there is suffering in their lyrical angularity. Blessedness occurred in the central section of the Credo; in the two arias of the mass's final section blessedness is contemplated after the event. Once more Bach sings from his apprehension of mortality: he has discovered what bliss and mercy mean, and makes from that knowledge a music purged. After the flowing triplets have been stilled to rest in the relative major, the tragic implications of the music become, in the middle section, manifest. Both voice and flute lines are more fragmented and more urgent, answering, chasing one another in downward flowing phrases and aspiring arpeggios that are cut off in silence:

Ex. 156

The middle section ends with a cadenza into F sharp minor, the voice's melisma agitated by tritones. And there is no vocal da capo, no restitution of the human spirit to its primordial state. The flute does, however, repeat its opening ritornello, truncated by two bars, its final painful descent through a major seventh being brushed aside by a repetition of the rumbustuous 'Hosanna'. In a sense, therefore, the whole of the Benedictus's purgatorial meditation is a 'middle section' to the worldly hubbub of the 'Hosanna': a moment outside time that man may occasionally discover or rediscover. The solo lines, both vocal and instrumental, seem, in their wide-ranging, long-leaping lyricism, to be seeking even as they're flying.

The last aria, the 'Agnus Dei', had been prophesied in the G minor end to the Credo's 'Et in unum Dominum'. The effect of purgation achieved by the appearance of G minor as home key at this point cannot be explained merely by the fact that it is a minor subdominant to the glorious D major of the 'Hosanna'. Subconsciously we must recall its relation to the mass's central mystery, which began to unfold in the 'Et in Unum' duet. Moreover, despite the aria's intimate scale, it is the consummation of the entire mass: a rebirth of the first Kyrie in that its melody fuses maximum lyrical expressivity with maximum harmonic tension, thereby fulfilling Bach's equation between passion and Passion. Bach directs that the obbligato should be played by all the violins in unison, thereby involving us all, purely yet gravidly, in this ultimate threnody. The instruments begin low in register, more wearily broken than the

Benedictus's flighting. At the same time the syncopation of the phrases suggests, as it does in earlier movements, an ardent expectation. The broken line is harmonically fraught, a falling seventh being balanced by a rising tritone, which presses to the dominant triad by way of a Neapolitan A flat:

Ex. 157

Weeping appoggiaturas in quavers sigh across the beats, to cadence in the dominant minor, which immediately falls sequentially to the subdominant. The melody, always in the syncopated rhythm, undulates in a series of tritonal ascents and descents, each harmonically more tense than the previous one, and returns to the tonic through diminished sevenths, similarly undulating. The anguish of the music is inherent in its harmonic stress and broken rhythm; its serenity accrues from its equilibrium. Rising and falling, the melody breathes, like a human creature.

The alto voice doesn't at first sing the syncopated phrase, but a figure derived from the weeping tailpiece. These sighs are freely echoed by the violins, still low and warm in tessitura. The voice takes up the syncopated phrase on the words 'qui tollis peccata mundi', more fragmentarily mirrored by the violins. The dominant modulation is approached circuitously, with tritonal arabesques for both voice and instruments, and with a dominant ninth of A minor before the cadence. A ritornello in the dominant minor stresses the Neapolitan E flat. Voice and violins are in dialogue on the weeping quavers, entwined with one another; but after seven bars what might have been a middle section fades out on a diminished seventh of G minor, as though from inanition. This occurs between bars 33 and 34—collateral to the precise year in which Jesus died in the flesh and ascended in the spirit. The da capo is heart-rendingly extended on the words 'miserere nobis', forming a cadenza wherein both voice and violins, for the only time, soar relatively high in range.

The violins leap from the low D to high C, drops in syncopation to the Neapolitan A flat:

Ex. 158

The postlude returns to the syncopated figure, riddled with tritones. Its range, however, is extended, moving in a great arch from the tritonal descent to the low A, up to the high B flat and down through wide plunges to the bottom G on the fourth string. The final descent through a major seventh carries the line to a rest the more final because it hasn't denied pain. This is a matter of rhythmic equilibrium, of melodic contour (try substituting a resolution on the upper G instead of the fall through the seventh), and of harmonic weight. The angularity recalls the postlude to the Benedictus, which also ends with a descent through a major seventh. In both passages the agony of the 'Incarnatus' and 'Crucifixus' seem to have become dismembered and disembodied. The Agnus distils *lacrimae rerum* into peace; and that Bach refurbished it from an earlier source only demonstrates his recognition of the inevitable. *This* he had experienced; this was demanded as the consummation of his greatest work.

The Agnus Dei attains peace for the individual spirit and does so, as had Christ, from an extremity of suffering. The mass ends, however, with a return to its public function: with a 'Dona nobis pacem' for which Bach uses the same music he had used for the 'Gratias agimus'. This has occasioned surprise, even dismay, as though Bach were skimping of effort. That seems improbable in view of the considerable length of time he gave himself to complete the work. It seems more pertinent to remember that 'Gratias agimus' ('we give thanks unto Thee') is an obeisance paid to God by man; whereas 'Dona nobis pacem' ('give unto us Thy peace') implies a divine answer. The peace petitioned for is neither worldly nor ephemeral. In the liturgy the priest continues, after the 'Dona nobis', with the prayer:

> O Lord Jesus Christ, who said to your apostles: 'Peace I leave with you, my peace I give to you', regard not my sins but the faith of your Church, and deign to give her peace and unity according to your will.

This image of Christ and his Church united by a giving and receiving is ratified by Bach's use of identical music for these two sections of the mass. The fusion of different texts into the same music is a representation of the hypostatic union of Christ. Because Jesus gave thanks when he broke bread, Christians called it the Holy Eucharist, 'our sacrifice in praise and thanksgiving'. The Christian believes that in the act of communion God, with all the treasures of heaven, comes down to dwell in him, effecting a union of the divine and human. The idea that the 'Dona nobis pacem' is a prayer *for* peace negates that efficacy; rather can it be considered as a laudation of that peace(ful union) that passes understanding. It becomes a solemn hymn of praise and thanksgiving, not because sacrifice consists of praise and thanksgiving, but because it is offered with those ends in view. The use of the same music for the 'Dona nobis pacem' and the 'Gratias agimus' thus rounds off the mass both theologically and musically, taking us back to the moment when the divine 'enactment' was first prefigured. After those two tragically purgatorial arias there could be no further climax; we leave the Church to resume our everyday lives, in renewed confidence and strength. In the deepest possible sense Bach's art is functional. The solidity and lucidity of his craftsmanship, whether in the grandeur of the mass's Kyries or the smallest two-part invention, is an artefact; and an act of making, *perfectum ex perfecto*, is of its nature godly. To compose for the good of the work was to 'com-pose'—to put things together—for 'the glory of God and the instruction of my neighbour'. Bach believed that his work, well done, could make people 'better'. And it does.

2. Codetta: The Prelude and Fugue in B minor from Book I of the '48'

As an appendix to our examination of the Mass in B minor let us consider the final Prelude and Fugue of Book I of the '48'. Since they are also in B minor, Bach's favourite 'dark' key of suffering, we're not surprised to find that, at once extraordinary and representative, they are deeply related to the religious experience of the mass. Superficially, the prelude is a three-part invention in binary form. Its structure is not, however, symmetrical, for the first 'half' consists of seventeen bars, the second of thirty; and although the rhythm is absolutely regular, the harmonic progression is conditioned by counterpoint. The bass line marches in equal quavers, interlocking rising and falling scales. They begin with two rises through a fourth, which might be construed as overlapping fifths; in the second bar the downward scale leads to a falling third; in the third bar the pattern is established as rising fourths moving from the second quaver across the beat. This 'pizzicato' bass supports two upper parts of which the basic pulse is a crotchet; they proceed quasi-canonically at half a bar's distance, leaping through a fourth and declining down the scale, thereby effecting chains of dissonant suspensions, in the manner of a trio sonata:

Ex. 159

It will be observed that the fundamental motive of the prelude is thus that cliché of ecclesiastical polyphony—the rising fourth followed by a drooping down the scale—which we have seen to dominate, in innumerable contrapuntal permutations, the B minor Mass. Although the prelude is a small-scale piece one might claim that it creates, from the rich sobriety of its counterpoint, a tragic grandeur and pathos related to that of the mass's first

Kyrie. Its awareness of pain consists in the highly dissonant texture produced by the chains of suspensions, especially on major seventh and minor second; indeed it begins with Bach's cross symbol, also manifest in the wedge-shaped Kyrie theme, and repeats it in bars 42 to 43. Anxiety and unrest are latent in the false relations of the rising and falling scales, which are sharp in the ascent, flattened in the descent—for instance the dominant modulation promised by the dorian G sharp in the first two bars doesn't materialize. Yet, as in the mass, suffering is balanced by confident strength, not merely in the equilibrium between B minor and its relative D major, which produces, in bars 6 to 8, a more clearly euphonious texture, but also in the stability of line and rhythm, which remain impervious to dissonant shocks. The single appearance of semiquaver figuration in the D major episode has a liberating effect; because of this the return to the tonic B minor by way of its dominant has at least a hint of triumph. The violin-style canon mounts higher; cross-rhythms make for tension within the counterpoint; and the expected 6–4 cadence is delayed by an extra bar wherein the bass's level quavers are for the first time modified. Augmented to crotchets, they descend through a trill to a half-close on the dominant, above which the upper voices ornamentally resolve.

After the double bar all three parts are pervaded by the rising fourth-falling scale motive, both in quavers and augmented to crotchets. The upper parts resemble the imitative writing of the ritornelli in the mass's first Kyrie; and although the bass preserves some of the characteristics of an ostinato in that its quavers are unremitting, it's now part of the contrapuntal warp and woof. The figure flows in threefold imitation; but the freedom and range of the bass's movement gives density to the texture:

Ex. 160

Modulation comes rapidly, first to the subdominant minor, then relative major, then dominant minor. Passing dissonances and false relations are here acute (bars 21–24), leading to a real cadence, by way of suspended ninth and seventh, into F sharp minor. The cadence is not, however, a cessation; the polyphonic flow is unabated, making sequential modulations to E and D minor, the latter cadence proving to be major after all. The basic motive now appears in its initial form and in other mutations: for instance, falling scale *followed* by rising fourth. The parts often proceed in contrary motion, creating a sonority rich as well as dissonant. In bars 36 to 37 chromatic passing notes in crotchets build a climax, and chains of suspended sevenths promote melodic growth, since the cadences don't resolve. Chromatics invade all three parts both in drooping quavers and in more animated syncopation:

Ex. 161

Yet this is not disintegrative, for the falling crotchets in the bass have gathered an energy which can support chromatic lamentation. The final 6–4 cadence is approached by a Neapolitan sob that is embellished with dissonant appoggiaturas of minor second and major seventh. Yet it's precisely this pain that has encouraged the lines to wing across the bars, and has made the tonic pedal so irrefutably fundamental to the *tierce de Picardie*. As in the mass, crucifixion *is* redemption. Harmonic anguish creates contrapuntal order; and that 'bondage' liberates unbroken song! The interrupted cadence, to use the technical term, has no analogy with coitus interruptus; far from being frustration, it's release.

The fugue is even more closely related to the first Kyrie of the Mass, though the public statement of the mass is here presented in intimately subjective terms. The theme is another wedge, whereby lines drawn through the heads of the notes create an ascent and descent representing the arms of the Cross:

Ex. 162

Though not atonal, the theme contains every note of the chromatic scale, extending in length to twenty-one notes — a multiple of three and seven, numbers of the Trinity and of the Creator. The forlorn effect of the melody comes from its harmonic indirection: beginning with a falling minor triad (ashes to ashes), it yearns up through minor sixth and diminished seventh, only to droop chromatically in an appoggiatura. We feel the dissonance as the traditional symbol of weeping even though, in the initial monodic statement, the harmony note is of course merely implicit.

When the second voice enters, in a tonal, not real, answer, the dissonant weeping is overt, and counterpoised by a rising semiquaver figure that is not unqualified alleviation, since it too tends to float into irresolute tritones and diminished fourths. Despite the chromatics, the four-bar theme modulates to the dominant, the four-bar answer back to the tonic. A two-part, two-bar episode mates the weeping quaver appoggiaturas to the semiquaver expansion. Though the entry of the third voice is real, the dissonance of the texture increases if only because there are now three parts to collide with one another in chromatic wandering. Moreover, there is more semiquaver movement; the texture grows clotted, so that the third entry's modulation to the dominant and the fourth entry's return to the tonic hardly provide props for the undulating chromatics. Whether or not one counts the semiquaver writhings as a countersubject, they gradually acquire a more independent existence, and lead to a section which we may relate to the ritornelli of the mass's Kyrie. The chromatics stabilize into harmonic and figurative sequences, the bass being an inversion of the first four notes of the tonal version of the theme:

Ex. 163

The top voice moves in syncopation up and down through a third, answered in inversion by an inner voice; this is a near-literal quotation of bar 24 of the prelude. Dissonant suspensions still abound but, ordered by the sequences, are no longer distraught, rather sensuously satisfying, even ceremonial. As with the mass's ritornelli the gracious nobility of these 'bowing' figures seems to sing of man's attempt at heroic resolution, which is recurrently undermined by memories of the lamenting (and more mysteriously ordered) chromatic fugue.

The broken false entry of the fugue subject in bar 19 sounds —unusually for Bach—almost like despair.

On the whole, however, this ritornello section is equably balanced in its sequences between F sharp minor and A major, B minor and D major. When the full fugue subject returns in the alto, the chromatic appoggiaturas make the texture claustrophobic, though the semiquaver roulades expand. As the fugue slowly unwinds, we realize that its structure is an alternation of the meandering, chromatic, 'personalized' theme with harmonically sequential, 'ceremonial' ritornelli. In bar 26 the grave, pendulum-like 'bowing' dissolves suspended dissonance into euphony, the bass being an inversion of the subject's tonal answer. The tonality oscillates in lovely relaxation between B minor and D major, G major and E minor —a subdominant complement to the dominant leaning of the first sequential passage. But there's another wistful false entry of the subject in bar 28; and when the fugue is re-established the sharpening tonality, moving from E to F sharp minor, is accompanied by increasing acridity of texture. Stretto entries induce unstable modulations to G, A and D minor as well as to tonic, dominant and subdominant. By this time the flow of semiquavers is continuous, though hardly affirmative —as are the prelude's quavers—because the chromatics create a plethora of passing dissonances. The angular intensity is somewhat released when the theme appears in the bass, now in stretto, in F sharp minor sharpening to C sharp minor, and momentarily to its relative, E major. As the lines mount higher, we return to chromatic-riddled B, F sharp and E minor; the semiquaver countersubject collides with sustained pedal notes that are steering us towards a long-delayed return of the ritornello. This time its appearance —poised between tonic minor and relative major —is fleeting; yet its effect proves positive since it's now absorbed into, rather than juxtaposed with, the fugal texture. If in European music gradations of harmonic tension and relaxation, 'architecturally' ordered tonality and symmetrical dance metres have tended to be associated with the man-made concepts of humanism, whereas the many-in-oneness of counterpoint has seemed to suggest analogies with the divine, then the B minor Prelude and Fugue again reflect Bach's apprehension of the interdependence, even to the point of reversal, of sacred and profane. For here it is the humanistically ceremonial elements that induce serenity, while in the near atonal fugue God indeed works in a mysterious way. None the less, he *does* perform his wonders, and the coda *is* consummatory, as the wandering countersubject wings in the treble, accompanied by chords over a chromatic bass that even suggest a rhetorical progression:

Ex. 164

The punctuating chords define decisive movements-in-time from tonic to subdominant to dominant, which changes to a dominant pedal as the theme sings in the alto with the countersubject flowing, rather than meandering, in the tenor. The *tierce de Picardie* is approached with chromatic enhancement, as it is in the prelude.

This prelude and fugue demonstrate that the epic and cosmic experience that Bach encompassed in ideally liturgical terms in his mass was inherent in his psyche, and may be in ours, if we have ears to hear. The microcosm of these pieces is more 'difficult', and therefore perhaps closer to us, than the public statement of the mass; indeed in so far as the chromaticism of the fugue becomes nearly total, it anticipates the Romantic subjectivism of Reger and early Schoenberg. None the less Bach's fugue, if less tensely serene that his prelude, is not in fact disintegrative; Romantic heat is cooled by a balance between harmonic lucidity and contrapuntal stress (the nouns and adjectives are reversible). The peace that passes understanding is attained within the mind and in the last resort needs the support neither of state nor Church, visible or invisible.

In this sense the B minor Prelude and Fugue prefigure the abstract fugal universe of Bach's last years, as does the F minor Sinfonia or three-part invention which, although part of a collection assembled for teaching purposes, is rightly accounted one of Bach's sublimest masterpieces. Only two pages long, it is not strictly a fugue but is pervasively contrapuntal, every note being thematic, derived from one of three related motives. The first (A) is simply the falling chromatic scale of the bass, which weeps across the beats. This is identical with the bass of the *Weinen, Klagen* cantata in the same key, traditionally associated in its flatness with what Mattheson called 'the deathly anguish of the heart; we've already noted that it reappears, a semitone lower, as the bass of the 'Crucifixus' of the B minor Mass. The second motive (B) is painfully fragmented: a rising minor third droops a semitone, breaks, strains up again through a tritone to the sharp seventh; resolves on the tonic; declines down the scale with the seventh flattened. This theme moves in quavers, against the crotchets of the 'Crucifixus' bass. The third motive (C) begins as a decorated version of B: the rise through the minor third and semitonic descent are garlanded with semiquaver and demisemiquaver roulades. The effect is both of diminution and of agitation, though four cadential quavers stabilize the fourth bar. Motives B and C are versions of Bach's 'Cross theme'; both are modified and intensified as the piece proceeds:

Ex. 165

Bach never wrote a movement more harmonically charged; yet his emotional fervency finds contrapuntal discipline and architectural order equal to it. The first four bars, for all their chromatic involution, modulate conventionally to the dominant. This positive progression is counteracted by bars 5 and 6, which appear to be episodic yet prove to be an inverted diminution of B, with the minor thirds sometimes tensely diminished. These two bars return to the tonic but with the parts changed over: A is now in the treble, B in the bass and C in the alto. This time the modulation ranges flatwards, in a cycle of descending fifths, from F to B flat to E flat to A flat: all darkly minor until the last, the home key's relative major, which effects the first full close, after twelve bars. The 'Crucifixus' motive A then moves to the alto; sequential movement is now rapid, every half-bar producing a key shift, if not a real modulation. The heat of this harmonic-tonal evolution begins to alchemize the motives themselves: a permutation of B appears in the top part, augmented to, and fused with, the crotchets of the 'Crucifixus' motive; the leaping tritone is stretched to a sixth, a seventh (minor, major, diminished) and even to an anguished minor ninth. In context this sounds and feels like a racking of the limbs, a physical crucifixion; yet again equilibrium, even grace, is preserved through the mirror-like stillness of the answers by inversion. The interlacing of the parts disarms, or absolves, their dissonant complexities. It would be an insensitive performance that ignored either the pain inherent in the dissonances (which demands a tempo at which the harmonies will tell) or the paradoxical serenity that the counterpoint attains from that laceration (which calls for a tempo that discourages lingering self-indulgence).

There's a comparable balance within the apparently agitated tonal movement. Lamentations in the dark flatness of B flat, E flat and A flat minor oscillate with the alleviation of G flat, D flat and A flat major, in which key occurs, in bar 27, a full close exactly paralleling the dominant cadence in bar 5, with the same stabilizing bass. The last eight bars are consummatory. The augmented permutation of the 'Cross motive' descends from treble to alto to bass, changing back in the process to the original 'Crucifixus' scale. The final cadence achieves, and deserves, the bliss of a *tierce de Picardie*. Harmonic agony is resolved (though probably only after a Cross-hung suspension), because throughout the piece the emotion has been deepened in the process of its contrapuntal objectification. More amazing still in so potently personal a work is that Bach combines experiential with intellectual allegory. That 'Cross motives' create the harmonic stress of false relation, that canonic processes bring the balm of mathematical certitudes that seem God-like because beyond human fallibilities: so much is evident to our ears and senses. But only after we've done some arithmetic do we discover that motive A (the 'Crucifixus' bass) contains eleven notes, which stand for sinning mankind—a notion Bach adapted from St. Augustine's *Transgressionem decalogi notat*, ten plus one being a trespass of the ten holy commandments; while motive B contains fourteen notes, the number that represent's Bach's name in the figure alphabet. It would seem that Bach identifies himself with man as sinner, and through his music intercedes with God on our behalf, for motive C extends to nineteen notes, an indivisible number and the sum of the holy numbers seven (which represent creation) and twelve (a quaternity of trinities and symbol of the Church). While these puzzles cannot affect our analysis of the musical events they may indirectly affect the way we perform the piece. They at least confirm our sense that this composition is peculiarly moving because it had for Bach a deeply personal significance and was at the same time concerned with abstract theological concepts. This conditions our response to the music of his final years, in which passion, though distilled, is certainly not spent.

IV

POSTLUDE

Dame Algebra

Praise Her because, mute but full of sentence, Her written structures exemplify the pattern it is their purpose to convey, and so are read the same by all minds. .

Praise Her because she can so elegantly summarize the average effect of anonymous and seemingly disorderly occurrences.

Hers the pure joy of knowing what at all times and in all places is the case: Hers the music, silent and uncarnal, of immortal necessity.

Woe to us if we speak slightingly of Her. Except Her grace prevent, we are doomed to idolatry, to worship imaginary gods of our own making, creatures of whim both cruel and absurd.

For She it is, and She alone who, without ambiguity or palter, can teach us to rejoice in the Holy Providence of our Creator and Judge.

Honour to Her then, and delight to those who serve Her faithfully.

Let music strike!

W. H. AUDEN

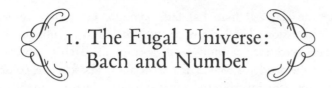

1. The Fugal Universe: Bach and Number

The final score of the B minor Mass was, as we have seen, copied out by Bach late in life, probably in 1747 or 1748. While some of the music may have been newly composed at that time, one cannot count the mass as a late work, but rather as a summation of Bach's lifelong experience: that is why its position in his oeuvre and in European history is crucial. The music renders incarnate the tenuous connection between fallible human passion and infallible divine order and attains that peace which passes understanding. One can hardly expect man to discover such peace except in a society wherein the Law is accepted as an act of faith. The blessedness of Beethoven's Benedictus, in his *Missa Solemnis*, might be accounted yet more miraculous in that it is a state achieved, and passed through, *within the psyche*—affecting the world outside because we listen to it and, in listening, experience it vicariously. None the less Beethoven differentiates in calling the 'Dona nobis pacem' a 'prayer for inner and outer peace', whereas Bach, in his mass, scarcely separates private experience from public act.

The musical manifestations of this act lie, we've noted, in the mass's consistent (however complex) rhythms, its continuous (however flexible) lines, its symmetrical (however intricate) figurations, its ordered (however dissonant) harmonies. Allied to these features is the basic moderation of Bach's tempi: the pulse or heart-beat, or the normal speed of a man walking, conditions most of Bach's tempi whether they sound, in final effect, fast or slow. Often we are thus prompted to speak of Bach's music as though it were 'pre-ordained'; and this in turn reflects the theological concept of Pauline predestination, which increasingly dominated Lutheranism. Predestination was not merely an admission that human actions are predetermined by or dependent on natural or, as we would say, psychological *causae secundae*. It rather involved the idea of election, of (some) men having been preordained by God for salvation. Because God's ways are *ipso facto* incomprehensible to men, man's free will is as naught. However vigorously pursued, the activity of the creature must inevitably be overborne by the Creator: 'God shall be all in all; he is potter, we the clay'. If man has faith enough, grace may come through personal intercession; but he can be justified only by faith, not by will or works. The certitude, stability and serenity of Bach's music, however responsive to the depths as well as heights of human experience, comes from its total — perhaps, remembering the 'vivos et mortuos' passage in the Credo, we should say almost total — acceptance of the will of God even if, or because, that will is intellectually inexplicable.

The *St. John Passion* and the B minor Mass effect a synthesis between a religious-mystical inheritance and the passionate humanism of the high Baroque. By the 1740s those elements were being undermined by rationalistic deism, with which Bach had little intuitive sympathy. Like Beethoven in the latter part of his life, he therefore increasingly sought a haven of quiet within the mind; and he too had a 'late period' in which, without abandoning his experiential and compositional principles, he was no longer directly tuned to the world outside, as represented by church and state. For this reason the theological dimension of Bach's predeterminism was modified by another dimension which we may call philosophical. Though we have no evidence that Bach himself knew Spinoza's writings, we do know that Spinoza deeply influenced both theologians and music theorists who played a part in Bach's formative years. In any case Spinoza's celebrated definition of the wise man as one who 'in so far as he is regarded as such is scarcely at all disturbed in spirit, but being conscious of himself, and of God, and of things, by a certain eternal necessity never ceases to be, but always possesses true acquiesence of his spirit', sounds profoundly Bachian. The ideal of both men was to achieve a system, philosophical or musical, which could be simultaneously free and determined, since man is in bondage 'in so far as his behaviour is guided by inadequate cognition, but free in so far as his cognitions are adequate'. Men who 'think themselves free, in so far as they are conscious of volitions and desires but are ignorant of the causes by which they are disposed to will and desire', may thus attain 'the greatest possible human perfection'. Whether or not this is capable of verbal formulation, it is clearly demonstrable in terms of Bach's music, implicitly throughout his life, explicitly in the compositions of his final years.

It has been said that Spinoza, defining a unitary view of the cosmos and of man's place in it, evolved an abstract metaphysical system as intellectually rigorous as a theorem in pure mathematics. The ultimate, unfinished masterpiece of Bach's last years, the *Art of Fugue*, is likewise an abstract *demonstratio* of contrapuntal principle, for which Bach does not even indicate which pipes, reeds, strings or keyboards should be 'instrumental' to the aural realization of the symbols: he plays to God and himself in an empty church, or becomes an instrument through which an angelic concourse 'intellectually sounds in the ears of God'—to use Sir Thomas Browne's phrase. What this means, in terms of Bach's 'late' technique, is that the ostensibly archaic elements in his art are reborn. Fashionably operatic rhetoric fades from the music of his last phase; musical science becomes associated with mathematical law in a manner that Spinoza would have recognized but which would have seemed obsolete and irrelevant to Bach's younger contemporary, Rameau, a professional composer with as much science and mathematics as he needed. For Rameau the laws of harmonic proportion, of tonal relationship, and of metrical symmetry reflected—in music as in architecture—a social order which was in turn dictated by God as master-mechanic. Bach's mathematics in his last works have become mystical rather than social, using the word mystical in the same sense as it is applied to Spinoza's philosophy. This is not (like Beethoven's) a mysticism by direct, visionary experience but a mysticism of logic and deduction. It has nothing to do with the Enlightenment, much to do with Bach's medieval heritage and with the 'logical' mysticism of some oriental philosophies of which Bach had, of course, no conscious knowledge. Somewhere beyond intellectual formulation Bach's mathematics slide off into pre-Christian numerology, and science and magic become inextricably confused. They do so not adventitiously, but because both proffer a law that is independent of human volition. That is a theme worth preliminary enquiry, before we tackle that of the intrinsic nature of Bach's final works.

In our introductory chapter we pointed out that in so-called primitive societies it is clear that—today and for several thousand years past—art has no affinity with our post-Renaissance notions of expression and communication. There is no I, attempting to contact Them; the artist is rather a medium, through whom or which an act of revelation occurs. The musician has thus no concern with evolution or development in time; supremely a functionalist, his purpose is to create the conditions in which revelation may happen. He would lose the self rather than find it; and repetition, whether in song, dance, basketwork or beadwork, is a means towards this relinquishment. Repetition involves counting; and the permutations of number often have magical associations. This becomes explicit in the sophisticated Oriental cultures, as we can see in the techniques of classical Indian music. Ragas are preordained series of pitch relationships which, in accord with the acoustically emotive properties of intervals, originally evolved from the instinctual behaviour of the human voice; talas are preordained metrical patterns that cannot but be permutations of mathematical law; and both raga and tala are considered to have cosmological significance. The infinitely subtle, variously human nuances of pitch in the sitar's melodic line—whimpering, whispering, sighing, crying, lilting, laughing—originate in given intervallic relationships, and create, under the stimulation and opposition of the drummer's numerical law, a sense of wholeness from their interaction. So in this music to lose the self is to find it; and without its numerology classical Indian music would be impotent. Number is not here an imposition; it is the law within which, and only within which, we live, move and have our being.

Comparable notions underlie the musics of most Oriental cultures; the musical instincts of the ancient Chinese and Arabians were inseparable from their mathematical genius. Similarly Greek music was related to the Pythagorean science of numbers, the mathematical laws of harmonic proportion being part of a developed cosmology. Indeed music's social importance lay in its power to 'keepe unstedy Nature to her Law', as Milton put it; reconciling ecstasis with the intellectual worship of number could satisfy the claims of mind and body equally. Something of this survives into the Christian theocracy of Europe's Middle Ages. The metrical modes of troubadour song are still imperfectly understood, occasioning academic disputation. They are probably based on the metres of classical prosody; since, however, troubadour song was probably directly influenced by Arabian music by way of the Crusades, it is remotely possible that in the modes vestiges of ancient permutation theory survive.

If this is speculation, it is fact that medieval musicians in general organized their music on principles of metrical proportion rather than of harmonic congruence; and that these proportions had doctrinal as well as mathematical significance. The association of 'perfect' rhythm (which is triple) with the Trinity dates back at least as far as Philippe de Vitry (1291–1361); nor can one disentangle this Christian symbolism from the magical, pre-Christian numerology rife in medieval alchemy. Disentanglement is hardly called for, since the mathematical structures work precisely because they are doctrinally credible; the fact of belief matters more than the logic of what is believed. And such doctrinal conceptions survived well into the Renaissance, when music became harmonically rather than metrically oriented. Harmonic perspective, based on the harmonic series which is in turn related to the solar spectrum, is itself scientific law, abortively investigated centuries back by the Greeks. So, after the revival of classical learning, the old numerology ran in harness with intervallic logic, which equated the 'perfect' fifth with God, the nefariously imperfect fifth with the Devil.

There is a fairly close structural analogy between the structure of a Machaut motet and that of a Gothic cathedral. The main structure of the cathedral is a feat of mathematical engineering (however intuitively arrived at), to which individual craftsmen add their contributions. Similarly the medieval motet is built on the rock of the plainsong cantus firmus (the word of God and the Church), the other parts being added separately, each meaningful in itself, more meaningful in relation to the whole. The linear-mathematical principles of Machaut's famous *Messe de Notre Dame* have clear affinities with the Oriental technique of the raga; while its device of isochronous rhythm—a metrical sequence which remains constant throughout a given part, though the pitch relationships change—is comparable with the Oriental tala, especially since the metrical patterns are complex and asymmetrical, and often have doctrinal as well as musical import. Harmonic dualities occur—there's a fierce coruscation of dissonances for the Crucifixion—but they are absorbed in the grandeur of the mathematical proportions, the godlike reiteration of the absolute consonances of fourth and fifth, the stark sonorities, and probably the supernal reverberation of bells.

At the very end of the Middle Ages, when a once stable world was in disintegration, preoccupation with the presumed certitudes of mathematics became obsessional. Both music and mathematics were considered as branches of philosophy, astronomy and theology, in which related disciplines most late medieval composers (who were often also clerics) had been trained. A puzzle-piece such as Machaut's *Ma fin est mon commencement* (wherein the tenor accompanies the cantus with the same melody backwards, while the countertenor proceeds to its middle point and then inverts itself) may be said to 'music' by mathematical permutation a philosophical concept. Yet humanity flowers—in the smooth lines and sensuously triadic harmony—through the acceptance of mathematical law; and can do so because that law is envisaged as philosophical, if not exactly theological. About a hundred years later, when the Renaissance has burgeoned, one finds a comparable equivocation in Dunstable's motet, *Veni sancte spiritus*. Here the harmony is consistently triadic, with the mellifluous sensuality of high Renaissance music. Yet the sensuality is passive, directionless; and the piece's structure is unambiguously medieval, linear and mathematical. The plainsong cantus firmus is repeated three times in notational values that decrease by (Trinitarian) thirds; the metrical structure is isochronous; the three liturgical texts are sung simultaneously. A Christianized version of raga and tala is thus still in evidence; and the rhythm of the lines dissolves the sense of temporal progression, largely because metrical proportions are complex, independent of an earthbeat. Again, the numerical elements in the music's structure are inseparable from its function, which was not to express Dunstable's attitude to the world in which he found himself, but to create an atmosphere through which an act of revelation might occur.

Later Renaissance composers, believing more in the validity of human passion, were more concerned with its incarnation through melodic appeal, rhythmic vivacity, instrumental colouring and harmonic tension and relaxation. Early Baroque composers turned such humanly expressive elements into operatic 'projection' and, as we have seen, it was partly in this tradition that Bach was trained. Yet, as we've also noted, the heart of his achievement was in combining this maximum awareness of 'the pain of consciousness' with the maximum command of an abstract spiritual order — or, in musical terms, the highest density of harmonic tension with the most perfect extension of contrapuntal science. What happens in the music of his last years is not that the human core of his art evaporates but that, no longer 'projected', it becomes one with the only science (mathematics) which is exact because it is founded on eternal verities. Pythagoras taught that there is a 'mysterious connection between gods and numbers, on which the Science of Arithmacy is based'. Pythagoras also called music 'an Arithmetic, a science of true numbers', and believed that music was of all human activities closest to mathematical law. Only those tones which are numerically determined according to the harmonic series are music; other sounds are noise. Moreover the harmonic spectrum parallels the movements of astral bodies. Number proceeds from unity; things originate from number: so there can be unity without things, but never things without unity. In this sense the Pythagorean aphorism that 'all is number' came to imply the Platonic doctrine of transcendent ideas, and was thus interpreted by the church fathers from Aquinas to Duns Scotus. In Bach's day Leibniz reinterpreted the notion, remarking in 1712 that 'musica est exercitum arithmeticae occultum nescientis de numerare animi'. Music is a hidden practice of the soul which deals in number without knowing it's so doing; in a confused perception the soul thus achieves that which, in clearer perceptions, it is unable to achieve. 'If therefore the soul does not notice that it calculates, it yet senses the effect of its unconscious reckoning, be this as joy over harmony or oppression over discord.' This goes to the heart of the matter. Bach's musical mathematics in his last works may be as exact as an exercise in dialectical logic of Leibniz or Spinoza, but it is 'truer' in that its intellectual rigour encompasses the total range of human experience. Paradoxically, mathematical abstraction liberates us from the tyranny of fact. As Walter Kaufmann has put it: 'In mathematics we experience a taste of freedom; the bondage of accident is broken; the soul is no longer the prisoner of the body; man is as a god.' The Swiss mathematician-philosopher Ferdinand Gonseth (quoted by Kaufmann) makes the same point in stating that 'mathematics exists between two complementary poles: one the world of reality, called exterior, the other interior. These two worlds are transcendental, that is, beyond consciousness. They cannot be perceived "in themselves" but only by the traces which they leave in the field of our consciousness.' In Jungian terms, 'number is an archetype of order which has become conscious'.

The theologians, philosophers, alchemists and music theorists whom Bach read encouraged an equation between mysticism, magic and number, absorbed from Greek and Oriental sources, from scholastic philosophy and, in pseudo-scientific form, from the metaphysicians of the then present. Such concepts exerted an increasing influence on Bach. As rational Enlightenment encroached, Bach ballasted his faith with hermetic truths that could be demonstrated, in terms of music, with an exactitude that leaves verbal language helpless; what results from Bach's *demonstratio* of the transcendental unity of number is liberation and joy. Of course since the universe is mathematically constructed there is a sense in which all music must be mathematics. 'Cum Deus calculet et cogitationem exercet fit mundus', said Leibniz; and in our own distracted day many composers have subscribed to such a view in reaction against post-Wagnerian, egocentric breast-beating. Even the felinely sensuous Debussy remarked that 'music is a mysterious form of mathematics whose elements are derived from the infinite'; and believed, or affected to believe, that artistic process is more beautifully manifest in Nature than in art itself. Varèse, Debussy's more radical expatriate successor, called Debussy a 'fantastic chemist', and likened his own compositional processes to alchemy and to crystal and rock formation. Webern, who was a scholar in the field of late medieval music, maintained that it was 'for a later period to discover the close unifying laws that are already present in the works themselves. When this true conception of art is achieved, then there will no longer be any possible distinctions between science and inspired creation. The further one presses forward, the greater becomes the identity of everything, and finally we have the impression of being faced by a work not of man, but of

Nature.' Not for nothing was Webern partial to serial rows whose second half is a mirror inversion of the first, an eternity symbol, wherein 'here is Necessity, here is God'. Such music attains that mystical 'light of the eye' (the title of one of his later cantatas) which is a haven within the mind; that it resembles the precariously desperate canonic unities of a late Gothic motet suggests that so fanatical a concern with mathematical law tends to occur in civilizations on the brink of disintegration. This 'Gothic desperation' is evident too in the early Stockhausen and Milton Babbitt; and since the number of possible permutations merely of the twelve equal tempered semitones was estimated as far back as 1920 to be 479,001,600 it is hardly surprising that an attempt to realize the implications of serialization had to wait until, in the age of electronics, the composer-scientist-priest could stand, as Varèse puts it, 'godlike above the material', which he hands to the mastermind of a computer.

Even with the computer's aid, however, an infinitely complex total determinism has proved inapprehensible by finite minds. The Greek composer Xenakis, who was trained as a mathematician and electrical engineer, has made an important contribution to the musical ambience of our time; yet it is unclear what precisely is meant when he claims to have 'constructed' musical compositions on the same fundaments as his buildings; to have 'illustrated' in music sundry scientific theorems; and in *Nomos* (which means rule or law) to have 'made music which possesses an extra-temporal architecture based on the theory of group transformations, and which utilizes the theory of sieves which annexes the congruence module Z and is the result of an axiomatic theory of the universal structure of music'. What, in the context of this—to the non-scientist—rebarbative quotation, is the exact meaning of the words *construct, illustrate* and *utilize*? Why should man spend thousands of years painfully aspiring to self-consciousness only in order to surrender it to the probability calculus? Whether or not such a total reliance on external law is a refuge from chaos, we can certainly say that for the Indian sitar player, for Machaut, Dunstable, Schoenberg, Webern, above all for Bach, the law was a superhuman means towards a human end, not an end in itself. For them, the search for infinity is finite: the perfection of mathematical law, having been attained, must lead again to a search for consciousness. In the words of Robert Duncan, 'Death is the condition of eternal forms'; from the infinite, the babe, taking breath, leaps into life with anguish, and the cycle starts again. This is equally true whether a composer thinks of music, as did Beethoven, as organic process, living and dying within the mind like plant or flower; or whether he thinks of it, as did Bach, as revealed truth. What matters is the equilibrium between human intention and divine pretension; and from this point of view the difference between Bach and Beethoven is one of degree, not kind. Beethoven's discovery of Self was a revelation of organic process; Bach's revelation of law led to a self reborn. An obvious starting point for the investigation of this is Bach's Goldberg Variations, a work that exists in limbo — using the term in its theological sense as 'a region where pre-Christian just men and infants are confined, pending admission to heaven'. If we say that these variations dangle one foot in the world of physical matter while the other takes off into the purity of mathematics the metaphor may seem grotesque. As we'll see, however, it is a not inaccurate description of the music's effect.

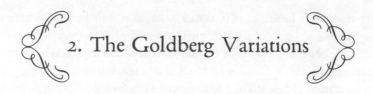

2. The Goldberg Variations

The Goldberg Variations were commissioned, but not by church or state for public performance. According to Forkel, Count Kaiserling, formerly Russian ambassador at the court of the Elector of Saxony, employed a harpsichordist called Goldberg as a household musician. For a while Kaiserling resided in Leipzig, and sent Goldberg to Bach for advanced musical instructions. The count, Forkel tells us,

> was often sickly, and then had sleepless nights. At these times Goldberg, who lived in the house with him, had to pass the night in an adjoining room to play something to him when he could not sleep. The Count once said to Bach that he would like to have some clavier pieces for his Goldberg, which should be of such a soft and somewhat lively character that he might be a little cheered by them in his sleepless nights. Bach thought he could best fulfil this wish by variations which, on account of the constant sameness of the fundamental harmony, he had hitherto considered as an ungrateful task. But as at this time all his works were models of art, these variations also became such under his hand. This is, indeed, the only model of the kind that he has left us. The Count thereafter called them nothing but *his* variations. He was never weary of hearing them; and for a long time, when the sleepless nights came, he used to say: 'Dear Goldberg, do play me one of my variations'. Bach was, perhaps, never so well rewarded for any work as for this; the Count made him a present of a golden goblet, filled with a hundred Louis d'or. But their worth as a work of art would not have been paid if the present had been a thousand times as great.

So although the Goldberg Variations were not, like the *Art of Fugue*, composed in abstract musical terms, they were created for private ears. Their function was therapeutic: Johann Goldberg played them to his count; Bach played, or at any rate composed, them to his God; and their mathematically preordained features encourage us to hear them within an eternal silence.

In creating the work Bach did not contradict the suspicion of variation form with which Forkel credits him: the Goldberg Variations are not variations in the sense that Haydn or Mozart, or any later composer, would have understood the term. The sarabande⁄aria which Bach uses as his theme is not a simple tune to be varied, but a complex and subtle melody already elaborately embellished. Beneath this melody, however, is a simple bass line and a thirty⁄two⁄bar tonal structure that affirms the fundaments of classical tonality:

Ex. 166

The first eight bars assert the tonic, G major; the second eight modulate to the dominant; the third eight proceed from dominant of the tonic to the relative (E minor); the last eight bars return to the tonic. This harmonic pattern is modified throughout the variations only in details. Sometimes root position triads are exchanged for first inversions; occasionally this happens with a second inversion. The third, sixth and occasionally fifth of the bass may be sharpened or flattened; this becomes inevitable, and has momentous consequences, when, halfway through the work, the minor key is substituted for major. The relative minor (E) then becomes the flat submediant, E flat *major*, a relaxation instead of increase in tension. Yet in essence the variations do not depart from the original harmonic bass and tonal scheme, over which they form, not melodic variations, but an immense passacaglia. This is a convention to which Bach had long been partial: not surprisingly, since it is the most radical example of the Baroque obsession with unity. In this late work, however, the metaphysical and mystical implications of unity take over from the social and autocratic. Though the unity isn't religious in affirming dogma or creed, it might be called such in a philosophical sense.

For all its metaphysical implications, the work finds its source in a piece of near⁄modern music: a sarabande which Bach had included, fifteen years earlier, in his notebook for Anna Magdalena. It is not even certain that Bach composed it; he may merely have copied it from a French source, or from a G major ground of Henry Purcell which is similar though not, I think,

strikingly so. Whether Bach composed it or not is unimportant. What matters
is that its bass offered him what he needed, and that its formal proportions and
elegant ornamentation were presumably in tune with Kaiserling's apartment.
Moreover, if Bach didn't write it he might have done, for its graciousness is
neither precious nor affected. This is partly because the bass is simple, songlike
and symmetrical, partly because the melody, beginning with repeated
crotchets and moving in gentle arches, is delicately balanced above it:

Ex. 167

Far from being disturbed by the tendrils of ornamentation, the line is thereby
rendered more fluid, the texture diaphanous. Even the sighing appoggiaturas
release rhythm from the shackles of time; so although the sarabande is gallant
and courtly, its effect is different from comparable movements in Handel. It
is profoundly Bachian in its fusion of physical with spiritual grace, though
of course such a synthesis is found also in French sarabandes from
Chambonnières to D'Angelbert to Couperin le Grand.

That the work won't remain rooted in this contemporary aristocratic world
becomes evident in the aria itself, since in the second half the filigree decorating
the melody gradually disperses. After the Lombard sobs and sighing upward
appoggiaturas that take us to the relative in bar 24, the melodic flow turns into
equable semiquavers (Ex. 168).

Despite the occasional dissonant passing note the sonority, with the parts
spaced in the middle of the keyboard, is radiant. We are reminded here that a
sarabande, though sensual, is also traditionally sacral.

Ex. 168

After the aria the variations fall into groups of three. Apart from Variation 2, which forms a contrapuntal bridge to the first canon, these groups follow a consistent pattern up to Variation 12. The first member of each 'trinity' is based on dance rhythm, even though there is a fair leavening of counterpoint, symmetrical mirror inversions of figurations and so on. The second member of the 'trinity' is a toccata for the two keyboards of the harpsichord (Goldberg's instrument seems to have been similar to one reputedly in Bach's possession). Here the physical movement breaks into arabesques, again disciplined by imitation and inversion of figuration. The third member of each group is a canon, first at the unison, then second, then third, then fourth, and so on, up to the ninth. Except for the final canon at the ninth the imitative parts unfold over a freely melodic version of the ground bass. In place of the canon at the tenth Bach substitutes, for the thirtieth variation, a quodlibet, a contrapuntal collage of popular songs.

The initial variation of each group, the dance, springs from the physical, with animated leaps in clearly defined rhythm. The first variation is however somewhat complex in effect since, although more earthily harmonic and metrically time-ridden than the rarefied sarabande, it's also more polyphonically self-contained in being a two-part invention. In the first four bars the ground bass is palpable on the first quaver of each bar; the left hand prances through tenths and octaves, the right hand rises in semiquaver scales, after a written-out mordent imitated between the parts. The dominant modulation hinted at in the aria really occurs in bars 3–4, but is immediately counteracted by the second four bars wherein the right and left hands are inverted. The second eight bars consist of four bars of flowing semiquaver arpeggios in the right hand, with bouncing quavers in the left, followed again by the two hands' inversion. In the last bar the scales glide in contrary motion to collide on the new tonic, D. The second half of the variation mirrors the first, though the right hand substitutes an openly rising third for the original mordent. The part-writing is more sinuous, with cross-accents at the modulations to the relative. In the approach to the cadence a subdominant feeling is more marked; chromatic passing notes effect a momentary modulation to A minor as well as C major. There's already a hint here as to how the mirror-like perfection of Bach's counterpoint will contain the many within its oneness, though this does not disturb the mood of quiet content:

Ex. 169

Perhaps Bach doesn't immediately establish his pattern of dance-toccata-canon because he wants us to sense an embryonic quality in the early variations. In any case Variation 2, though it changes the time signature from 3/4 to 2/4 and the number of parts from two to three, is the same kind of music as Variation 1, if less sensuously resonant, more cantabile. The ground bass is still defined on the first beat of the bars; and the bass's figuration begins with equal quavers moving up and down a step, then down a third—an augmentation of the semiquaver figure in the upper parts, which are consistently imitative, beginning in canon at the sixth. This main theme rises a fourth, is tied across the bar-line, and falls in semiquavers. Though the tied notes are often dissonant suspensions the music creates, from the symmetry of its proportions and the lucidity of its texture, a sober grace. After the double bar the imitative theme is stretched from rising fourth to octave, and then appears, at the modulation to the relative, in stretto, leaping fifth answered by fourth. This coagulates the texture slightly; certainly it's more difficult to hear, as well as to play, the parts. There are, however, no real modifications to the original harmony; and the variation leads inevitably to the first strict canon, at the unison. Bach notates this in long bars of 12/8, a time signature which, as we've several times noticed, he tends to reserve for celestial matters, since although its triplet-rhythm quavers spring from bodily movement, such movement is sublimated in the spacious arching of the dotted crotchet pulse.

The canonic parts move mainly by step, dotted crotchet tied over to an undulation of quavers; and there's a long bar's distance between the unisonal entries. Especially on a keyboard instrument, where there can be little contrast of tone colour (such as is provided by violin and harpsichord in the sublime canonic first movement of the A major violin sonata), canon at the unison cannot be easily heard. Bach doesn't help in this when he directs that this canon, like all the others except the last, should be played on one manual, not two, in different registrations. He is prepared to sacrifice ready audibility in order to make a philosophical point, since it's precisely the oneness that embraces the many with which the music is concerned. None the less Bach helps us in another and subtler way, by introducing a small irregularity into the bass. At first the harmonic notes of the ground occur on alternate beats, two a bar; halfway through the third bar they are speeded up to three or four a bar and are compensatorily repeated, to fill out the 'architecture'. The repetitions of the harmonies underline the repetitions of the unisonal canon, and make it more audible than it would be otherwise:

Ex. 170

The point is not to recognize the theme, but simply and profoundly to know that it is there. Even after the double bar, when the canonic entries occur on the off-beat and passing dissonances complicate the texture, the music still flows in pastoral simplicity, in the style of an organ trio sonata. Though the canon is just apprehensible, its twoness is scarcely discernible from its oneness. It has purged the two previous variations of their metrical assertiveness; and considering the first three variations as a 'trinity', one might say that their techniques are cellular. Each strand embryonically emerges and, without climax, is dovetailed into the 'perfection' of the unisonal canon. The technical manifestations of this canon, as described above, are thus complementary to the magical-philosophical implications of the First Number, which is not only unity but, as Jung puts it in *Psychology and Alchemy*, 'The unity, the One, All-Oneness, individuality and non-duality . . . an archtype and attribute of God, the monad'.

The next 'trinity' of variations returns to the earth in that its first member

(Variation 4) is a fugal dance, with the ground bass more simply stated than in
the three previous variations, or even in the aria itself. Its metre is 3/8:
conventionally that of the quick, round-dance section of the French overture.
That may emphasize its worldliness, though the flavour of the music is far
from courtly. Its arpeggiated tune and rigidly metrical rhythm rather evoke a
stomp on the village green; or perhaps—since there's artifice in the
contrapuntal entries answering one another by inversion—a burgomaster's
junketing:

Ex. 171

Certainly, the rhythm is vigorous, the texture relatively thick, the counterpoint
solid; the many dissonant suspensions on the strong beats become a means of
marking the metrical accent. The stockiness and sturdiness, reinforced in the
last four bars of each half by the doublings in parallel thirds and sixths, is the
more striking after the 'timeless' fluidity of the unisonal canon. Again,
however, the contrapuntal and tonal symmetry of the variation distances its
impact in the context of the whole work. It's a moment in the here-and-now of
Bach's world, and at the same time another 'grain of sand' in his musical
cosmos.

Variation 5 is the first toccata-style piece exploiting the two keyboards. The
ground bass is clearly defined on the first beats of the left hand part which,
back in 3/4, jauntily leaps through tenths. The right hand swirls in
semiquavers, mingling scales with broken chords, in violin style:

Ex. 172

In the second eight bars hands and figurations are again inverted. After the double bar the part-writing mirrors the first half: the leaping tenths are inverted in the right hand, the semiquavers inverted in the left. Since the tenths are decorated, the passage-work is more complicated, the harmony more involved. In total effect, however, the variation is a release of high spirits through keyboard dexterity. And this physical energy spills over into the next canon (Variation 6) which, being at the second, naturally lends itself to dissonant suspensions on the strong beat, in the manner of a trio sonata. The metre returns to a gentle 3/8; the bass flows in semiquavers, with the harmonic ground-notes disguised; the two canonic parts clingingly overlap. As the parts come close together, the texture is enriched with parallel sixths and thirds, while the canon creates false relations between B flat and B natural, C natural and C sharp:

Ex. 173

This minor tinge to the dominant modulation is counteracted by an enhanced dominant approach to the cadence, the original F sharp G A D progression being intensified to G G sharp A D. At the cadence the bass's semiquaver flow is punctuated by falling octaves in quavers. After the double bar chromatic passing notes intrude for the first time in the variations. Inevitably the suspended seconds, sevenths and ninths toughen the texture as the modulation to the relative is approached by *its* enhanced dominant:

Ex. 174

The final eight bars, however, return to equability. The bass falls through quaver sevenths, instead of rising through octaves; the effect is almost ceremonious, as the bottom notes balance the wide falling intervals with a scalewise ascent to the dominant-tonic cadence.

Philosophically, the number two is the archetype of duality, and in some primtive languages the word for two is related to words meaning to split, but also to follow and to accompany. Since Pythagoras the number two has been symbolically equivalent to matter as *increatum*; representing repetition, it implies rhythm, pulsation, oscillation, and therefore forms the basis for our perception of time. In the natural philosophy of the Middle Ages, Jung maintains,

> one is not a number at all; two is the first number. Two is the first number because separation and multiplication begin, which alone make counting possible. With the appearance of the number 2, Another appears alongside the One, a happening so striking that in many languages 'the other' and 'the second' are expressed by the same word. The other can have a sinister significance—or one feels it at least as something opposite and alien. Therefore, argues a medieval alchemist (Gerhard Dorn), God did not praise the second day of creation, because on this day, Monday (the day of the moon) the binarius, alias the devil, came into existence. In other words, as soon as the number 2 appears, a unit is produced out of the original unit, and this unit is none other than the same unit split into two and turned into a 'number'. The One and the Other form an opposition. . . . The One, however, will not let go of the Other because, if it did, it would lose its character; and the Other pushes itself away from the One in order to exist at all. Thus there arises a tension of opposites between the One and the Other.

Now it would, of course, be ludicrous to suggest that Bach deliberately illustrated these psychological-numerical truths by way of this canon; it is, however, valid to say that canon at the second in European harmonic music is related to such concepts. Perception of it is more than usually dependent on temporality, since each entry is a dissonance that proceeds to a consonance; and the pain of the dissonance can be construed as a devilish other, only conceivable within time—which neatly accords with Christian doctrine. Nor is it fortuitous that the canon at the second offers the first intimation of harmonic development in the Goldberg Variations. At the end of this second 'trinity', we begin to sense what the work's inner pattern may be. The dance pieces start from the earth; the toccatas spring from the physical excitation of virtuosity, but increasingly lose contact with 'the Sea of Space and Time', as Blake called the material world. They thus provide a transition to the canons which, always vocal in texture, tend to negate metre, and therefore the temporal sense. In the level, impersonal flow of their two-in-oneness they approach a metaphysical rather than physical state of being, though from the canon at the second onwards each canon tends to absorb into its impersonality an increasing degree of melodic-rhythmic passion and of harmonic contrariety.

Variation 7, played on two keyboards, is again a dance, earthy, if less rudimentarily so than Variation 4. Its 6/8 rhythm is that of a loure, not so merry as a gigue, nor so graceful as a siciliano. The ornamentation, especially the demisemiquaver roulades, is perky rather than elegant; the sonority of the two real parts, in which the ground bass is no more than latent, suggests a rustic oboe and bassoon. Only when, in the second half, the relative minor modulation encompasses a hint of A minor is rural innocence compromised; though the effect of the right hand's yearning augmented fifth is momentary, the return to the tonic unambiguous:

Ex. 175

The toccata variation (no. 8) reaffirms the ground bass on the first note of each 3/4 bar. Like the first toccata, its mood is ebullient, its technique virtuosic, exploiting crossed figurations on the two manuals. During the first four bars the right hand springs up in semiquaver arpeggios, while the left hand bounces down in arpeggiated quavers. The second four bars, in a manner by now familiar, invert the figuration: semiquavers descend and quavers rise. In the second eight bars the hands too are inverted, and the descending quaver arpeggios are filled in with scalic semiquavers. The modulation to the dominant is insistent, fizzing into demisemiquavers at the final cadence. After the double bar the opening of the variation is mirrored in the new key; soon all the figuration is filled in with passing semiquavers. The texture of crossing semiquavers bristles, the excitement being intensified as the modulation to the dominant is insistent, fizzing into demisemiquavers at the subdominant (Ex. 176).

The final four bars, however, return to the original foundation, with both hands in inversion. Again, the contrapuntal and figurative symmetries depersonalize the virtuosic physicality, and so can lead to the next canon, at the third, wherein the two imitative parts move equably in vocal style, over a free

Ex. 176

bass in which the metrical form of the ground is dissolved in asymmetrical melody. Being at the third, at one bar's distance, the canon naturally creates euphony, though the independence of the lines encourages sequential ·modulations (to E minor and major) subtler than any tonal movement thus far. Immediately after the double bar the theme modifies its step descent to a third. Passing modulations created by polyphonic flexibility grow abstruse, with a Neapolitan F major at the approach to the basic modulation to the relative:

Ex. 177

The semitonic suspensions in the canon are piercing.

None the less one can appreciate—especially if one writes the variation out in open score—how the 'perfection' of the counterpoint generates radiance from the dense texture. Number symbolism is again relevant: for Jung says that tension between the One and the Other inherent in the number two culminates in release, out of which comes the Third, wherein the lost unity is restored. 'Unity, the absolute One, cannot be numbered, it is indefinable and unknowable . . . Three is an unfolding of the One into a condition wherein it can be known.' In alchemical terms, 'Out of One comes Two, but from the pairing of these two comes the Third.' The Son proceeds from the Father; the unity of Father and Son is the *vinculum amoris*; and this constitutes the Holy Ghost, the Third. It's not surprising that three (as we remarked in connection with the Sanctus of the B Minor Mass) should be so significant in most religions. Translated into psychological terms, it represents the flow of psychic energy, in relation to time and fate. It concerns progression and resolution, which are inevitably implicit in the sonorously harmonic texture generated by canon at the third.

Variation 10 is called 'Fughetta', and is a small, strict, three-part fugue. But it's also a binary dance movement that relies on metrical accent and syncopation rather than on quasi-vocal polyphony. The theme combines repeated notes and trills with arpeggiated crotchets; the fundamental harmonic progression is evident. Nothing disturbs the assured, bucolic march of the first half from tonic to dominant; the trio-sonata-like suspensions at the cadence are grand, in Handelian style, rather than painful. After the double bar the suspensions are sharper, the marching gait less rigid, since the bass is diminished into quavers. The final eight bars return however to the original movement and texture, sounding homely as well as affirmative.

The next toccata variation (no. 11) exploits crossing scales, rather than arpeggios, on the two keyboards. The music is notated in flowing bars of 12/16: a time which in Bach is friskier, less seraphic, than 12/8, though it often (as here) has levitating implications. Scale movement is of its nature less earthbound than harmonically rooted arpeggios, especially when the scales dissolve into extended trills. In the second four bars arpeggio figurations are, however, added to the scales and are, moreover, tritonal, since the dominant modulation is approached by way of its minor and subdominant minor. As so often in Bach this hint of harmonic pain enhances ecstasy, inducing wonder into the toccata's joy. After the double bar the texture is yet more airborne. The scales flow in quasi imitation, in contrary motion; the modulation to the relative is again intensified by a Neapolitan approach. And again human passion proves a gateway to heavenly bliss. The cross-rhythms of the contrary motion scales are so fluid that the bar-lines seem to evaporate; the final cadence takes off and, in so doing, is without finality:

Ex. 178

Variation 12 is the canon at the fourth. Four is the first non-prime number and the first square number. In Euclidian geometry four points produce the first three-dimensional body; in physics quaternions control the rules for rotating a body in space. Qualitatively, a four-fold structure dominates all models of the universe and concepts of the divine, up to the four-dimensional universe of modern theoretical physics. Even in Europe's Middle Ages — despite Christian obsession with the Trinity — the number four prevails in alchemy and in the disposition of the points of the compass, of the seasons, of the elements, and of the temperaments or 'humours'. Psychologically, the difficult step from three to four is the progression from the infinitely conceivable to finite reality; four is the number of fulfilment. Bach signifies the special nature of his canon at the fourth by making it a mirror canon by inversion. Twice two is four, and the two images, within and without the mirror, make a whole, poised over the repeated crotchets of the ground which is, to begin with, firm as a rock. In the canonic parts the balance of rising and falling scales makes the two-in-oneness easy to hear; the mirror-like stillness seems to disembody the texture's sensuality. None the less sensuality is latent since canon at the fourth lends itself to alternating tonics and dominants; there's even something like whimsy in the hiccuping entries in bars 5 and 6:

Ex. 179

while after the double bar wit deepens to mystery, as the canon flows into chromatic passing notes. When the canonic scales droop in A minor and rise in G minor-major, melodic permutation yields harmonic alchemy:

Ex. 180

The 'cross' between horizontal flow and vertical harmony—and between disparate, even contradictory, modes of feeling—is Incarnation: the point at which human and divine are interfused. Mirror canon is a synonym for that many-in-oneness.

Certainly a climax comes—in so far as it is valid to use the word with reference to a work concerned with being rather than becoming—in the 'trinity' of variations 13–15. For the first time the initial member is not based on dance or body movement, nor on our mundane world. True, the slow 3/4 pulse recalls the original sarabande; and the original version of the ground is clearly discernible in the bass. But it's the sacral rather than sensual implications of sarabandes that flower in this music: an aria wherein a highly ornamented line floats asymmetrically over the bass. The melody begins with a written-out turn, and soars in demisemiquaver arabesques. G major becomes that key of seraphic bliss which was the goal of the B minor Mass and, as the convolutions of line float across the beats in tied syncopation, the bar-lines dissipate:

Ex. 181

The sensuality of the Baroque becomes celestial. In the last four bars stepwise movement turns into broken-chord, violin-style figuration which enriches the harmony, and perhaps implies a whiff of mortality in the chromaticized cadence in the last bar:

Ex. 182

In the second half the arabesques are still more extended, winging through the slow pulse. Complementarily, harmonic pathos is deepened, since the weeping semiquavers that appear in the first half's cadential bar become thematic at the modulation to the relative. They are extended, moreover, through sequences to B and A minor; even the bird-soaring roulades of demisemiquavers at the return to the tonic are affected by chromatic passing notes in tenor and bass. In the final bar the weeping semiquavers and the touch of minor in the chromaticized cadence evoke *lacrimae rerum*. Bliss is inseparable from the apprehension of pain.

This is why the joy of the next variation (no. 14) is different from that of the previous virtuosic toccatas. The first four bars have cascading arpeggios in the left hand and in the right an inverted mordent that bounds through three octaves on to a trill! The second four bars settle into quaver and semiquaver arpeggios crossing on the two keyboards, only to flicker through the next four bars in a written out version of the original mordent. The sonority glints and rustles, like mutation stops on a Baroque organ. In the final four bars the twittering mordents swirl into demisemiquavers, with a mysterious minor flattening in the approach to the dominant cadence:

Ex. 183

The mordents chirrup in parallel thirds and sixths, disrupting the accents. In the second half right and left hands are inverted. The Neapolitan approach to the relative casts a minor shadow which extends into the cadential bars, with an effect similar to that of the '*lacrimae rerum*' cadence to the previous variation. *That* had made the aria's bliss real; *this* transmutes the toccata's crackling laughter into mirth — in the medieval as well as modern sense.

Up to this point all the variations have been in the 'benediction' key of G major. Variation 15 introduces the tonic minor, with an effect proportionate to its long delay. The fifteenth variation is a canon at the fundamental tonal relationship of the fifth. This interval was, we've frequently remarked, traditionally a musical synonym for the absolute concord which is God, since if one admits harmony at all, the fifth is the closest interval to the unison and octave, which are non-harmonic. Psychologically, Jung tells us that 'four forms a frame for the one, accentuated as the centre. By unfolding into four it acquires distinct characteristics, and can therefore be known. . . . So long as a thing is in the unconscious it has no recognizable qualities and is consequently merged into the universal unknown, with what the Gnostics called "a non-existent all-being". But as soon as unconscious content enters the sphere of consciousness it has already split into four; that is to say it can become an object of experience only by virtue of the four basic functions of consciousness. . . . The splitting into four has the same significance as the division of the horizon into four quarters, or the year into four seasons. Through the act of becoming conscious the four basic aspects of a whole judgement (perception, recognition, distinction and evaluation) are rendered viable.' The Hebrew word for five, *chumish*, means facultative comprehension; the Greek word *pente* is derived from Pan, who represents Nature and the All. Five is the mind of God that, brooding 'over the waters', brings what *sub*sists in matter into *ex*istence.

Such speculations, however arcane, bear on the effect of the fifteenth variation in the context of the whole work. From the quiet content of the first variation we have reached this tragic statement, which resolves an infinity of suffering into calm. Yet the variations have not progressed or developed; they have simply *revealed* more, brought more that subsists into existence. Again the metaphor of a cell or grain of sand seems pertinent. In this variation the ground is *sub*sistent in a bass line of considerable flexibility, melodically an equal partner to the two canonic parts. They are based on the weeping pairs of semiquavers first heard in the cadences to Variation 13; their appoggiaturas and passing notes weave dissonances — German sixth, augmented fifth, minor ninth and major seventh — into the most humanly expressive music thus far. Yet at the same time this *ex*istent passion is objectified since the canon is in mirror inversion. The sighing descents of the appoggiaturas are answered in the ascent, thereby creating the lines of a cross; and this equilibrium is still more movingly evident in the second half when the bass becomes thematic in taking over the weeping semiquavers, while the canonic parts move in stepwise syncopated quavers, with suspended seconds.

Ex. 184

In the minor the original modulation to the relative becomes a modulation to the flat submediant, E flat major, a relaxation of tension which, we recall, Bach uses at the same pitches, and with profound effect, in the *St. John Passion*. The return to the tonic is by way of C minor, with chromaticized semiquaver tears, at first declining, answered in the ascent. In the final bars the lower canonic part falls to G, rounded off in an inverted mordent, while the upper part drifts to D *in alt*, fading on the bare fifth:

Ex. 185

Despite the pathos, this is no subjective lament; there could be no sublimer image for the whole that makes man hale and holy.

Both chronometrically and spiritually this is the halfway house in the work. With the sixteenth variation we return to the 'real' world, though not to the society in which Bach was nurtured, nor even to the aristocratic chamber where Goldberg is playing the variations. The venue is rather a high Baroque court, for the two halves of the variation form between them a French overture, the first part pompously ceremonial with shooting scales, stilted double-dotted rhythms and cadential trills, the second part a fugal round dance notated conventionally in 3/8. The texture of the first part is sinewy, that of the second regularly affirmative. The ground bass is fairly clear through the textural complexities of the heroic first section, less clear in the round dance, wherein each two bars equal one bar of the basic harmony. After the tragic canonic Variation 15, the ostentatious splendour of the sixteenth variation sounds faintly ironic; all that peruked stomping seems more vainglorious than glorious. None the less the next toccata variation (no. 17) suggests that a return to this majestic if wish-fulfilling apotheosis of the World, the Flesh and the Devil may be to *reculer pour mieux sauter*. The left hand figuration in rising thirds is derived directly from the bass of the round dance (bars 24 *et seq.*), is counterpointed against a figure in cross-rhythm and combined with reverberating parallel sixths (Ex. 186).

Again excitation is controlled contrapuntally by inversion of figuration; and again after the double bar hands and motives are inverted. Corporeal energy becomes a whirlwind that theatens the prideful assurance of the French overture, though this toccatta is not itself transcendent.

Ex. 186

Neither is the next canon, for Variation 18, the canon at the sixth, differs from previous canons in that it remains 'worldly' in temper, and this despite the fact that it is notated *alla breve*, in archaically scholastic counterpoint. For the Greeks six, the doubled triangle, was the number of harmony, of friendship, health and justice; as Thomas Taylor put it in his *Theoretick Arithmetick*, it is 'the harmonic conjunction of that which is known with that which knows'. Such a concept may be interpreted on many levels and we've seen that in the Sanctus of the B minor Mass Bach gives it the sublimest possible reading. Here he interprets it, validly enough, in homely terms. Canon at the sixth lends itself to suspensions in trio-sonata style, demanding a regularly metrical beat. Metrical rigidity, combined with solid part-writing and rich suspensions, create an effect of stability, even cosiness:

Ex. 187

So although variations 16 to 18 remain a 'trinity', the pattern seems to have changed as compared with the first half of the work. And Variation 19 preserves this human simplicity, over the most rudimentary statement of the ground thus far. Semiquavers babble through a 3/8 pulse, with a minimum of interior dissonance. It's as though after the vainglory of the French overture, the earthy vigour of its toccata and the *alla breve* canon at the sixth which imprisons counterpoint in the academic establishment, Bach is sailing home. Being where he has his true being, he can again plumb depths and scale heights. Variation 20 certainly does the latter, for it is a cross-handed toccata for two keyboards, wilder than any of the previous toccatas, both because its contrary motion arpeggios cover an immense range and also because they coruscate in triplets that sound like laughter or even, in higher register, like giggles:

Ex. 188

As Blake put it, 'He who catches a joy as it flies Lives in Eternity's sunrise'. Such merriment simultaneously echoes human joy and the chuckle of the Deity, especially when, in the second half, the triplets are chromaticized. There's bacchic tipsiness in these cross-handed roulades. Since the binary structure preserves the usual mirror-like symmetry, inhibition is not totally released, but the acceptance of bondage becomes itself liberation. Such ecstasy is precarious, like that of a tightrope walker.

Not surprisingly, danger finds summation in tragic pathos. The twenty-first variation is the canon at the seventh; and the relation of seven to six is similar to the relation of three to two. If six is the number of harmonious conjunction, seven is a disturbance of balance, movement that may either produce catastrophe (like the Flood in the seventh chapter of Genesis), or that may, returning on itself, complete a cycle ('three score years and ten'). Bach's canon at the seventh brings the second appearance of the tonic minor, over a chromaticized version of the ground. The canonic theme consists of an undulating scale followed by leaping fifth and fourth; gradually the bass's chromatics creep into the canon. After the double bar the rhythm of the bass is syncopated and the canon inverted. The modulation to the flat submediant brings only momentary relief, since in the last four bars the canonic parts are fragmented, the passing dissonances acute, culminating in a Neapolitan approach to the cadence:

Ex. 189

This canon does not attain the equilibrium between human and divine typical of the canon at the fifth. Though its potentially operatic intensity is distanced by the counterpoint, its textures are, as befits the number seven, uneasy, vacillatory.

Variation 22 begins the next 'trinity' with a return to species counterpoint, *alla breve*, but mundane, safe, even comfortable, in much the same style as the canon at the sixth. The bass, after the chromaticism of the canon at the seventh, is in its most rudimentary form; the duple metre is regular; imitative entries are always on the off-beat, suspended across the bars. Dissonances are rich, not anguished, with double suspensions such as sound well on Baroque organ. The manner suggests an equation between the civic and the ecclesiastical, which is a different matter from the fifteenth variation's identity of the human with the divine. Again, this social music explodes into a whirlwind toccata alternating semiquaver scales in parallel thirds with demisemiquaver scales, sometimes crazily fragmented. Dionysiac drunkenness spurts, in the second half, into a flurry of parallel thirds and sixths in contrary motion:

Ex. 190

This is the most sensuously tempestuous of the toccatas, and that in which contrapuntal control is least rigorous. Variation 24, however, the canon at the octave, is both rigorous and simple. The number eight is the reflection or double of four, the symbol of foundation. It therefore represents the repetition of process; and the Hebrew word for eight has a dual root, meaning either the act of placing one thing on another, or a distribution by parts. The original shape of the written letter was two squares, one above the other: which turned into the modern 8, the only completely closed figure. Bach's canon at the octave moves, over a melodic bass that is freely thematic, at two bars' distance. It seems to 'complete' the irresolution of the canon at the seventh in a noble calm, moving mostly by step in 9/8 (three times three), in a manner reminiscent of Bach's Christmas music. During the second half the texture grows more complex at the modulation to the relative, yet the long trills and reiterated dotted crotchets reinforce the sense of affirmation. Some players perform it in full registration, triumphantly celebrating the canons' attainment of the 'perfet diapason' of the octave. This fits the character of the pastoral music less well than a calm presentation: which creates repose and at the same time foretells a birth.

If the first half of the Goldberg Variations manifested a slow evolution towards the simultaneously divine and human canon at the fifth, the second half—beginning with the French overture—has on the whole been earth-rooted if capable, in the toccatas, of corybantic revel. The work's second climax, the twenty-fifth variation, should, as the first member of a 'trinity', be dance-like, and *is* a sarabande. Yet nothing could more deeply reveal how for Bach the poles of flesh and spirit are inseparable: this sarabande could not be danced, and although vehemently human, even rhetorically operatic, is also tragically purgatorial (Landowska christened it 'the Crown of Thorns'). That a secular music of the passions can become Passion music depends partly on the slowness of the pulse, which allows time for a chromaticized version of the ground to communicate its tensions to the other parts. The music returns darkly to the tonic minor; the melody is highly decorated, in arioso style. Upward-aspiring grace notes, sobbing appoggiaturas, shattered syncopations create music as densely charged as the arioso of the *St. John Passion*; and although the 3/4 pulse is continuous, the melodic line is agonized by cross accents and by its variety of figuration, from syncopated semiquavers and demisemiquavers to chromaticized triplets:

Ex. 191

Though on a long view the tonal scheme is unchanged, the very slow movement permits what appear to be wanderingly, wonderingly 'lost' modulations, provoked by the chromatics. During the second eight bars of the first half the bass rises chromatically to balance its earlier declension while the arioso line painfully stretches to A, B flat and C, before cadencing in a double appoggiatura. The second half begins in D minor instead of major, moving in sequences through G, C and F minor. These pseudo-modulations follow the pattern of the minor version of the ground; the arioso line grows more tortuously convoluted as both tonality and metre seem to dissolve. At the expected modulation to the flat submediant Bach introduces his only real irregularity, substituting E flat minor for the major:

Ex. 192

The dark flatness evokes the gloom of Golgotha, as imitative chromatics press up through the two lower parts while the arioso leaps through octaves and sevenths, pitifully to droop. In the twenty-fourth bar the cadence shifts, by way of a double appoggiatura, into E flat major; but in the final eight bars the slowly drooping chromatic bass effects sequential modulations to C minor and B flat minor before arriving, exhausted, at the tonic. Yet exhaustion is far from being an adequate account of the effect, since during the last four bars the chromatic bass wearily climbs *upwards* while the arioso, though consistently *falling* across the bar lines, does so in an unbroken surge of demisemiquavers:

Ex. 193

The ultimate sob of the double appoggiatura in the last bar can thus be heard as a *consummatum est*, surviving pain that would seem well-nigh insupportable.

The climactic significance of the twenty-fifth variation is unmistakable, both because of the music's intensity and because of its length. The number of bars (thirty-two) is of course the same as in the original sarabande aria; the tempo of their unfolding, and the complexity of their musical events, are however unparalleled. Man, dancing, *becomes* divine through suffering; whereas in the central climax, the fifteenth variation, the 'divinely' impersonal counterpoint of a canon at the fifth *reveals* a maximum charge of human passion. This twenty-fifth variation, although so slow and apparently free in its arioso figuration, is still recognizably a sarabande. The next toccata (Variation 26) preserves the sarabande rhythm, with a stress on the second beat, though it has speeded up the tempo of the original aria, not to mention that of the G minor arioso. The left hand enunciates the sarabande rhythm, again in G major, in 3/4; the right hand whirls in a scurry of triplets, notated in 18/16. In the second eight bars the hands are inverted; and the process is repeated after the double bar, with the usual basic modulations so that, as compared with the melodic-rhythm and tonal-harmonic undermining of Variation 25, we feel reassured. After such an extraordinary experience as the twenty-fifth variation assurance can, however, hardly be complete: in the last five bars the dotted sarabande rhythm disappears, and the variation flickers out in semiquaver triplets, mostly in two, instead of three, parts.

And there are two parts only in the last canon, which is at the ninth, the ground now becoming itself one of the imitative parts. Because it approaches completion within the decad, nine was called the horizon by the alchemical writers: 'It is not possible there should be any elementary number beyond the nine . . . because all numbers are comprehended by and revolve within it.' It represents the final interrelation of the world of forms, of the knower, the known, and knowledge itself, preparatory to the act of completion in the ten. Bach's canon at the ninth functions in a consummatory manner through its sheer simplicity. The ground bass (and the ground is the earth) has dissolved into the canonic two-in-oneness; and the answer at the ninth is never treated, though like canon at the second or seventh it readily could be, as a dissonant suspension. Even passing dissonances are minimal, as the gentle 6/8 rhythm flows in upward scales. When, after the double bar, the canon is inverted we accept its inevitability:

Ex. 194

This is the only canon which Bach directs to be played on two keyboards.

This cannot be because it is complex —euphoniously spaced, it is perhaps the most contrapuntally simple of the canons —but must be rather because, on separate keyboards, with the ground now intrinsic to the canon, the 'twoness' of the parts is admitted without their ceasing to be one. The variation suggests acceptance, and its acceptance seems an end: a cycle is completed, after which there can be no more transcendent suffering or 'ecstasis'. Joy, however, is still possible: the next two variations are both toccatas for two keyboards. Variation 28 exploits, during the first four bars, leaping tenths in the left hand, written out trills in the right, these figurations being inverted in the second four bars. The next eight bars are a tintinnabulation of parallel thirds, sixths and tenths: a sonority that evokes the glitter of angelic wings —as Beethoven may have intuitively felt when he recalled this passage in the variations of his piano sonata op. 109. The second half follows the usual tonal sequence but presents the material in a different order. The first four bars alternate quaver leaps with dancing semiquavers; the second four return to the glinting trills; while the last eight have the original figurations the other way up. Chromatics in the upper part and in the tenor somewhat agitatedly increase the jubilation:

Ex. 195

The last toccata re-establishes a clear, energetic version of the ground, supporting powerfully resonant 6—3 chords alternating with prancing triplet figuration:

Ex. 196

The second half has the material in reverse order, with sizzling chromatics: once more we find an architectural symmetry. Yet the variation, though brilliant in virtuosity and sumptuous in sonority, is sensual rather than ecstatic, and lacks the counterpoint and cross-rhythms that typify the 'metaphysical' variations. One might say that the 'trinities' in the second half of the work — from the sixteenth variation onwards — tend to reverse the pattern of the first half. The evolution from corporeal dance to potentially ecstatic toccata to metaphysical canon, reaching its apex in the canon at the fifth (Variation 15), is no longer adhered to. On the contrary the dance pieces, though still metrical, may be fugal, the canons dance-like. The climax to the second half turns out to be a dance (the first member of a 'trinity') which has been metamorphosed into an aria of purgatorial Passion (Variation 25). This human apotheosis weighs no less, indeed exactly balances, the divine apotheosis of the canon at the fifth, for the corporeal has become spiritual. Perhaps for this reason the last 'trinity' substitutes an extra toccata for its dance and Bach, having written a canon at the ninth wherein the lower part becomes the ground bass, does not move over this 'horizon' to complete the decad, which brings all digits back to unity and combines the one with zero. The *human* approach to completion is seven; ten is the completion of God — 'heaven unwearied', 'eternity' and 'necessity' according to the Pythagoreans, and according to the alchemists 'the boundary of all things'. Probably Bach thought that ten was, cosmologically, inapprehensible to man. In any case he did not compose a canon at the tenth but substituted for it a dance, and a low one at that.

Certainly in Variation 30 we're back in the world—and not in a count's nocturnal palace but at Bach's domestic hearth where, Forkel tells us, members of the family were wont to meet with cantors, town musicians and organists and would strike up a chorale. 'From this devout beginning they would proceed to jokes which were frequently in strong contrast. They sang popular songs, partly comic and partly of indecent content, all mixed together on the spur of the moment so that the different improvised voices indeed constituted a kind of harmony, but so that the words in every voice were different.' Bach's quodlibet uses a straightforward version of the ground to support three upper parts in metrical counterpoint, incorporating two popular songs, *Ich bin so lang nicht bei dir g'west* and *Kraut und Rüben*. The counterpoint is

Ex. 197

ingenious, as no doubt it was when the Bachs improvised; and can be so
because harmony, tonality and rhythm are all at their simplest (Ex. 197).

The quodlibet makes us genially laugh, as Forkel said it did and should.
Yet in taking us back to the simplicities from which the variations emerged
and in rooting these not in contrapuntal abstraction but in the everyday
realities of Bach's community, the quodlibet reminds us that, in Sir Thomas
Browne's noble words:

> there is musicke where-ever there is a harmony, order or proportion; and thus
> farre we may maintain the musick of the spheares. . . . Even that vulgar and
> Taverne Musicke, which makes one man merry, another mad, strikes me into
> a deepe fit of devotion, and a profound contemplation of the first Composer;
> there is something in it of Divinity more than the eare discovers. It is an
> Heiroglyphicall and shadowed lesson of the whole world, and Creatures of
> God; such a melody to the eare, as the whole world, well understood, would
> afford the understanding. In brief it is a sensible fit of that Harmony, which
> intellectually sounds in the eares of God.

Though the quodlibet was meant to be a joke, it is—as we'd expect of
Bach—a joke with philosophical implications. In 1934 Fritz Müller
claimed to have solved the enigma of the folksong quotations. In English the
words say 'I've not been with you for so long. Come closer, come closer.
Cabbage and beet drove me far away. Had my mother cooked some meat, I'd
have stayed much longer.' *I* is the theme, *you* the player; and if mother (Bach)
had cooked more meat (stayed closer to the theme) you and I would have been
together rather than lost. This I don't find very convincing; but the homely
quodlibet certainly heralds the longed-for return of the aria, as it was in the
beginning. All experience is one in the microcosm which is the Goldberg
Variations. As the aria sounds da capo, totally unchanged except for what we
can now hear within it, the cycle starts again. In context, in the timeless
stillness of the night, the effect of this da capo is indeed out of this world: for
although it brings us back to the immediate moments of Goldberg's (or
Bach's, or our) performance, we now hear this gracious sarabande—originally
composed for an eighteenth-century wife, later offered to an eighteenth-century
count—as it 'intellectually sounds in the Ears of God'.

The Goldberg Variations are poised between being and becoming. Their
structure is 'completed in all directions, like the mass of a well-rounded sphere,
equally great in the middle from all directions'. These words are Parmenides'

description of Unity, which is Being, which is God; and when the Pythagoreans went on to say that all is number they meant that any movement from unity was a process of becoming. The word 'number' is etymologically related to the word 'name': *num* in Hebrew represents a coming forth, a change from universality to differentiation; *nam* means to individualize and to make distinct. Unity (God) is pre-existent to consciousness; numbers are the principles (*archai*) of the world on which all Nature is founded. Action and reaction, movement and resistance, evolution and growth move, throughout Nature, in rhythms and permutations that would seem to be mathematically exact. This is why, with its circular form, the work —though it encompasses a profound awareness of the complexities of human experience and has focal points (such as variations 15 and 25)—appears to be timeless. The precision, even in small details of figuration, of its architectural symmetries complements the many-in-oneness of its contrapuntal mathematics. The centre and the periphery of Parmenides' sphere become interchangeable; smallest equals greatest, since 'God' is manifest in the minutest particular, which He at the same time embraces and transcends in his whole. In this sense the Goldberg Variations bear on the ancient hermetic riddle of the identity of 'everywhere' and 'nowhere' (*sphaera cuis centrum ubique, circumferentia nullibi*) in the infinity of God. Such musical abstraction, which withdraws from the world, yet contains the world within itself, becomes the mainspring of Bach's creativity in his final works.

When Bach corrected the proofs of the published version of the Goldberg Variations he not only emended errata but also appended, in a *Handexemplar*, a set of 'fifteen divers canons on the first eight bass notes of the preceding aria'. As though to emphasize their abstraction, Bach did not write them out in score, but presented them in riddle form, with clues as to their solution. Beginning with a 'Canon Simplex', which none the less works two ways — either as a straight canon with the second entry beginning on the fifth note, or as a theme accompanied by itself backwards —the procedures grow gradually more complex. A 'Canon a 4, per Augmentationem et Diminutionem', presents the theme at half-speed, transposed and inverted; at quarter-speed differently transposed; and in its original version as bass. At the maximum point of elaboration two chromatic themes proceed in consort with the eight-note bass. Above, Bach writes the words 'Canone sopr'il Sogetto', and below 'Symbolum Christus Coronabit Crucigeros'. The alliterative Cs give the clue that the canon must be completed with *crossing* parts and that the note C is the plane of the mirror on either side of which the themes are reflected. Finally there's a 'Canon Triplex' which brings in the numerology of the figure alphabet, in which the sum of Bach is 14 and that of J. S. Bach is its retrograde, 41. Moreover, although there are fifteen canons in all they are numbered only from 1 to 14, two being telescoped in number 10. They fall into groups of 4 1 4 1 4—a play upon Bach's 41 plus 14 'signature'.

It is improbable that Bach intended these canons to be performed as an epilogue to the Goldberg Variations which are, as we've seen, superbly planned as a circular whole. None the less their abstraction, 'all passion spent', is oddly affecting; for if the variations contain the contradictions and complexities of the world, purged into pure form, the canons, which seem to be form *in essentia*, reveal through their abstract meditation flashes of light, shadowy depths. In so doing they provide a link to the final works of Bach's 'mathematical' phase, the *Art of Fugue* and the *Musical Offering*, in which the canons are at once more complex and more mysterious.

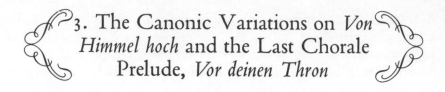

As instances of Bach's final phase we will examine not the immense *Art of Fugue* nor the comprehensive *Musical Offering* but two relatively small works which form an appendix to them. Being of modest dimensions, they lend themselves more readily to analysis; and one of them, said to have been dictated on Bach's death-bed, is as profound as it is valedictory.

The Canonic Variations on *Vom Himmel hoch* exist in two versions. One, printed in open score and with only the entries indicated in the canonic parts, is a pedagogic abstract presented as evidence of technical skill to the Mizler'sche Societät, to which august institution Bach applied for admission in 1747. Characteristically, he delayed his entry until that year so that he could become its fourteenth member, that number being, as we have seen, his signature in the figure alphabet. The other version of the Canonic Variations is in short score, with the canons written out, so that we have a performing score for an organist. Scholarly disputation rages as to whether the printed abstract or the autograph score came first. The point would be unimportant, were it not that there are slight differences in text between the two versions, and a significant difference in the order of the movements. In the open score the variations are grouped in one of those chiastic structures to which Bach was partial. Variations I and II are three-part canons at the octave and the fifth, with the cantus firmus in the pedal. Variations IV and V are in four parts, with the cantus firmus in the soprano in Variation IV, in the bass in Variation V. In Variation IV the canon is at the seventh, with one free part; in Variation V the canon is at the octave by augmentation, also plus one free part. Variation III, standing in the middle, is in four sections, the first two in three parts with canon by inversion at the sixth and third respectively, the second two in four parts with canon by inversion at the second and ninth respectively. In this multiple variation the canonic theme *is* the cantus firmus. In the three-part sections the pedal part is free, whereas in the four-part sections the canon is between pedal and tenor and between pedal and soprano, the remaining two parts being free. The multiple variation in the middle thus harks back to the two three-part variations, while looking forward to the two four-part variations.

Though this looks impressive, both architecturally and musically, there are arguments in favour of the short score also. This ends with the multiple variation, which incorporates Bach's signature —the notes B-A-C-H —in the last bar, the appropriate place for a signature. Moreover, it seems logical for the variations to proceed towards their point of maximum contrapuntal ingenuity and to end when the cantus firmus has itself become the canonic theme, as happens with the final canon of the Goldberg variations. The chiastic version is typical of Bach and gives intellectual delight when diagrammatically represented:

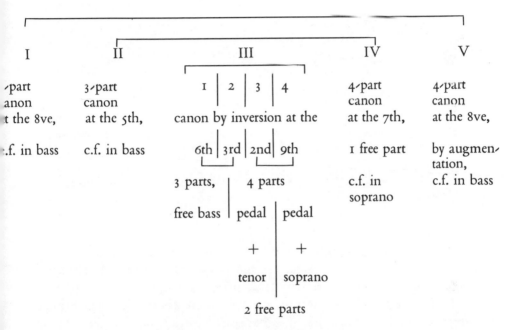

Bach may have considered the two versions equally valid, for different occasions: obviously the short score is for the use of organists; writing the work out for presentation to a learned society, Bach suggests a more theoretical permutation. We must leave the matter open, but will here discuss the variations in the sequence in which they appear in the autograph.

Like the Goldberg Variations, the Canonic Variations are not really variations at all, and are formally archaistic. The earlier work is a complex passacaglia; the Canonic Variations are a chorale fantasia — contrapuntal embroideries on a hymn tune, in the manner practised by Bach in his youth, after the prototype of a seventeen-century organist-composer such as Scheidt. A technique that in Scheidt is usually effective and sometimes beautiful becomes, with Bach, 'the height of human perfection', to adapt Spinoza's phrase. The hymn tune, *Vom Himmel hoch, da komm ich her*, is a Christmas song, and therefore a song of joy and of birth. The first two three-bar phrases balance one another: the first moves by step, the second opens in arpeggio. The third clause alternates stepwise movement with rising and falling thirds; the final clause is a resolutory descent by step through an octave:

Ex. 198

For his first variation Bach has the chorale unadorned on the pedals, supporting two parts, on two manuals and in canon at the octave. The canonic theme has its own identity, yet sounds like an emanation of the hymn, beginning with the downward-flowing scale with which the chorale ends, then rising through an arpeggiated octave which expands the hymn's second clause. That the canon is strict is self-evident since in the open score version Bach merely indicates the point of entry; that it also 'fits' with a 'perfection' that seems supernal though created by a human being is the miracle of Bach's art. The chorale is the Word that sings to us, in an almost popular vein, of a divine birth; its metre is the simplest 4/4. Above it the two canonic parts, enacting the two-in-oneness of Father and Son, Spirit and Flesh, lilt in a radiant C major; their metre is a spaciously floating 12/8, a time signature we have seen to have seraphic connotations. Though the canon occasionally produces passing dissonances and suspensions, these never become dramatic events; nor do we hear the basic modulations to dominant and relative as occurrences in time. The level flow of semiquavers, the white lucidity of C major, the appropriately *dove*-tailed perfection of the canon two-in-one generate a sublime content. When the canon's final arpeggiated phrase is echoed in the lower octave it's as though God himself were laughing:

Ex. 199

The second variation is also in three parts, with the cantus firmus on the pedals. The chorale takes on a syncopation in its opening bars, but is not otherwise modified. The canonic parts are at the fifth (the most absolute consonance after the octave) and are at first thematic, presenting the hymn in double diminution. Perhaps because of this subdominant-flavoured opening the modulations to dominant and relative are less well defined than in Variation I. Unity is the more deeply affirmed since the canonic theme is so closely related to the chorale, incorporating the descent by step, the rising thirds, and the final fall through an octave. Significantly, Bach doesn't here make use of the arpeggiated segment of the chorale; all is a flowing, with cross accents syncopated over the beats. In the cadence there is a subdominant, plagal flavour with flattened seventh before, in the last bar, the octave scale drifts *upwards* with will-less inevitability:

Ex. 200

Variation III (in the short score version) completes the three in the four, being in four parts, two for the player's right hand, one for his left, and one for his feet. The chorale, in its original time values, is in the soprano, unadorned; the other right hand part is free, and quite elaborately decorated. The canon, at the seventh, is between left hand and pedal, beginning with the first clause of the chorale in double diminution. Compared with the first two variations, this music sounds more humanly complex, partly because canon at the seventh invites dissonant suspensions, partly because the free part has a considerable variety of rhythmic pattern and of expressive, rather than merely decorative, embellishment. In this variation the Word sings on top, and flows in tenor and bass into canonic permutations that are rhythmically regular but harmonically tense; between the cantus firmus and the canon melody flowers:

Ex. 201

One might construe this as a Spinozan compromise between freedom and determinism; certainly the free melody—which none the less intermittently refers to fragments of the cantus firmus—is emotive in a way the melodies of the previous variations hadn't been. Yet though paired semiquavers softly sigh, syncopation suggests physical energy, and suspended seconds and sevenths gently sob, we hear them all within the contrapuntal dialectic. They sound, as it were, *sub specie aeternitatis*. And there is surely a link between this Bachian equilibrium and Spinoza's definition of the wise man previously quoted; this is beautifully evident at the close of the variations, for after the canon has been discreetly chromaticized in its third clause, this slight heat is counteracted by the plagal cadence, with flat sevenths that effect a real subdominant modulation in the penultimate bar.

In the fourth variation more humanly expressive features appear, balanced by a still greater degree of contrapuntal predetermination. The cantus firmus, in its basic form and tempo, is again on the pedals. The canon is at the octave, as in Variation I, tenor imitating soprano in augmentation. There's an additional part in the alto, free yet partially determined in being involved with, and sometimes echoing, the canon. The character of the variation depends on the fact that the canonic theme is as linearly and metrically elaborate as was the free part in the previous variation; and because it's answered in augmentation a multiplicity of figurations coexist. Moreover, the augmented theme takes twice as long as the original version, thus creating a hierarchy of speeds. As the lines melismatically unfold, with floating demisemiquavers tied across the beats and paired semiquavers drooping in appoggiaturas or rising in thirds, the music develops the levitating quality we've frequently observed in Bach's aria-like movements:

Ex. 202

This apparent freedom is strictly determined: for although the augmented version of the canonic theme sounds too dissimilar to, and strays too far from, the original version for their relationship to be aurally apprehensible, it is this relationship that conditions the character of the music. We apprehend it, perhaps intuitively, as the deep tonic pedal allows time for the original canonic theme to catch up with its augmentation. The contrapuntal apotheosis is harmonic too, since in the penultimate bar the free part is chromaticized as well as plagal. The alto weighs down through B flat and A flat, and in so doing seems to release the upward spring of the soprano's last demisemiquaver scale, with sharp sixth and seventh (Ex. 203).

Four bars from the end Bach introduces his signature—B-A-C-H into the alto. It's a fleeting moment in the polyphony, and he doesn't here identify the notes by name, as he does later.

The final variation, in the short-score version, is the most complex in that it is divided into four sections. The first two echo variations I and II in being in three parts, while the other two similarly echo variations III and IV in being in four. The cantus firmus is no longer independent of the canons since they are now strictly thematic. The canons are always by inversion, the two sides of the mirror forming a whole, like Parmenides' sphere. In the first section canon is by inversion at the sixth, with pulse diminished from minims to crotchets; the pedal part moves freely in quavers, making reference to the arpeggiated motive in the hymn. The second section inverts the right and left hand parts to make a canon by inversion at the third; the texture is unchanged, even in minor details such as the cadential trills. In the third section canon by inversion is at the second, between pedal and tenor; two free but thematically allied parts are added in alto and soprano, the latter shimmering in continuous semiquavers:

Ex. 203

Touches of D minor and E minor, first evident in Variation IV, here threaten to become real modulations, and even after the return to the tonic there's a faint flutter of G minor. The disturbance remains, however, latent; the G minor triad shifts to major, becoming a dominant of C, thus leading into the last section. Here canon is at the ninth, between pedal and soprano. Running semiquavers resume in the tenor; the alto is at once free and in syncopated bondage to the soprano. This multiple variation concludes with a coda in a stretto in which all the figuration is thematic. Segments of the chorale appear simultaneously at three different speeds—in crotchets, quavers and semiquavers, though it's the semiquavers that are pervasive, as if the Word were alchemized into heavenly bells. In the four final bars Bach adds a fifth part for the only time in the work, so that the four-part canonic texture survives after the bass has descended to a low tonic pedal. Here is another argument in favour of placing this variation last, especially since Bach uses the extra part to sign his name, enigmatically divided between voices, but with the notes identified in score. In the alto the name-notes also appear almost (but not quite) backwards—H-C-B-A:

Ex. 204

The contrapuntal ingenuity of this coda is breath-takingly beautiful. As Tovey once pointed out, if technical ingenuities are not beautiful they are not really ingenious, since (almost) any fool can write double invertible counterpoint, or what-else, if he doesn't care how it sounds. The miracle of Bach's counterpoint here is that the mathematical abstraction is also the Christmas message. The dancing angels of the first variation are reborn in the lucent semiquavers; and the celestial music ends, as Bach signs his own name, with the clash between cadential B naturals and figurative B flats. It is the most harmonically acute cadence in the whole work; and the dissonance is produced by the flat B in Bach's own name! Yet at the same time this momentary pain created by Bach's own (inevitably sinful) humanity makes the resolution of the suspended fourth on to the third the more heart-easing; and it's not blasphemous to say that in this sense Bach's role is Christ-like. The collocation of his personal identity with the unity of God's mathematics may be compared to the portrait of the donor, usually tucked away in a discreet corner, in late medieval and Renaissance paintings. Though the point of the artefact is its divine message (in this case the tidings of Christmas), the humanly sinful donor made it possible. Bach is the donor in a fundamental sense. He paid for the piece materially, in offering it for the glory of God to an academic society; but he also created the artefact, and through it became an instrument of revelation.

The Canonic Variations have a coda in Bach's last complete composition, which is a totally canonic and thematic chorale prelude. During his Weimar days he had set the hymn *Wenn wir in höchsten Nöten sein* in his *Orgelbüchlein*, ornamenting the tune richly, in Buxtehude's style, and accompanying it with simple harmonies. At the end of his life he made this other setting, drawing its title from another stanza of the hymn — *Vor deinen Thron tret' ich.* Clearly he regarded the piece as a last testament which, his eyes failing, he dictated to a copyist from his sick-bed, if not at death's door. The autograph, which appears in the same volume as the short score of the Canonic Variations, breaks off at the twenty-sixth bar. But there must have been another manuscript since C. P. E. Bach published the chorale prelude complete, in open score, as an appendix to his posthumous edition of the *Art of Fugue*, restoring the original title. Today both titles are used, and either is apposite.

In this last composition, as contrasted with the *Orgelbüchlein* setting, the cantus firmus is presented in a simple, readily recognizable form. Bach added a few ornamental notes to the first clause of the hymn, in order to bring the number of notes up to fourteen which, we recall, represents B-A-C-H in the figure alphabet. He also managed to include forty-one notes in the complete chorale melody; and 41, we'll also recall, is 14 backwards and stands for J. S. BACH. While Bach revelled in the permutational complexities he could extract from such puzzles, he did not do so in the spirit of a game; or if he did, it is because games are magic, and it would not have escaped his notice that *his* number is twice seven. As we have noted in reference to the Goldberg Variations' canon at the seventh, seven was, for the Pythagoreans, a peculiarly significant number, there being seven colours in the solar spectrum and seven tones in the diatonic musical scale, the pitches of which are not arbitrarily but mathematically determined. Whereas six represents harmony and concord, seven is not a closed circle but a spiral, preparatory to the completion of a process. In alchemical theory seven is the gateway between earth and heaven; the rainbow in its seven colours, appearing after the Deluge, was a sign of the meeting of the terrestrial and celestial. The process of 'sevening' is like the Flood in the seventh chapter of Genesis that 'covered the earth', or like a withdrawal of the spirit of death. On the seventh day, after the six days of creation, God breathed into man's nostrils the breath of life, 'and man became a living soul'. Seven is the number of new departures, and of reincarnations.

Such hermetic speculations were not foreign to the alchemically oriented ·theologians and mystics, nor even to the music theorists, whose works Bach read. Though they cannot of course modify the musical effect of Bach's double sevens, they do condition the frame of mind in which he created his *opus ultimum*: wherein there *is* a dissolution of the body, a return to Nature, and a union of finite man with the infinite. And that Bach's last composition should be a chorale prelude for organ is movingly appropriate, for the chorale, the organ, and polyphony are the fundaments of his art. The Lutheran hymns, we've noted, embodied the faith and the life of a people; polyphony was both a philosophical concept and a musical and religious heritage; and the organ reached the apex of its evolution in Bach's time and place. Having two keyboards and pedal, the organ of Bach's day was ideally adapted to contrapuntal 'science'; it could sustain tone as long as the player's fingers or feet remained in contact with the keys, thereby enunciating savagely 'crucified' dissonance as easily as the blandest consonance; and it could differentiate melodic strands in varied tone colours. All this is manifest in the last chorale prelude. Basically its technique is that of a vocal motet in four parts; even so, the spacing is instrumental, and only a Baroque organ could so completely absorb harmonic stress into linear flow.

The key, we're not surprised to discover, is the benedictory G major. Each phrase of the hymn is stated in the soprano as cantus firmus; the Word always rides on top, but is never obtrusive. It's a simple, beautifully balanced melody in 4/4, moving entirely by step after the initial repeated tonics; and its first phrase is presented with discreet ornamentation which not only (as we've observed) makes up the notes to the symbolic fourteen but also, in musical terms, gives the line a serene flexibility. This initial phrase of the hymn appears after a prelude which, inevitably, covers seven bars; and each clause of the chorale is separated from the previous one by a seven-bar ritornello, though ritornello is hardly an appropriate term, since every note in this composition is thematic. We accept the cantus firmus as such only because it is in longer notes values, registered on a solo stop, and at first differentiated from the other parts by the bloom of its ornamentation. These other parts are three in number, presenting the theme in diminution and in canon by inversion. Ex. 205 is the complete chorale prelude.

Thus in the first clause the theme *rectus* in the tenor is answered *inversus* in the alto. A chromatic tail to the tenor line modulates to the dominant, which immediately declines to the tonic, with a suspended seventh tenderly resolved. The pedal entry, *rectus*, is answered by the alto *inversus*; the sharpwards modulation, with chromatic parallel thirds, is repeated, and still more exquisitely resolved in ornamented suspensions. At this point the hymn enters in the soprano, its note values twice as long as those of the other parts. The alto and tenor move, *rectus*, in parallel thirds; the pedal answers by inversion. There's a

Ex. 205

5

10

15

20

touch of E minor before the first clause cadences in the tonic. The suspended seventh between alto and tenor resolves chromatically, by way of F natural, E and E flat, anticipating the final cadence (bars 10–11).

The second clause of the hymn begins with an undulation up and down from the third. In the seven-bar interlude it appears *rectus* in the tenor, *inversus* in the alto, *rectus* on pedals. The drooping chromatics that conclude the first clause are now balanced by a chromatic rise, which again resolves in ornamented suspensions, euphoniously spaced. This effects a real modulation to the relative E minor (bar 14); the suspensions and passing notes are dissonant but, given the disposition of parts, tenderly so. When the second clause of the hymn enters in the soprano it is unornamented, making it more assimilable into the contrapuntal texture: it sounds like canonic augmentation, which, indeed, it is. The two inner parts start off *rectus*, in parallel thirds, answered by the pedal *inversus*. The music preserves its calm linear equilibrium, since each slowly arching phrase is mirrored by its inversion. This balance extends to the tonality, for the touch of subdominant at the beginning of the clause is complemented by the gentle dominant modulation at its end. Even visually, in score, we may observe a delicate equipoise between stepwise movement and the quiet fourths and fifths that support the cadential suspensions (bars 18–19).

The unuttered words of the first two clauses of the hymn are: 'Vor deinen Thron tret' ich hiermit, O Gott mit inniglicher Bitt; Beschere mir ein selig End; nimm meine Seele in deine Hand'. The music, moving almost imperceptibly yet with a deep charge of emotion within its canonic inevitability, emulates a slowly pulsing heart. The tempo, as Hermann Scherchen remarked in a perceptive analysis, is about quaver equals 72, the *integer valor* of the Middle Ages, which gives seventy-two pulse beats and eighteen full respirations to the minute. So each 8/8 bar corresponds to one deep inhalation and exhalation, at about the rate produced in deep sleep. The breath of life, with which God made man 'a living soul', faintly expires; yet in so doing becomes again the breath of God, as creature returns to Creator. For this chorale prelude's structure is not a dissolution. Tonally, the second clause, which ends *in* the dominant, slightly increases the momentum; and the canonic entries follow one another at closer intervals. This heightened temperature continues into the next clause of the hymn, the words of which are 'Ach, kehr dein liebreich Angesicht von mir blutarmen Sünder nicht; dass ich dich schau dort ewiglich. Ja, amen, ja, erhöre mich!' Immediately, in the seven-bar interlude, the consciousness of sin imparts harmonic tension beneath apparent tranquility. There are four entries by inversion, at the fourth or fifth;

and the tenor's falling phrase, answered by alto in ascent, creates both false relation between the declining C natural and ascending C sharp and also rapid modulation up a cycle of fifths from G to D major and, with the pedal entry, to A and E minor. The tritones and passing dissonances — for instance the major seventh between tenor and bass — are acute; yet the passion is still 'recollected in tranquillity', since the level movement is undisturbed, the canons *rectus et inversus* are still mirrored in stillness, and the harmony and tonal movement remain in equilibrium. If there is a climax at all, it occurs when, at the entry of the third cantus firmus clause, the spacing between the parts is widest, covering three octaves between the soprano and pedal Ds. This re-establishes the tonic, as the cantus firmus declines down the diatonic scale, gradually effacing the dominant C sharps (bars 27–29).

In the final seven-bar interlude the tenor entry is in crotchets, *rectus* answered *inversus* in quavers by alto. The pedal enters *rectus*, in quavers, in dissonance with the tenor. Although the tune merely undulates by step, a chain of ornamentally resolved suspensions modulates to those 'suffering' keys, E minor and B minor, modulations which are, however, immediately counteracted by sequences moving positively to D and A major. Modest chromatic alterations — the Cs and Ds being flat in the descent, sharpened in ascent — make the music hover between tonalities, threatening declension, aspiring upwards, yet never quite relinquishing the blessedness of G major (bars 33–34).

Surrender and resignation are one when the pedal has the augmented theme in inversion, answered by cantus firmus in the soprano, with the two middle parts at the original (preludial) speed. And again bondage becomes freedom: the cadence to the hymn's last phrase is interrupted, a modulation to E minor being substituted for the tonic resolution. This interrupted cadence carries a lacerating suspended minor second, which is immediately cancelled by an F natural in the alto leading into an extended plagal cadence — a longer version of the cadence to the hymn's first clause. Again, the sharpwards modulations of the previous section are flattened. Undulating 6–3 chords, with both F and E flattened, remain strictly thematic, though the melodic identity and metrical definition dissolve, in the counterpoint's hierarchy of speeds, into this seemingly endless 'Amen'. The music runs down as the pulse flags, beneath the immobile yet sustained inverted pedal on which the hymn tune has found rest. There could be no more precise musical synonym for the acceptance of death identified with the will of God.

Spinoza, whose affinity with Bach has already been referred to, maintained that there were three kinds of knowledge. The first, which he called *imaginatio*, is cognition 'perceived from things represented to our intellect fragmentarily, confusedly and without order, through our senses'. The second kind of cognition, which Spinoza termed *ratio*, is that 'based on notions common to all men and on adequate ideas of the properties of things'. These kinds of cognition are roughly synonymous with unscientific and scientific knowledge. But there is a third kind of knowledge which Spinoza called *intuitio*; this 'proceeds from an adequate idea of the absolute essence of certain attributes of God to an adequate knowledge of the essence of things'. Such knowledge is given to prophets and to some artists who, in understanding things by this third type of knowledge, attain

> the highest endeavour of the mind and the highest virtue. In proportion as we understand things more in this way we better understand God. He who understands things by this kind of knowledge passes to the summit of human *perfection*. From the third kind of knowledge arises the highest possible mental *acquiescence*. Whatsoever the mind understands under the form of eternity, it does not understand by conceiving the actual existence of the body, but by virtue of conceiving the essence of the body under the form of eternity. Whatsoever we understand by the third kind of knowledge we take *delight* in, and delight is accompanied by the love of God as cause. From the third kind of knowledge necessarily arises the intellectual *love* of God. The intellectual love of God is *eternal*.

No more relevant comment on Bach's last chorale prelude is verbally conceivable. 'Perfection', 'acquiescence' and 'delight' are, as we've seen, incarnate in this music; and within those qualities are the atemporal notions of 'eternity' and of 'the intellectual love of God'. As late as 1950 Fred Hamel was the first to point out that Bach's musical signature, the B-A-C-H motive, is not merely an autobiographical identity: 'if one draws lines between the two middle notes A and C, and the outer ones B and H, the sign of the Cross appears'. That Bach found this satisfying we cannot doubt: he knew that he was able, through his music, to carry that Cross on our behalf. He must also have known that he was the 'brook', the fountain of life, linguistically signified by his name; and the Cross and the welling brook are simultaneously manifest in every aspect of his technique. In this last chorale prelude we do not need the gloss of the latent text of the hymn to tell us that 'brook' and Cross are interdependent, that the intellectual love of God transcends, but does not efface, human suffering as well as joy. Bach, dictating this music, was dying into beatitude: this is inherent in the abstract musical events, which tell us, as Spinoza puts it, that 'death becomes less hurtful in proportion as the mind's clear and distinct knowledge is greater and, consequently, in proportion as the mind loves God more'. Those parts of us which 'perish with the body are of little importance when compared with the part which endures'. Like God, the 'perfection' of the last chorale prelude persists: at once an epiphany and an epitome of Bach's life-work.

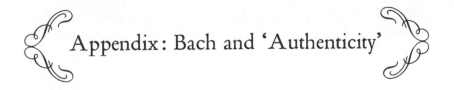

Appendix: Bach and 'Authenticity'

Nowadays—as any one attending a festival, even a mini-festival, of 'early' music will know—most performances of pre-nineteenth-century music make some attempt at 'authenticity' and, given our lack of confidence in what we ourselves believe, the arguments for this are obvious. Though valid creation is generated from a tension between private experience and public assumptions, an artist has no choice but to start from the conventions his age offers him. These conventions, being the common parlance of the day, are not arbitrary: an artist couldn't ignore them, even if he thought he wanted to, and creative sparks are most likely to ignite if he's an abrasive agent, working within their limitations. A good composer writes as effectively as possible for the resources available; in this sense the spirit of the music is inseparable from the letter, and few people who have heard Dowland or Bach performed on contemporary-styled instruments, with some deference to contemporary conventions of tempo, phrasing, ornamentation and timbre, will want again to hear them performed on modern instruments, in nineteenth- or twentieth-century styles. Authenticity makes better sense. Everything 'sounds', where much was opaque; and sounding is, inevitably, the first step towards understanding.

It is, however, *only* the first step; and the statement contains a recognition that authenticity, though desirable, is a complex ideal. In referring to the artist as abrasive I've implied a distinction between his experience and that of the world that made him; and the more he has to offer, pertinent to the human condition in general, the less dependent will he be on the topicalities and localities of his group. Confining myself to the Baroque period—the 'old' music closest to us in time and probably, though not necessarily, closest in spirit—I would say that a representative composer such as Telemann, much of whose vast output sounded so dreary in the unauthentic performances of my youth, may acquire unexpected vivacity and grace, even pathos, when the accumulations of aural varnish are cleaned off. In its own terms, the music makes modest sense to us today. Even a greater composer, Couperin, may be so closely tied to a past time and place that it's only since the elaborate stylizations he worked within have been partially understood that his relevance to us — his human significance beyond the elegant confines of Versailles — has become apprehensible. We reach a third stage with a still greater composer, Handel, since although he, being representative, must profit, like Couperin, more or less unambiguously from authentic performance, the public values in which he believed were those to which all sensible men could and can subscribe. Couperin's values are, I think, profound, but are latent within the exceedingly subtle conventions of a world that has vanished; Handel's Reason, Truth and Nature, with the musical conventions in which they're formulated, are values still recognizable. Moreover when Handel, driven to express extravagance of madness or intensity of suffering, departs from these conventions it's clear that he knows what he's doing and why: miraculous moments such as Saul's frenzy or (in *Messiah*) Christ's broken heart are shattering precisely because we experience their melodic, harmonic and tonal audacities in reference to a norm. Their boldness becomes the more striking in a context wherein contemporary stylization has been respected.

Yet because Handel is a very great, not merely representative, composer authenticity is not *essential* to the performance of his music, as it now seems to be to that of Telemann or Couperin. Great works of art, which are those most likely to survive, are also those most likely to override the ephemeral; which is why they may be re-interpreted in terms of a later age, so long as that age has the courage of its convictions. Mozart, accepting — somewhat critically — his society philosophically as well as musically, had no doubt that his rescoring of *Messiah* for the current classical orchestra improved the music; and for his public it undoubtedly did so. Mendelssohn, reinterpreting and to a degree rescoring the *Matthew Passion* in terms of a nineteenth-century ethic, believed enough in what he was doing for his performances to make a memorable impact on his public: so memorable, indeed, that forgotten Bach became once more modern music, being reborn in being rediscovered. Mammoth performances of *Messiah* in the Albert Hall stirred the vitals of Victorian common men; what they got from the music may not have been what Handel was aware of putting into it, yet some such stability, sobriety and affirmative sense, if not sensibility, must have been latent in music that is not merely historically interesting, but is a human document with at least some pretension to 'universality'. Perhaps one might even say that Beecham's brilliant orchestrations of Handel, if not Stokowski's of Bach, had an Edwardian swagger that sprang from self-confident conviction. Thousands of people, attending the orchestral concerts that were the staple musical diet of the rapidly expanding middle classes, found zest in Handel-Beecham, though it vulgarized Handel's rich social solidarities. Demotic ebullience is not totally alien to Handel; and although one may think that Stokowski's theatrical rhetoric was inimical to Bach's religious heart, at least he offered a Bach that could be relished by common men who were agreeably, and justifiably, as unashamed of their relish as they were of their commonness.

We today lack both relish and self-confidence. Not knowing what we believe in, we have uncommon intelligence and sophistication, and need them because the accumulations of knowledge are now immense. It's no longer simply a question of fairly recent 'old' music which preserves some, however distorted, continuity with our own traditions; the frontiers of 'early' music have been pushed back into times past, and the further back we go, the more dificult the evidence is to interpret. With much medieval and Renaissance music we cannot begin to translate the signs without palaeographic research; but although by studying contemporary sources one may learn much, the information one garners is as contradictory as it is voluminous. The rules governing musica ficta or proportional rhythm, for instance, are capable of many varied readings; so even to establish a text, before tackling its 'interpretation', is a difficult, sometimes insoluble, problem. Similarly, information about medieval and Renaissance instruments, though copious, is contrarious and confused; even when we can examine authentically ancient instruments we have to recognize that knowing how they were constructed doesn't necessarily tell us how they were played, let alone when and where. Moreover a scholar may be tempted to make of his knowledge a shibboleth, forgetting that our performances cannot possibly be identical with the original and shouldn't be, since we're radically different creatures with radically different needs. Authenticity has two related aspects, one of which pays tribute to what we know of historical evidence, while the other respects a given sequence of musical events. The two may coincide, but need not. When they don't, it must be music that makes history, not the other way round.

It follows that authenticity must involve an ability to do as well as to know. In my youth viols, in the hopeful hands of knowledgeable amateurs, tended to sound like vile primitive fiddles, seraphic lutes to cavort like bucking broncos. It was artists like Landowska and Bream, rather than scholars *per se*, who first made early music sound like music, though we now know that they played it 'wrong'. Today technically adept players of viols, lutes and harpsichords, not to mention rebecs and rackets, are legion; yet technical competence allied with historical knowledge cannot guarantee conviction.

That comes only from experiencing music as a way of life; if we can't, like Mozart rewriting Handel, re-experience the past in *our* terms, we must make it ours vicariously, in being reborn. Bach, the latest and greatest of 'old' composers, offers the biggest challenge precisely because his art is least stringently tied to a specific time and place. We regard his position in European history as crucial because while being firmly rooted in his Baroque present, he harked back to a remote medieval past and anticipated a future which is nineteenth-century Romanticism — and us. He is not the greatest of religious composers because he was a good eighteenth-century Lutheran; historical probity cannot be an adequate key to the interpretation of Bach for the obvious reason that he was demonstrably, in the techniques of his music, not of an age but for *all* times. Though archetypal elements must be manifest in any human creation, even a transient news-sheet, they have never been more powerful and pervasive than in the work of Bach.

His archetypal, rather than merely historical, veracity bears on the fact that with Bach an equilibrium between historical and musical authenticity is harder to achieve than it is with Handel. It's interesting that of the recorded performances of that in every sense difficult work, the Goldberg Variations, two seem to me supremely memorable; and neither is authentic though each, in different, even opposed, ways is sublime. Rosalyn Tureck plays the work on the wrong instrument, the piano, in a manner that emphasizes its hieratic and mystical qualities. Her tempo for the aria is so slow that it bears little relation to a sarabande and, for this historical shortcoming, might be said to deny part of Bach's intention, which is to start from the elegant artifice of a contemporary court only to reveal 'all Heaven in a grain of sand'. Yet in total effect Tureck does fulfil Bach's *musical* intention, for the Goldberg Variations *is* a hieratic work which touches on realms of experience we call mystical, and Tureck's da capo of the sarabande-aria at the end, so slow as to seem almost immobile, really does transport us 'out of this world'. One might even make out a case that to start from the ideality, in the Platonic sense, of Bach's sarabande makes better sense, for us, than to start from a courtly convention which we cannot share.

Wanda Landowska, on the other hand, played the work, on the harpsichord, with romantically passionate humanity. The richness of sonority and complexity of texture she attained weren't authentically Bachian, and her instrument bore not much more resemblance to an eighteenth-century harpsichord than does Tureck's piano. Yet such richness and complexity are demonstrably not alien to the music; and Landowska arrives at the same goal as Tureck by the opposite route. Tureck's lucid pianism *reveals* 'all passion spent' through its very limpidity; Landowska's extravagant, exuberant, vehement plucked-string sonorities discover, through the whirligig toccatas and the mysterious arioso of Variation 25, the still centre at the heart of 'the fury and the mire of human veins'. Her sarabande-aria, the same at the end as it was in the beginning, is not so much heaven as the temporal moment in which we find ourselves, in the still night, as harpsichordist Goldberg embarks again on the cycle of the variations to while away time for an insomniac prince. The temporal moment is also eternity, which contains all that the variations have encompassed.

An ideal performance of the Goldberg Variations would, I suppose, synthesize Tureck's heaven with Landowska's earth, revealing that the borderline between them is illusory. I've not heard such a performance, but have encountered many that attempt historical authenticity but don't come within light years of the truth. Helmut Walcha's may be taken as representative, in that its virtues serve best when the letter may be substituted for the spirit. When historical knowledge is pertinent, he uses it effectively: for instance, he makes a brilliant sound in the French overture that forms Variation 16, for the sharply articulated double dots, the shooting scales and coruscating trills and turns appropriate to the convention are excitingly executed, and an aristocratic past is vividly re-created. Walcha is good, too, given his crisp finger technique and metrical precision, at evoking the non-aristocratic, Lutheran, burgomaster-like aspects of Bach's world: scholarly exactitude paradoxically makes the quodlibet jollier. Yet although aspects of the past are thus reborn, the experience remains 'historical' in the limiting sense because Walcha has the same approach to the corybantic toccata variations, and even to the slow canons at the fifth and seventh and to the amazing twenty-fifth variation. To believe that when Bach's music is elaborately canonic it is necessarily and merely impersonal is a foolish heresy, which ignores the musical evidence — in the fifteenth variation, for example, the sequence of arching melodic gestures, which create harmonic and rhythmic tensions that are absolved in the stillness of mirror inversion. However complex the mathematics involved, this is not music of the computer that Walcha emulates, but of a human being inspired with the breath of God. Similarly to play the twenty-fifth variation with Walcha's metrical rigidity is to obliterate the effect of those logical yet miraculous tonal modifications that cause earth *and* heaven to open as the passacaglia's law is, if only apparently, threatened. Kirkpatrick's performance, though far more intelligent, seems to me similarly prosaic, lacking the incandescence that, in their different ways, Tureck and Landowska achieve. In this case I doubt if there's a failure to reconcile historical with musical authenticity, for one can question neither Kirkpatrick's learning nor his musicianship. One can't say much more than that Kirkpatrick's performance is as intelligent as one could hope for; but that though neither Landowska's nor Tureck's performance is authentic, each has a streak of genius as far beyond intelligence as Bach's art is beyond his superlative craft.

The Goldberg Variations are perhaps a special case; so let us turn to a general, basic, ostensibly simple matter — the interpretation of the chorales. Everyone knows that nineteenth-century tradition grievously distorted them; they were sung too slowly, wallowing in a Romantic rubato. Now we know that the chorales were in origin congregational hymns, often founded on secular popular tunes; secure in this knowledge modern performers canter briskly through them, asserting the eighteenth-century Lutheran's sturdy independence. Now this may be part of the truth, but it cannot be the whole truth; if it were, Bach's chorale harmonizations would be no different from those of any other composer, as they demonstrably are. No other composer, whether a hack or a man of talent, harmonized these melodies with Bach's luxuriance, his fusion of vertical density with horizontal independence. The technique, combining a maximum of dissonant tension with continuously flowing lyricism, conditions, indeed is, the unprecedented experience; and it cannot be adequately audible, and therefore apprehensible, unless the complexities of harmony are allowed time to speak. A funereal gait, with extravagant rubato, is not called for; but the tempo must arise from the nature of the musical events, not from any prior knowledge which, even if historically valid, may be extraneous to those events. The proper tempo of Bach's chorales will vary within comparatively narrow limits and will tend to a basic *moderato* rather than *adagio*. None the less the eventfulness of the music, in terms of harmony and texture, won't encourage an *allegro*; nor would jauntiness be appropriate to the texts which generate these events. Deference to Bach's musical authenticity is a tribute to his comprehension of the words he set, or rather of their implications. Both theologically and musically this comprehension was of a different order from that of other representatives of his church.

But although respect for Bach's authenticity is more important than respect for the authenticity of history, we cannot deny that our increased knowledge of historical conventions and resources has contributed immensely to our understanding of Bach. In particular the Bach performances of Nikolaus Harnoncourt and the Concentus Musicus have been a revelation. Much work and devotion have gone into Harnoncourt's act of recovery and rediscovery, as a result of which we're able to listen to Bach with something resembling contemporary immediacy. In one of his prefaces Harnoncourt, defending his use of boy soloists even in vocally demanding music, points out that for Bach and his public all music was contemporary and most of it was by Bach himself. When we remember that it was performed by the same relatively few musicians, who habitually worked under Bach's direction, it seems less remarkable that they should have been able to negotiate such difficult music with apparent aplomb. Admittedly Bach's music was different from and more complex than the currently fashionable music of his time; even so, his singers and instrumentalists didn't have to learn to cope with a strange idiom, since there was, for them, no other. This music was their bread and butter — as well their (and our) bread and wine.

Harnoncourt's recordings manage to create this sense of rediscovery and at the same time to suggest that the music is being performed by people born and bred to a modern idiom. It sounds like eighteenth-century Bach, but as fresh as a daisy; and at the same time like twentieth-century music, which of course it is, in so far as it speaks to us. The affirmative passages in Bach usually come off magnificently in Harnoncourt's performances. The 'Cum sancto Spiritu' of the B minor Mass is, for instance, electrifying; the lines in their glowing colours dance and sing simultaneously, instead of stumping and thumping, so their earthy virility becomes also an ecstasis. As our analysis suggested, they're a rite of spring as well as a Christian resurrection, and Bach's identification of the physical and metaphysical, buried under the sanctimoniousness of nineteenth-century tradition, is triumphantly reaffirmed. In some solo arias, for instance the 'Laudamus te', Harnoncourt also achieves exactly the right balance between metaphysical radiance and physical passion. The tempo is fast, yet the phrasing and articulation are gracious, redolent with social *cortesia* and with spiritual grace. In the limpid sonority of the Baroque violin, the lark of the soul ascends etherially — from his nest on the turning earth.

Yet despite such delights Harnoncourt's Bach recordings sometimes leave me with a sense of dissatisfaction, which mostly springs from a conflict between historical and musical evidence in the performance of the slower movements. It is with the greatest music that I feel the deepest unease; and Harnoncourt's performance of the 'Crucifixus' from the B minor Mass may serve as *locus classicus*. Now the 'Crucifixus' is, we recall, a passacaglia notated in 3/2 time. Historical evidence tells us that in Bach's day 3/2 was a metre certainly no slower than 3/4, and probably faster, since the old triplex notation discourages small note values. Harnoncourt has just played the 3/4 'Et incarnatus' at a fair pace, which might be justified on the interior evidence of the movement *per se*, since it emphasizes the music's dramatic, even theatrical, fire. What is impossible to justify is that, having taken the 'Et incarnatus' at this pace, he has to conduct the 'Crucifixus', for historical reasons, as fast or faster; at that speed it ends up sounding inane. There are solid, incontrovertible musical reasons for this. The mystery of the 'Crucifixus' depends not only on its chromaticism, in which many Baroque composers indulged in comparable situations, but also on its enharmony—for instance the way in which the chromaticized sharp A functions as a Neapolitan B flat—which only a composer of Bach's genius could have envisaged. Enharmony implies ambiguity, which imparts wonder and awe. At Harnoncourt's gabble there's no time for the puns to register aurally, so no wonder is evoked. A performance which is thus musically and humanly insensitive cannot in the deepest sense be authentic even historically. If the 3/2 time signature means that Bach wants the 'Crucifixus' to go faster than the 3/4 'Et incarnatus'—and this might be a historically valid deduction—then the 3/4 of the 'Et incarnatus' must go slower than Harnoncourt's. And it can, without impairing the music's intensity. On the contrary, a slower pace, at which we can really hear the momentous harmonic events which the quasi-polyphony engenders, can sound more rather than less urgent. There is another possibility: Bach may have used the old-fashioned 'triplex' notation, along with the number symbolism whereby he repeats the passacaglia bass thirteen unlucky times, as a means of stressing the liturgical solemnity of the movement, while not expecting the tempo convention to be adhered to rigidly. This is feasible, though perhaps unnecessary, since the conventional relationship of 3/4 and 3/2 works admirably if the 3/4 is only a little slower than Harnoncourt's.

The first Kyrie of the mass is a case comparable with, if less flagrant than, the 'Crucifixus'; and here Harnoncourt's interpretation of the historical evidence is puzzling. Admittedly, the movement is very long, its inexorable movement 'planetary', so there's an excuse for not letting it drag. Yet though Baroque tempi were faster than those current in the nineteenth-century, it would be dangerous to build much on the lively tempi that, according to only one contemporary authority, Bach adopted in rehearsal. In any case ₵ was not conventionally fast, even when unqualified by Bach's verbal directive of *largo*;

and the tempo of this movement is surely to be found in the intrinsic musical evidence. The Kyrie theme owes its painful grandeur to the evolutionary tension of its implied harmony and the vast rhythmic span needed for its manifestation. Beginning with rock-like repeated notes, with assertive dotted rhythm, it expands, as we've seen, in wedge form, striving from tone to imperfect to perfect fifth, to major sixth, followed by a flattened Neapolitan descent and a stabbing diminished seventh in the approach to the cadence. True, a sense of corporeal movement must survive, especially in the sequential, ceremonially bowing ritornello phrases. Even so, those phrases must preserve dignity; and a tempo that will allow for dignity will also allow time for the anguish latent in the chromatically expanding Kyrie theme to make its impact. At Harnoncourt's tempo, this doesn't happen. If one does find precisely the right tempo the movement will seem, as so often with Bach's music, to be playing itself. Maazel comes closest to it, among the recordings I'm acquainted with.

Klemperer's version is also worthy of comment because, though patently unhistorical, it is not patently wrong. It is prodigiously slow — the total timing of the Kyrie is nearly twice as long as Harnoncourt's! At first it sounds impossible, even grotesque; yet because it maintains an inner momentum, the cumulative effect becomes overwhelming. At that tempo the human expressivity of the melodic gestures and the grinding tensions of the harmony have time and space in which to operate. With a lesser conductor, the line would have sagged, the harmony fumbled. Yet Klemperer brings it off, even though Bach might not recognize his music. If I had to choose the more Bachian performance, Harnoncourt's or Klemperer's, I'd opt for the latter. Harnoncourt seems to me musically wrong, whatever historical evidence he may adduce for his tempo. Klemperer offers no historical validation for his tempo, since there is none; but he might have claimed that he penetrated to the heart of the music through a personal act of empathy. His prefatory note suggests that a perfect performance of the B minor Mass is today impossible. He was probably right, and if so a personal reinterpretation, on this level, is legitimate. But if his reinterpretation works in the more hieratic movements, it's unconvincing in the corporeally rumbustious sections of the Gloria. Those aspects of Bach which can be allied to late Beethoven — and there are such aspects — are susceptible to Klemperer's genius; those apsects which celebrate the physicality of the audible, visible and tactile world are not thus susceptible.

The second Kyrie is similarly problematical. We've seen that, being notated in archaic *alla breve* style, it should probably be faster than the first Kyrie, especially since there are few small note values. Klemperer accepts this but, since his first Kyrie has been so monumental, can take the second at a pace that preserves nobility, while exploiting the pressure of the diminished third; this imbues the theme's apparent stepwise movement with harmonic ambiguity and intensity. Maazel adopts a fastish tempo, but revels in the Romanticism inherent in the chromatics, to the extent of concluding with a long ritardando and diminuendo. The effect is moving and beautiful, yet is unacceptable, not so much because it's unhistorical as because it belittles the music's passionate power. Its unhistorical musicality does distort; but it distorts less than Harnoncourt's historical authenticity, for having taken the first Kyrie so briskly, he has to take the notationally faster second Kyrie at a preposterous lick. At this speed the tensions in the theme, in its harmonies and textures, cannot hope to register. One looks for a balance between Klemperer's devotional solemnity and Harnoncourt's insouciant immediacy. It is hard to come by.

As a final example from the B minor Mass I'll refer to the penultimate movement, the Agnus Dei. Harnoncourt's tempo is not absurdly fast, though it is certainly far from languorous; he could probably educe contemporary evidence to 'prove' that an aria thus notated should go at this speed. I think it's demonstrably wrong for two reasons. The first is intrinsic: the music is so highly charged, melodically, harmonically and rhythmically, so much happens in so short a space, that the tones need and deserve all the weight one can give them, without sundering the total design. And 'weight' is an appropriate metaphor, for — as we observed in our analysis — the contours of that fragmented, wandering, wondering melody, yearning upwards through sixths and diminished sevenths, plumbing down through broken arpeggios and chromatically thrusting Neapolitans, seem to seek their centre of gravity at the world's heart: the low G which is the violin's open fourth string. This intrinsic reason for a slowish tempo is therefore related to the second reason, the aria's position in relation to the mass as a whole. Liturgically, the Agnus is the ultimate moment of mystery towards which the rite has proceeded; musically, it's the only movement notated in G minor, a key significantly hinted at in reference to God's potential incarnation. So although not chronometrically a long movement, and thinly scored, it must seem to contain the temporal burden of the human conditions, as well as its atemporal alleviation. Klemperer, with a funereally limping tempo, may at first seem perverse; yet again he succeeds in justifying himself in relation to his time scheme for the whole work. This time-scheme is certainly slower than Bach's would have been, and I'm not recommending it for conductors other than Klemperer. Accepting its premises, however, one recognizes that its proportions are right. In this context, the Agnus could not go faster; and at this tempo the burden of suffering breaks the heart, even as the rhythmic equilibrium heals. Too little historical knowledge must lead to distortion for which only genius, such as Klemperer's, can compensate. Too much historical knowledge, on the other hand, imbibed at second or third hand, may make it difficult to see the wood for the trees. One may miss the intrinsic nature of a sequence of musical events in worrying about their historical identity. Still more, one may fail to respond to the relationship of parts to the whole. This too is distortion. Without historical knowledge sensitivity may mislead; but without sensitivity historical knowledge is impotent. What it amounts to is that to perform the music of any past period is simply, and profoundly, to seek the life that is within death. Thoreau put it beautifully more than a hundred years ago:

> The living fact commemorates itself. Why look in the dark for light? Critical acumen is exerted in vain to recover the past; the *past* cannot be *presented*; we cannot know what we are not. But one veil hangs over past, present and future; and it is the province of the historian to find out not what was, but what is. Where a battle has been fought, you will find nothing but the bones of men and beasts; where a battle is being fought, there are hearts beating.

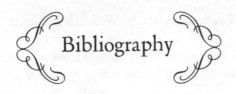

Bibliography

Boehme, Jakob, *Works*, ed. G. Ward and T. Langcake (London, 1764–81)

Bosman, Leonard, *The Meaning and Philosophy of Numbers* (London, 1932)

Chiapusso, Jan, *Bach's World* (Bloomington, Indiana, and London, 1965)

Collingwood, R. G., *The Principles of Art* (London, 1938)

Crossley-Holland, Peter, *The Sacred Dance* (London, 1972)

Curtis, Natalie, ed., *The Indians' Book* (New York, 1907, repr. 1950)

Eliade, Mircea, *The Myth of the Eternal Return*, trans. W. R. Trask (London, 1955

Erikson, Erik, *Young Man Luther* (London, 1959)

Geiringer, Karl, *Johann Sebastian Bach: the Culmination of an Era* (New York, 1966)

Hollander, John, *The Untuning of the Sky* (Princeton, 1961)

Jung, Carl Gustav, *Answer to Job*, trans. R. F. C. Hull, (London, 1954)

Jung, Carl Gustav, *Psychology and Alchemy*, trans. R. F. C. Hull, (London, 1953)

Kaufmann, Walter, *Critique of Religion and Philosophy* (London, 1959)

Langer, Susanne, *Feeling and Form* (London, 1953)

Luther, Martin, 'Table Talk', in *Selected Writings*, ed. John Dillenberger (Chicago, 1961)

Paz, Octavio, *The Labyrinth of Solitude*, trans. Lysander Kemp (London, 1967)

Róheim, Géza, *The Eternal Ones of the Dream* (New York, 1945)

Sachs, Curt, *A World History of the Dance*, trans. B. Schönberg (New York, 1937)

Scherchen, Hermann, *The Nature of Music*, trans. William Mann (London, 1950)

Schmitz, Arnold, *Die Bildlichkeit der wortgebundenen Musik J. S. Bachs* (Mainz, 1950)

Spinoza, Benedictus de, *Ethics*, trans. R. H. Elwes (New York, 1936)

Vaughan, Thomas, 'Anthroposophia theomagica' (1650), in *The Magical*

Writings of T. Vaughan, ed. A. E. Waite (Edinburgh, 1888; repr. New York, 1968)

Whone, Herbert, *The Hidden Face of Music* (London, 1964)

Watts, Alan, *Myth and Ritual in Christianity* (London, 1954)

Index